Comparative Grammar of Italian and French

Learn and Compare 2 Languages Simultaneously

MIKHAIL PETRUNIN

MIKHAIL PETRUNIN

Copyright © 2019 Mikhail Petrunin

All rights reserved.

To all Italophiles and Francophiles of the world.

MIKHAIL PETRUNIN

CONTENTS

Preface To the Learner	xvi
Acknowledgements	xx
Symbols	xxi
Introduction: Alphabet	1
Letter names and Pronunciations	1
Digraphs	4
Diacritics	6
Diphthongs	8
Chapter 1: Nouns	10
Gender of Nouns	10
Forming the Feminine	16
Plural Forms of Nouns	19
Special Cases of Forming the Plural Nouns	20
Nouns which are always Plural	23
Nouns which are always Singular	24
Chapter 2: Adjectives	26
Gender of Adjectives	26
Forming the Feminine	27
Plural Forms of Adjectives	31
Peculiarities of Adjective Use	32
Italian Bello	35
Italian Grande	35
Italian Buono and Nessuno	36

Chapter 3: Adverbs — 37

Use of Adverbs — 37

Forming Adverbs from Adjectives. Adverbs Ending in -mente (-ment) — 37

Peculiarities of Adverb Use — 38

Other Adverbs — 38

    Adverbs of manner — 38

    Adverbs of place — 39

    Adverbs of time — 40

    Adverbs of intensity — 41

    Adverbs of doubt — 42

    Adverbs expressing affirmation — 42

    Adverbs expressing exclusion — 42

    Adverbs composed of several words — 43

    Adverbial phrases — 43

Position of Adverbs — 44

Comparison of Adjectives and Adverbs — 45

Irregular Comparatives and Superlatives — 48

Chapter 4: Articles — 51

Origin of Articles in Romance Languages. Definite and Indefinite Articles. Gender — 51

    French — 52

    Italian — 52

Use of the Article — 53

    General Use of the Indefinite Article — 53

    General Use of the Definite Article — 54

    Omission of the Definite Article — 59

    Omission of the Article — 60

The Partitive	61
Contraction of the Article	63

Chapter 5: Pronouns — 65

Personal Pronouns	65
Subject Pronouns	67
Overview	67
Use of Subject Pronouns	68
Omission of Subject Pronouns	71
Direct Object	72
Use of Direct Object Pronouns	74
Word Order of Direct Object Pronouns	75
Divergent Aspects in Word Order	76
Indirect Object	76
Use of Indirect Object Pronouns	77
Common Verbs Used with an Indirect Object in Romance Languages	79
Word Order of Indirect Object Pronouns	80
Contraction. Using Direct and Indirect Object Pronouns in the Same Sentence	80
Italian ci, ne and French y, en Special Pronouns	82
Italian ci and French y Pronouns	82
Use of ci and y	82
Italian ne and French en Pronouns	86
Use of ne and en	87
Prepositional (Disjunctive) Pronouns	89
Use of Prepositional (Disjunctive) Pronouns	89
Use of Prepositional (Disjunctive) Pronouns in French. Special Cases	90

Reflexive Pronouns 91
    Use of Reflexive Pronouns 92
    Word Order of Reflexive Pronouns 92

Possessive Adjectives and Pronouns in Romance 93
Languages
    Possessive Adjectives 93
    Possession with de (French) and di (Italian) 95
    Omission of Possessive Adjectives 96

Possessive Pronouns 97

Demonstrative Adjectives and Pronouns in Spanish, ... 98
Portuguese, Italian and French
    Demonstrative Adjectives 98
    Forms of Demonstrative Adjectives 99
    Demonstrative Adjectives this and these in Romance ... 100
    Languages
    Demonstrative Adjectives that and those in Romance ... 101
    Languages
    Word Order of Demonstrative Adjectives 102

Demonstrative Pronouns 102
    Forms of Demonstrative Pronouns 103
    Possession with the Demonstrative Pronoun and de ... 104
    (di)

Interrogative Pronouns and Adjectives 104

Exclamations with Interrogative Pronouns 113

Relative Pronouns 116

Indefinite Adjectives and Pronouns 126

Chapter 6: Verbs 144

Overview 144

The Indicative Mood 147

The Present Tense	147
Irregular Verbs in the Present Tense	157
Verb Spelling and Vowel Changes	159
Use of the Present Tense	180
Special Use of the Present Tense and Prepositions	182
The Past Participle	183
Overview	183
Formation of Past Participle of Regular Verbs	184
Irregular Past Participles	184
Use of Past Participle	185
The Present Perfect	186
Formation of the Present Perfect	186
Formation of the Present Perfect with the Verb to be in Italian and French	188
Agreement of the Past Participle	189
Agreement of the Past Participle with avoir in French	189
Use of the Present Perfect	190
Special Use of the Present Perfect in Italian and French	191
Fr. venir de + The Infinitive	191
The Preterite	191
Formation of the Preterite	191
Irregular Verbs in the Preterite	193
Irregularities in Formation the Preterite	195
Use of the Preterite	204
Special Use of the Preterite in French	205
Difference between the Preterite and the Present Perfect in the Romance languages	205
Asking Questions	206

Peculiarities of Interrogation in the Romance languages	207
Negation	209
Formation of Negation in Simple Tenses	210
Omission of Pas in French	211
Negation of the Infinitive	211
Negation with Adjectives and the Adverb Very	212
Formation of Negation in Compound Tenses	212
Other Negative Expressions	213
The Imperfect Tense	221
Formation of the Imperfect	221
Irregular Verbs in the Imperfect	224
Use of the Imperfect	224
It. da; Fr. depuis + The Imperfect Tense	228
Difference between the Preterite and the Imperfect in the Romance Languages	229
Compound Tenses in The Past	229
Overview	229
The Pluperfect Tense	230
Formation of the Pluperfect	230
Use of the Pluperfect Tense	232
Peculiarities of Use of the Pluperfect in the Romance Languages	232
The Past Perfect (Anterior) Tense	232
Formation of The Past Perfect (Anterior)	233
Use of the Past Perfect (Anterior) Tense	235
The Future Tense	236
Regular Formation of the Future	236
Irregular Verbs in The Future	237

Irregularities in Formation of the Future in French	239
Use of The Future Tense	240
The Informal Future	241
Special Use of the Future	241
The Future Perfect Tense	242
Formation of the Future Perfect	242
Use of the Future Perfect Tense	244
Special Use of the Future Perfect	245
The Conditional Tense	246
Overview	246
Formation of the Present Conditional	246
Irregular Verbs in the Conditional	247
Irregularities in Formation the Conditional in French	249
Use of the Conditional Tense	250
The Conditional Perfect Tense	251
Overview	251
Formation of the Conditional Perfect	251
Use of the Conditional Perfect Tense	253
Conditional Clauses	254
The Subjunctive Mood	256
Overview	256
Basic Rules for Indicative and Subjunctive	256
The Present Subjunctive	258
Formation of the Present Subjunctive	258
Irregular Verbs in the Present Subjunctive	259
Use of the Present Subjunctive	261
Hope or If Only in Italian and French	262
Use of the Present Indicative instead of Subjunctive	268

Subjunctive with Subordinate Conjunctions	269
Indirect Commands in Romance languages	273
Subjunctive after Affirmation in Romance Languages	274
Subjunctive in Relative Clauses	274
Subjunctive with the Superlative and It. solo, unico; Fr. seul, unique	275
Subjunctive with Indefinite Words	275
The Present Perfect Subjunctive	276
Formation of the Present Perfect Subjunctive	276
Use of the Present Perfect Subjunctive	278
The Imperfect Subjunctive	279
Formation of the Imperfect Subjunctive	279
Irregular Verbs in the Imperfect Subjunctive	280
Use of the Imperfect Subjunctive	280
The Pluperfect (Past Perfect) Subjunctive	281
Overview	281
Formation of The Pluperfect Subjunctive	281
Use of the Pluperfect Subjunctive	283
The Sequence of Tenses with the Subjunctive	284
The Imperative Mood	286
Irregular Imperative	288
The Negative Imperative	289
Softened Commands in the Romance Languages	290
The Present Participle (Gerund)	291
Overview	291
Formation of the Present Participle (Gerund)	292
Irregularities in Formation of the Present Participle (Gerund) in Italian	292

Use of Present Participle (Gerund)	293
No Use of Present Participle (Gerund)	295
How to Avoid Using the Present Participle (Gerund)	296
The Compound Present Participle (Gerund) in Italian	297
Formation of the Compound Present Participle (Gerund) in Italian	297
Use of the Compound Present Participle in Italian	298
The Continuous Tenses	298
Formation of Continuous Tenses	298
Use of Continuous Tenses	300
The Present Continuous	300
The Imperfect Continuous	300
The Infinitive	301
Overview	301
Use of The Infinitive	301
Make in Causative Constructions in The Romance Languages	312
Let and Verbs of Perception + the Infinitive in the Romance Languages	315
The Compound Infinitive	317
Use of the Compound Infinitive	317
Reflexive Verbs	318
Overview	318
Formation of Reflexive Verbs	318
Reflexive Verbs with a Reflexive Meaning	320
Italian and French Compound Tenses with Reflexive Verbs	322
Reflexive Verbs with Parts of the Body	323
Reciprocal Reflexive Verbs	323

Reflexive Verbs Versus Non-Reflexive Verbs	326
Reflexive Verbs in the Infinitive in the Romance languages	327
Reflexive se (French) and si (Italian) as an Indefinite Subject	328
Frequent Reflexive Verb of Becoming	329
Affirmative Imperative of Reflexive verbs in the Romance Languages	329
Negative Imperative of Reflexive Verbs in the Romance Languages	330

The Passive Voice — 330

Overview	330
Formation of the Passive Voice	331
French Passive Voice with de	337
Alternatives to Passive Voice in the Romance Languages	337

Chapter 7: Numbers, Time and Dates — 340

Numbers — 340

Overview	340

Cardinal Numbers — 340

Peculiarities of Spelling Rules of Cardinal Numbers in the Romance Languages	345
Phrases of Approximation Used with Cardinal Numbers	346
Use of Cardinal Numbers	347

Ordinal Numbers — 350

Adverbial Ordinals in the Romance Languages	355

Fractions — 355

Arithmetical Operations	357

Collective Numbers — 357

Multiple Numerals	358
Dates	359
Days	359
Months	360
Ways to Ask the Date in the Romance Languages	362
Seasons	362
Time	363

Chapter 8: Prepositions — 370

Overview	370
Simple Prepositions	371
Uses of Simple Prepositions	372
Compound Prepositions (Prepositional Phrases)	423
Contraction of Prepositions with Article	434

Chapter 9: Conjunctions — 435

Overview	435
Coordinating Conjunctions	435
Subordinating Conjunctions	436
Correlative Conjunctions	440
Functions of Conjunctions	441
Copulative conjunctions	441
Adversative conjunctions	442
Disjunctive conjunctions	443
Consecutive conjunctions	444
Causal conjunctions	445
Concessive conjunctions	446
Conditional conjunctions	447
Final conjunctions	448

Temporal conjunctions	448
Comparative conjunctions	450
Complementizer	451

Chapter 10: Interjections — 452

Overview — 452

Types of Interjections — 452

Interjections with Exclamatory Words — 464

Verb Charts — 465

Regular Verbs — 465

Irregular Verbs — 468

Index — 472

MIKHAIL PETRUNIN

PREFACE TO THE LEARNER

This new edition of Comparative Grammar of Italian and French is a complete reference guide to all the aspects of Italian and French. It is the ideal reference book for those who would like to learn and compare Italian and French simultaneously.

It is designed not only for beginners who do not have an extensive knowledge of grammar, yet need a guide through the grammatical concepts of all mentioned above languages, but also intermediate and advanced students who would like to have a reference book of several Romance languages at once. Comparative Grammar of Italian and French can also be used for either independent study or for learners in classes of all types.

It presents a clear and easy-to-read description of the Italian and French grammar with chapters divided into nouns, pronouns, verbs, prepositions, articles, etc. detailing how each of the two Romance languages operate. The book is well-organized, neatly tabulated, with separate subheadings for topics that require a little more language-specific discussion.

This edition features:

- Detailed contents section and index for easy access to information.
- Hundreds of illustrative and authentic examples.
- Coverage of all the grammatical aspects and useful expressions.
- Sections on the geographical, historical and cultural facts of the Italian and French-speaking world.

This book is written for learners who are particularly fond of or would like to concentrate on learning Italian and French or just to get an all-round knowledge of these two Romance languages.

Furthermore, I have aimed to create a useful and must-have book for all those interested in these two Neo-Latin languages - Italian and French with concise and clear explanations of all grammatical areas and numerous practical examples taken from current Italian and French usage.

Lexical Similarities of Italian and French

Below are some examples that demonstrate apparent lexical similarities between Italian and French.

Count from one to ten

Italian	French	English
uno, una	un, une	*one*
due	deux	*two*
tre	trois	*three*
quattro	quatre	*four*
cinque	cinq	*five*
sei	six	*six*
sette	sept	*seven*
otto	huit	*eight*
nove	neuf	*nine*
dieci	dix	*ten*

Several common verbs

Italian	French	English
sonare	sonner	*to ring*
avere	avoir	*to have*
fare	faire	*to do*
sentire	sentir	*to feel, to sense*

Some other commonly used nouns

Italian	French	English
uomo	**homme**	*man*
pane	**pain**	*bread*
cielo	**ciel**	*sky*
erba	**herbe**	*grass*
vivo	**vif**	*alive*
bianco	**blanc**	*white*
venire	**venir**	*to come*

Tips on How To Use This Book

In order to avoid mess and confusion in learning, I suggest 8 tips on how to effectively study these four languages:

1. To make the process of learning better structured and more effective, learn the grammatical rules and phrases of these four languages in a fixed and strict sequence. These languages have already been put in a strict order for you to learn. The sequence is this: at first you read a rule or phrase in Italian => and then in French. You should get used to this particular sequence in order to avoid confusion.

2. As Leonardo da Vinci once said, "Study without desire spoils the memory, and it retains nothing that it takes in." Motivate yourself and develop an overwhelming and strong desire to learn and master Italian and French. Motivation and understanding of how important the knowledge of these languages is to you is the key to success. Constantly remind yourself why you need to learn several or all of these languages and where you are going to use them.

3. Try to read and memorize the rules of each chapter at least twice before starting with the next one. If you genuinely wish to improve your Italian or French, return and revise each chapter over again. Practice makes perfect. Remember that.

4. While reading new rules, phrases and constructions, try to make up your own sentences and examples using the rules that you just learned.

5. Use this book with a pencil to underline rules or constructions that you feel are important and which you may use later on in conversation.

6. Revise comparative grammar of Italian and French from time to time. Because our brain tends to forget all the grammar rules we've learned so rapidly, we constantly need to refresh our memory by reviewing and repeating them at times.

7. Practice your Italian and/or French in real conversations with native speakers no matter how good or bad you know those languages. Use these language every day and at every opportunity both in the streets and on the internet, on social networks or different online chats. Learning is an active process. You will never learn a language until you practice it with people.

8. Your final goal is to speak Italian and/or French. Therefore, use your notebook or any device to record all the new words and phrases you hear while practicing your languages with people or watching TV or listening radio in Spanish, Portuguese, Italian or French.

Why you should learn Italian and French.

Nowadays over 90 million people speak Italian and around 270 million speakers of French in Europe, South and North America and Africa. Italian and French are spoken in in France, Switzerland, Belgium, Italy, San Marino and other European countries.

French has official status in a wide range of countries in Africa. In Arabic countries of North Africa (mostly Morocco, Tunisia and Algeria) French is the second spoken language. People of Western and Central African countries (Guinea, Ivory Coast, Gabon, Central African Republic, Cameroon, Republic of the Congo, Democratic Republic of the Congo, Togo, Benin, Senegal, Mali, etc.) speak French as their native or second language.

There is a large number of television programs and radio programs broadcasting, countless books, newspapers, magazines and journals are published worldwide in Italian and French.

Furthermore, Italian and French are official languages of the European Union, the United Nations (French), as well as many other international organizations, communities, congresses and conferences.

In conclusion, I would like to thank you for purchasing the book and your interest in it. I hope it will help you improve your languages.

Mikhail Petrunin

ACKNOWLEDGMENTS

I am grateful to my relatives, friends and colleagues for their useful advice and invaluable assistance in the writing of this book.

First of all, I would like to sincerely thank my parents Marina Petrunina and Mikhail Petrunin, as well as my sister Oxana Petrunina for their encouragement and support in this venture.

My special thanks go to my competent reviewers Kai Tang, Peter Mitchell, Ben Hack, Richard Graham, Falonne Placidia Nkounkou Babingui, Julya Veronica Pereira Lazzarotto, Wassila Oudinache, Cristina Becerra Bustamante, Francesco Lubinu, Simona Itro, Pamela Pacheco, T. Adam Forbish, Milagros Miracles and Taísa Crespo, Alexandra Offlaville and Stefania Tantimonaco, for their corrections, remarks and observations, which helped me to avoid many mistakes.

Many more people, my dearest friends Neyri Matos, Lina Benavides, Marina Drotsenko, Nimo Khenissi, Houssem Chaaouri and Taynara Leme offered their kind support in the form of comments, advice and suggested examples.

Despite the care and attention that has been involved into producing this book, there are, undoubtedly, errors, oversights and inaccuracies for which I take full responsibility.

Mikhail Petrunin, 2019

SYMBOLS

> – becomes, changes to

/ – or, alternative forms or meanings

It. – Italian

Fr. – French

Lat. – Latin

Masc. - Masculine

Fem. - Feminine

Pl. - Plural

Cons. - Consonant

INTRODUCTION: ALPHABET

Letter names and Pronunciations

The alphabet of the Romance languages is based on the Latin alphabet with several specific letters. The Italian alphabet has 21 letters and French alphabet includes 26 letters.

Remember that Italian and French pronunciation of some of the letters differ between particular regions and areas. The only way to pronounce and understand Italian and French correctly is to listen and try to copy native speakers.

However, below is the table that shows letters, their names and pronunciation in Italian and French:

\multicolumn{3}{c	}{Italian}	\multicolumn{3}{c}{French}
Letter	Name	Phoneme	Letter	Name	Phoneme
Aa	a	/a/	**Aa**	a	/ɑ/
Bb	bi	/bi/	**Bb**	bé	/be/
Cc	ci	/tʃi/	**Cc**	cé	/se/
Dd	di	/di/	**Dd**	dé	/de/
Ee	e	/e/	**Ee**	e	/ə/

INTRODUCTION: ALPHABET

	Italian			French	
Ff	*effe*	/ˈɛffe/	**Ff**	*effe*	/ɛf/
Gg	*gi*	/dʒi/	**Gg**	*gé*	/ʒe/
Hh	*acca*	/ˈakka/	**Hh**	*ache*	/aʃ/
Ii	*i*	/i/	**Ii**	*i*	/i/
—	—	—	**Jj**	*ji*	/ʒi/
—	—	—	**Kk**	*ka*	/kɑ/
Ll	*elle*	/ˈɛlle/	**Ll**	*elle*	/ɛl/
Mm	*emme*	/ˈɛmme/	**Mm**	*emme*	/ɛm/
Nn	*enne*	/ˈɛnne/	**Nn**	*enne*	/ɛn/
—	—	—	—	—	—
Oo	*o*	/ɔ/	**Oo**	*o*	/o/
Pp	*pi*	/pi/	**Pp**	*pé*	/pe/

INTRODUCTION: ALPHABET

Italian			French		
Qq	cu	/ku/	**Qq**	qu	/ky/
Rr	erre	/ˈɛrre/	**Rr**	erre	/ɛʁ/
Ss	esse	/ˈɛsse/	**Ss**	esse	/ɛs/
Tt	ti	/ti/	**Tt**	té	/te/
Uu	u	/u/	**Uu**	u	/y/
Vv	vi, vu	/vi; vu/	**Vv**	vé	/ve/
—	—	—	**Ww**	double vé	/dubləve/
—	—	—	**Xx**	ixe	/iks/
—	—	—	**Yy**	i grec	/igʁɛk/
Zz	zeta	/dzɛːta/	**Zz**	zède	/zɛd/

NOTE:

Italian

The letters *j*, *k*, *w*, *x* and *y* are used for loanwords and foreign names.

3

French

The letters **w** and **k** are used only in loanwords and regional words.

Digraphs

The Romance languages use digraphs. Digraphs are pairs of letters that symbolize a single sound and are usually not included in the alphabet.

Study the following digraphs that exist in Italian and French:

	Italian	French
Grapheme	sc	ch
Pronuncia-tion	1) /ʃ/ (before -i and -e); 2) /sk/ (before other letters)	/ʃ/
Example	1) **sc**ialo; 2) **sc**alo	**ch**at
English approxima-tion	As the English 1) **sh**ip; 2) **sk**y	As the English **sh**ip
Grapheme	gli	ll
Pronuncia-tion	/ʎ/ (before -i)	/j/

INTRODUCTION: ALPHABET

	Italian	French
Example	mi**gli**ore	bi**ll**e
English approximation	As the English mi**ll**ion	As the English **y**es
Grapheme	**sch**	**qu**
Pronuncia-tion	/k/ (used before i, e)	/k/
Example	**sch**erno	**qu**and
English approximation	As the English **sc**an	As the English **sc**an
Grapheme	**gh**	—
Pronuncia-tion	/g/ (used before i, e)	—
Example	**gh**iro	—
English approximation	As the English a**g**o	—

	Italian	French
Grapheme	gn	gn
Pronuncia-tion	/ɲ/	/ɲ/
Example	guada**gn**are	ga**gn**er
English approxima-tion	As the English can**y**on	As the English can**y**on
Grapheme	—	—
Pronuncia-tion	—	—
Example	—	—
English approxima-tion	—	—

Diacritics

A diacritic (diacritical mark or diacritical sign) is a glyph which is added to a letter.

Below are all the diacritics that are used in Italian and French:

INTRODUCTION: ALPHABET

Diacritics	Italian	French
The acute	é, ó	é
The grave	à, è, ì, ò, ù	à, è, ù
The circumflex		ê
The cedilla		ç
The diaeresis		ë

NOTE:

Italian

In Italian, **the acute** and **the grave** are used to mark a stressed syllable. Moreover, **the acute** can also be used to distinguish between words that are spelled identically, for example: *e* - and; *è* - is.

French

In French, **the grave** indicates the sound /ɛ/ when over *e* - *è*, for instance: **mère** - mother. Also, it can be used to distinguish words that have similar pronunciation, for instance: *a* - has and *à* - to. **The acute** can only be used over é in order to make the sound /e/: **épée** - sword. **The circumflex** normally marks an **s**, which once followed the vowel in Latin. Observe the following: **fête** - party in French used to be festum in Latin. **The cedilla** transforms hard **c** (before the vowels a, o and u) into **ç**, which is pronounced as /s/, for example: **ça** - that. **The diaeresis** means that two adjacent vowels should be pronounced separately (without diaeresis they would be pronounced as one). Study the following: **baïonnette** - bayonet.

INTRODUCTION: ALPHABET

Diphthongs

Diphthong is a combination of two different vowels sounds within the same syllable, for example: **ow [əu]** -> low. Knowing diphthongs will help learners with pronunciation and spelling.

The table below demonstrates diphthongs used in Italian and French:

Italian		French	
Diphthong	Pronunciation	Diphthong	Pronunciation
falling		*diphthongs	
ai	/ai/	ai	/ɛ,e/
au	/au/	au	/o/
ei	/ei/	ei	/ɛ/
eu	/eu/	eu	/œ,ø/
oi	/oi/	oi	/wa/ /wɛ/
—	—	ou	/u,w/
ui	/ui/	ui	/ɥi/ /ɥɛ/
rising		—	—
ia	/ja/	—	—
ie	/je/	ie, iè	/jɛ/ /jɛ/

8

INTRODUCTION: ALPHABET

Italian		French	
io	/jo/	—	—
iu	/ju/	—	—
ua	/wa/	—	—
ue	/we/	—	—
ui	/wi/	—	—
uo	/wo/	—	—
—	—	—	—
—	—	—	—
—	—	—	—
—	—	—	—

NOTE:

French diphthongs are also considered to be vocalic digraphs in some grammar books.

CHAPTER 1: NOUNS

A noun is a word that names a living being, different things or ideas, for instance, man, prosperity, shop.

Gender of Nouns

Latin, as a forefather of modern Romance languages, had three genders, which were masculine, feminine and neuter. After Latin ceased its existence most words that belonged to masculine and feminine retained the same gender later on in French and Italian, although there are still some exceptions. The Latin neuter gender most often became masculine in today's modern Romance languages.

Thus, unlike Latin, the daughter languages, which are Italian and French, ended up having only two genders: masculine and feminine.

Nouns in Italian and French referring to a man, such as brother, son, father, etc., are generally masculine. Those that were associated with a woman, such as sister, daughter, mother, etc., are generally feminine.

Did you know?

Rome is known as the "Eternal city" and also "Caput Mundi", coming from Latin and meaning capital of the world.

However, there is a general rule helping to identify the gender of nouns, as they are classified into gender groups in accordance with their endings. In Italian most nouns that end in *–o* are masculine, and almost all nouns ending in *–a* are feminine.

NOTE:

In French, unlike the above-mentioned languages, it is not so easy to identify gender by noun ending. However, most nouns form their feminine gender by adding –e to the end of the noun (in this case the last consonant is pronounced). To learn gender effectively one should memorize nouns along with their definite article in French.

CHAPTER 1: NOUNS

Below is the table demonstrating masculine and feminine endings in Italian and French:

Italian		French	
masc.	*fem.*	*masc.*	*fem.*
-o	-a	N/A	-e

Example:

	Italian	French	English
masc,	edifici**o**	bâtiment	building
femi.	port**a**	port**e**	door

Nevertheless, this rule has a number of exceptions:

1. Words derived from Greek and ending in *–ma*, *–ta* (in Italian) and *–me*, *–at* (in French), are masculine:

Italian	French	English
l'aroma	l'arôme	*aroma*
il clima	le climat	*climate*
il diagramma	le diagramme	*diagram*
il dilemma	le dilemme	*dilemma*
il diploma	le diplôme	*diploma*
il dogma	le dogme	*dogma*

CHAPTER 1: NOUNS

Italian	French	English
il dramma	le drame	*drama*
l'emblema	l'emblème	*emblem*
l'enigma	*l'énigme	*enigma*
lo schema	le schéma	*scheme*
il fantasma	le fantôme	*ghost*
l'ologramma	le hologramme	*hologram*
l'idioma	l'idiome (le langage)	*language*
il poema	le poème	*poem*
il poeta	le poète	*poet*
il problema	le problème	*problem*
il programma	le programme	*program*
il sintomo	le symptôme	*symptom*
il sistema	le système	*system*
il telegramma	le télégramme	*telegram*
il tema	le thème	*theme/topic*

CHAPTER 1: NOUNS

Italian	French	English
il trauma	le trauma	trauma

NOTE:

In French the noun **l'énigme** is feminine. Such French words as **map** and **planet** are <u>feminine</u> (Fr. **la carte** – map, **la planète** – planet). While **day** and **sofa** are <u>masculine</u> (Fr. **le jour** – day, **le sofa** – sofa).

In Italian the word **map** is feminine (It. **la mappa** – map), whereas **day**, **sofa** and **planet** are <u>masculine</u>: (It. **il giorno** – day, It. **il sofa** – sofa, **il pianeta** – planet).

1. Several nouns ending in **–o** or a **consonant** are <u>feminine</u> in Italian and French:

It. la ma**no**, Fr. la mai**n** – hand;

It. la mo**to**, Fr. la mo**to** – motorcycle;

It. la fo**to**, Fr. la pho**to** – photograph;

It. la ra**dio**, Fr. la ra**dio** — radio.

Italian and French nouns that end in **–e** or a **consonant** are <u>either gender</u>. This is mainly owing to the fact that there is a vast number of both masculine and feminine nouns that end in **–e** or a **consonant**. Below are examples of some common masculine and feminine nouns ending in **–e** or a **consonant**.

For instance, the following words ending in **–e** or **consonant** (**l**, **r**, **s(-i)**, **n**, **m**, **d**) are <u>masculine</u>:

Italian	French	English
il caff**è**	le caf**é**	coffee
il pon**te**	le pont	bridge

CHAPTER 1: NOUNS

Italian	French	English
il mese	le mois	*month*
l'animale	l'animal	*animal*
il paese	le pays	*country*
il piede	le pied	*foot*
il mare	*<u>la mer</u>	*sea*

NOTE:
In French the noun **la mer** is <u>feminine</u>.

Conversely, the following nouns that end in **–e** or **consonant** (**l, r, s(-i), n, m, d**) are <u>feminine</u>:

Italian	French	English
la base	la base	*base*
la classe	la classe	*class*
la fame	la faim	*hunger*
la morte	*<u>la mort</u>	*death*
la notte	*<u>la nuit</u>	*night*
la parte	la partie	*part*
la crisi	la crise	*crisis*
l'ellissi	l'ellipse	*ellipsis*
la tesi	la thèse	*thesis*
la carne	la viande	*meat*
*<u>il fiore</u>	la fleur	*flower*

CHAPTER 1: NOUNS

NOTE:

In Italian the noun **il fiore** is <u>masculine</u>. Even though French nouns **la mort** and **la nuit** end in **t**, they retain the <u>feminine</u>.

The above demonstrates that French words ending in **–e** are mostly <u>feminine</u>, which proves the general rule.

Nouns having the following endings, which are predominantly common and typical for Italian and French, are usually <u>masculine</u>:

Italian	French
-o (il vento)	N/A (le vent)
-ismo (il giornalismo)	**-isme** (le journalisme)
-asmo (el sarcasmo)	**-asme** (le sarcasme)
-ment, -mento (il momento)	**-ment** (le moment)
-ale (il generale)	**-al** (le général)
-acolo (lo spettacolo)	**-acle** (le spectacle)
-ino (il giardino)	**-in** (le jardin)
-on, -one (il camion, il limone)	**-on** (le camion, le citron)
-age (il garage)	**-age** (le garage)
-ore (l'interruttore)	**-eur** (l'interrupteur)

The French system of noun flexion is considered to be more difficult than similar one of Italian. It is worth considering the endings

CHAPTER 1: NOUNS

that refer to masculine gender in French: **-eau, -ier, -teur, -ail, -ard, -as, -at, -et, -is, -on, -aire, -oir.**

Nouns with the following endings are usually *feminine*:

Italian	French
-zione, -sione (produzione, formazione, decisione)	**-tion, -sion** (production, formation, décision)
-tù, -tà (verità, virtù)	**-té, -tude** (vérité, certitude)
-ce (pace, voce)	**-x** (paix, voix)
-enza (conoscenza, concorrenza)	**-ance, -ence** (connaissance, concurrence)
-cie (specie)	**-èce** (espèce)

Forming the Feminine

Did you know?

France is the largest country in the EU (almost 1/5th of the total EU area) and known as "the hexagon" (Fr. l'hexagone) because of its six-sided shape.

Most Italian nouns that end in – **o** form their feminine by changing the ending into **–a**. The French feminine is formed by changing endings into **–e**.

Nouns ending in a consonant form the feminine by adding **–a** in Italian and **–e** in French.

The table shows the ways of forming the feminine in Italian and French.

Italian		French	
masc.	*fem.*	*masc.*	*fem.*

CHAPTER 1: NOUNS

Italian		French	
-o	-a	N\A	-e
-cons.	+a	-cons.	+e

It is extremely important to pay particular attention to the formation of the feminine in French, as it requires the alteration of a noun stem.

Masculine	*Feminine*
-eur un dans**eur** - *danser*	**-euse** une dans**euse** - *danser*
-teur un institu**teur** - *teacher*	**-trice** une institu**trice** - *teacher*
-f un veu**f** - *widower*	**-ve** une veu**ve** - *widow*
-x un épou**x** - *spouse*	**-se** une épou**se** - *spouse*
-eau un jum**eau** - *twin*	**-elle** une jum**elle** - *twin*
-t un chat - *cat (male)*	**-tte** une cha**tte** - *cat (female)*
-er, -ier un écol**ier** - *schoolchild*	**-ière** une écol**ière** - *schoolchild*

NOTE:

In French nasal vowels that end in **-en, -ien, -on, -ion, -an** stop being so, and while forming the feminine the final consonant doubles: **-nne** (ex. Fr, le ch**ien** - la ch**ienne** - *dog - bitch*).

We can see from the table that French differs in terms of forming the feminine of nouns from the other three Roman languages.

Many words designating titles and professions form the feminine gender by the use of typically feminine endings: It. **-essa, -ina, -trice**; Fr. **-esse, -ïne, -trice, -teuse**.

CHAPTER 1: NOUNS

Duke– Duchess

It. (*-essa*) il duca – la duch*essa*;
Fr. (*-esse*) le duc – la duch*esse*.

Hero - Heroine

It. (*-ina*) l'eroe – l'ero*ina*;
Fr. (*-ïne*) l'héros – l'héro*ïne*.

Actor - Actress

It. (*-trice*) l'attore – l'at*trice*;
Fr. (*-trice*) l'acteur – l'ac*trice*.

Poet - Poetess

It. (*-essa*) il poeta – la poet*essa*;
Fr. (*-esse*) le poète – la poét*esse*.

There are also pairs of words denoting male and female:

Italian	French	English
l'uomo	l'homme	*man*
la donna	la femme	*woman*
il marito	le mari	*husband*
la sposa	l'épouse	*wife*
il ragazzo	le garçon	*boy*
la ragazza	la fille	*girl*
il padre	le père	*father*
la madre	la mère	*mother*
la regina	la reine	*queen*
il cavallo	le cheval	*horse*
la giumenta	la jument	*mare*
il toro	le taureau	*bull*
la vacca	la vache	*cow*

CHAPTER 1: NOUNS

Italian	French	English
il montone	le mouton	ram
la pecora	la brebis	ewe
il gallo	le coq	cockerel, rooster
la gallina	la poule	hen

Plural Forms of Nouns

Did you know?

Italian isn't only spoken in Italy. It has official or co-official status in Switzerland, San Marino, the Vatican City and Slovenia.

Most French nouns form their plural by adding an **-s**. In Italian, nouns form the plural by changing the masculine ending **-o** to **-i**, and the feminine ending **-a** is changed to **-e**. There are also some nouns ending in **-e**. The plural forms of these nouns is formed by changing the **-e** to **-i** (regardless of the gender).

	Italian	French
masculine singular	libr**o**	livre
masculine plural	libr**i**	livre**s**
feminine singular	pagin**a**	pag**e**
feminine plural	pagin**e**	page**s**

Besides the general rules presented the above, there are also other ways of forming the plural in Italian and French. Each of these considered Romance languages has its special cases of forming the plural, which require particular consideration, as this phenomenon significantly distinguishes one from the other without leaving any possibility of simultaneous comparison.

CHAPTER 1: NOUNS

Special Cases of Forming the Plural Nouns

Italian

The Italian language also has various peculiarities while forming noun plurals. It is necessary to consider them as it prevents the learners from spelling and grammatical mistakes.

- There are many nouns ending in *–ista* that refer to professions. If these nouns refer to a man they take the ending *–isti* in the plural and when they refer to a woman these nouns end in *–iste* in the plural. Below are the examples demonstrating this rule:

Masculine	Feminine
Il giornal*ista* – i giornal*isti*	la giornal*ista* – le giornal*iste*
Il dent*ista* – i dent*isti*	la dent*ista* – le dent*iste*
il farmac*ista* – i farmac*isti*	la farmac*ista* – le farmac*iste*

- Nouns ending in *–ca* and *–ga* form their plural in *–chi* and *–ghi* if masculine, in *–che* and *–ghe* if feminine, thus retaining the velar consonant \k\ and \g\ of the singular.

Masculine	Feminine
Il monar*ca* – i monar*chi* – monarch	la bar*ca* – le bar*che* – boat
Il patriar*ca* – i patriar*chi* – patriarch	la basili*ca* – le basili*che* - basilica
	l'ami*ca* – le ami*che* – friend
il colle*ga* – i colle*ghi* – colleague	la mos*ca* – le mos*che* – fly
lo strate*ga* – gli strate*ghi* - strategist	la pes*ca* – le pes*che* - peach

NOTE:

In Italian **Belga** *(the Belgian) loses the hard sound in the masculine plural:* **Belgi**; *but keeps it in the feminine:* **Belghe**.

CHAPTER 1: NOUNS

- Feminine nouns that end in *–cia* and *–gia* (with an unstressed *i*) form their plural in *–ce* and *–ge*.

> **Did you know?**
>
> *Kinshasa (12 million) is the world's largest French speaking city, ahead of Paris (over 11 million), Abidjan (4.8 million) and Montréal (3.6 million).*

la bo**cia** – le bo**cce** – carafe

la do**ccia** – le do**cce** – shower

la pio**ggia** – le pio**gge** – rain

la provin**cia** – le provin**ce** – province

la vali**gia** – le vali**ge** – suitcase

- Nouns ending in *-cia* and *-gia* (with a stressed *i*) form regular plurals with *-cie* and *-gie*:

la farma**cia** – le farma**cie** – drugstore

la s**cia** – le s**cie** – trail

la bu**gia** – le bu**gie** – lie

l'aller**gia** – le aller**gie** – allergy

Below is a table showing the summarized information for the three previous rules of forming the plural:

Singular	Plural	
	masc.	*fem.*
-co, -go (masc.); -ca, -ga (fem.)	-chi, -ghi	-che, -ghe
-cia, -gia (*i* unstressed)		–ce, –ge
-cìa, -gìa (*i* stressed)		-cìe, -gìe

- Some masculine and feminine nouns that end with a stressed vowel do not alter in the plural:

Did you know?

The highest peak in Europe is located in Italy. Monte Bianco (White Mountain) is 15,771 feet high and is part of the Alps.

la città - le città – *city*

la tribù – le tribù – *tribe*

la verità – le verità - *truth*

la virtù – le virtù – *virtue*

l'università – le università – *university*

French

The plural determinant of the Romance languages is the morpheme **−s** for all the nouns. However, since in modern French the ending **−s** is not pronounced at all, the formation of the plural involves by vowel gradation or change of phonetic form of determiners.

The table below shows the divergent ways of forming the plural of nouns.

Singular	Plural	Example
-eu	**-x**	un j**eu** - des jeu**x** (*game - games*)
-eau		un tabl**eau** - des tableau**x** (*picture - pictures*)
-au		un noy**au** - des noyau**x** (*kernel - kernels*)
-al	**-aux**	un journ**al** - des journ**aux** (*newspaper - newspapers*)
-ail		un trav**ail** - des trav**aux** (*work - works*)

NOTE:

Some nouns ending in **-eu, -al, -ail** form their plural by adding **-s**:

un pn**eu** - des pneu**s** (*tyre - tyres*)

un b**al** - des bal**s** (*ball - balls*)

CHAPTER 1: NOUNS

un év**ail** - des év**ails** (fan - fans)
un carn**al** - des carn**als** (carnival - carnival)
un fest**al** - des fest**als** (festival - festivals)
un r**ail** - des r**ails** (rail - rails)

Nouns which are always Plural

Did you know?

French is the second most spoken language in Europe, after German and before English, and is expected to become number one by 2030 owing to the country's high birth rate.

Despite the fact that Italian and French have a number of divergent ways of forming the plural of nouns, they still combine convergent ways of using nouns.

In Italian and French there is a wide range of nouns that are used in the plural only and do not have their singular forms:

Italian	French	English
i dintorni	les environs	surroundings
le carabattole	les biens	belongings
gli annali	les annales	annals
gli occhiali	les lunettes	glasses
i ferri	les fers	shackles
i dolciumi	les douceurs	sweeties
i pantaloni	les pantalons	pants

NOTE:

In French, **les pantalons** (pants) can be used in the singular form as well, for example: **le pantalon**.

CHAPTER 1: NOUNS

Nouns which are always Singular

There is also a range of nouns that are used in the singular. They are:

A. **Proper names**: Juan, María, el Nevá, Moscú, España.

B. **Corners of the earth and things that are the only ones in their way**:

Italian	French	English
il sud	le sud	*south*
il nord	le nord	*north*
l'orizzonte	l'horizon	*horizon*
il sole	le soleil	*sun*
la luna	la lune	*moon*

C. **Matters, materials and precious metal**:

Italian	French	English
l'oro	l'or	*gold*
il latte	le lait	*milk*
il pane	le pain	*bread*
il carbone	le charbon	*coal*

D. **Abstract conceptions, human qualities**:

Italian	French	English
l'esistenza	l'existence	*existence*
l'allegria	l'allégresse	*joy*
l'orgoglio	l'orgueil	*pride*

E. **Collective nouns:**

Italian	French	English
il popolo, la gente	le peuple	people, nation
*i soldi	l'argent	money
la gioventù	la jeunesse	youth, young people

NOTE:
In Italian **i soldi** is used in plural.

F. **Some nouns that usually have the suffix –*ismo* meaning scientific, political, literary, etc. directions, names of sciences and religions:**

Italian	French	English
l'impressionismo	l'impressionnisme	impressionism
la logica	la logique	logic
il buddismo	le bouddhisme	buddhism
la medicina	la médecine	medicine

CHAPTER 2: ADJECTIVES

An adjective is a word that describes a person or thing, such as their size, shape, appearance, colour and other qualities, for instance, big, round, beautiful, red.

Gender of Adjectives

Did you know?

Italian is the fourth most studied foreign language in the United States after Spanish, French and German.

Unlike in English, in Italian and French adjectives usually agree with nouns in gender and number. Just like nouns, masculine forms of adjectives in Italian end in *–o*, and those of feminine have the ending *–a*. In French, in comparison with above-mentioned languages, it is not so easy to identify gender by adjective ending. However, most adjectives form their feminine gender by adding *–e* to the end of the adjective (in this case last consonant is pronounced).

Below is the table demonstrating the endings of adjectives and some examples supporting the rule.

Italian		French	
masc.	*fem.*	*masc.*	*fem.*
-o	-a	N\A	-e
Ex. It. bianc**o**	Ex. It. bianc**a**	Ex. Fr. blanc	Ex. Fr. blanch**e**
(*white*)	(*white*)	(*white*)	(*white*)

It should be noted that adjectives in Romance languages are usually placed after the noun rather than before.

Masculine (singular)	**Feminine (singular)**
It. il libro ***nero***, Fr. le livre ***noir*** – ***black*** book.	It. la casa ***bianca***, Fr. la maison ***blanche*** – ***white*** house.

CHAPTER 2: ADJECTIVES

Forming the Feminine

> *Did you know?*
>
> French is a working language of the UN, the EU, NATO, the International Red Cross, the African Union, the Arab League and other international organizations.

Just like nouns, Italian adjectives ending in −*o* form their feminine by changing the ending into −*a*. French feminine is formed by changing endings into −*e*. Nouns ending in consonant form the feminine by adding −*a* in Italian and −*e* in French.

However, it is extremely important to give particular attention to the formation of the feminine in French, as there are some special ways of forming it.

French

A. Adjectives that end in -*on*, -*en*, -*el*, -*eil*, -*il*, -*et*, and in -*s* double the final consonant before adding -*e*:

Masculine	*Feminine*	
b**on**	b**onne**	*good*
parisi**en**	parisi**enne**	*Parisian*
cru**el**	cru**elle**	*cruel*
par**eil**	par**eille**	*similar*
gent**il**	gent**ille**	*nice*
mu**et**	mu**ette**	*silent*
gro**s**	gro**sse**	*big, fat*

B. Adjectives that end in −*et* alter their −*et* to −*ète* in order to form the feminine:

Masculine   *Feminine*

CHAPTER 2: ADJECTIVES

compl**et**	compl**ète**	*complete*
discr**et**	discr**ète**	*discreet*
secr**et**	secr**ète**	*secret*

Exception

prêt	prête	*ready*

C. Adjectives that end in **–er** change their **–er** to **–ère** in order to form the feminine:

Masculine	*Feminine*	
ch**er**	ch**ère**	*dear, expensive*
derni**er**	derni**ère**	*last*
enti**er**	enti**ère**	*entire*
fi**er**	fi**ère**	*proud*
premi**er**	premi**ère**	*first*

D. Adjectives that end in **–x** change the **–x** to **–se** while forming the feminine:

Masculine	*Feminine*	
amoureu**x**	amoureu**se**	*in love*
courageu**x**	courageu**se**	*courageous*
curieu**x**	curieu**se**	*curious*
ennuyeu**x**	ennuyeu**se**	*boring*
heureu**x**	heureu**se**	*happy*
jalou**x**	jalou**se**	*jealous*
sérieu**x**	sérieu**se**	*serious*
dou**x**	*douce	*sweet*

rou**x**	rou**sse**	*reddish brown*
fau**x**	fau**sse**	*false*

> **NOTE:**
> Remember that the word **doux** is **douce** in the feminine.

E. Adjectives that end in **–eur** usually form their feminine by changing the **–eur** to **–euse** if such adjectives are derived from verbs. Otherwise the ending is **–rice**:

Masculine	*Feminine*	
ment**eur**	ment**euse**	*lying*
flatt**eur**	flatt**euse**	*flattering*
tromp**eur**	tromp**euse**	*deceitful*
act**eur**	act**rice**	*acting*
protect**eur**	protect**rice**	*protecting*

Exception

antéri**eur**	antéri**eure**	*anterior*
extéri**eur**	extéri**eure**	*exterior*
meill**eur**	meill**eure**	*better, best*
maj**eur**	maj**eure**	*major*
min**eur**	min**eure**	*minor*
supéri**eur**	supéri**eure**	*superior*

> **NOTE:**
> The exception words form the feminine according to the general rule of forming the feminine by adding **-e** to the masculine.

F. Adjectives that end in *–f* in the masculine alter their *–f* to *–ve* in order to form the feminine:

Masculine	Feminine	
acti*f*	acti*ve*	*active*
attenti*f*	attenti*ve*	*attentive*
br*ef*	brè*ve*	*brief*
neu*f*	neu*ve*	*new*
sporti*f*	sporti*ve*	*athletic*
vi*f*	vi*ve*	*alive*

G. Adjectives ending in *–c* change their *–c* to *–che* in order to form the feminine:

Masculine	Feminine	
blan*c*	blan*che*	*white*
fran*c*	fran*che*	*frank*
se*c*	sè*che*	*dry*

Exception

gre*c*	grec*que*	*Greek*
public	publi*que*	*public*

NOTE:
The exception words add the ending **-que** *to the masculine in order form the feminine.*

H. Irregular adjective which are different in the feminine:

Masculine	Feminine

30

CHAPTER 2: ADJECTIVES

long	longue	*long*
favori	favorite	*favorite*
malin	maline	*sly*
frais	fraîche	*fresh*
beau	belle	*beautiful*

Plural Forms of Adjectives

French adjectives form their plural in the same way as nouns i.e. by adding an *–s*. In Italian adjectives form the plural by changing the masculine ending *–o* to *–i*, and the feminine ending *–a* is changed to *–e*. There are also some nouns ending in *–e*. The plural forms of these nouns is formed be changing the *–e* to *–i*.

Masculine (plural)	**Feminine (plural)**
It. i libr*i* ner*i*, Fr. les livre*s* noir*s*. – black *books*.	It. le cas*e* bianch*e*, Fr. les maison*s* blanch*es* – white *houses*.

Did you know?

About 60 million tourists a year visit Italy. Tourism is essential to Italy's economy and provides around 60% of the country's national income.

Below is the comparative table demonstrating similarity of masculine and feminine endings along with the singular and plural number of adjective in Italian and French languages.

Endings of masculine and feminine gender and singular and plural number of adjectives in Romance languages.

	Spanish		Portuguese		Italian		French	
	masc.	*fem.*	*masc.*	*fem.*	*masc.*	*fem.*	*masc.*	*fem.*

CHAPTER 2: ADJECTIVES

	Spanish		Portuguese		Italian		French	
Singular	-o	-a	-o	-a	-o, -e	-a	N\A	-e
Plural	-s	-s	-s	-s	-i	-e	-s	-s

Besides general rules presented the above, there are also other ways (special cases) of forming the plural of adjective in Italian and French, which tend to follow the same rules as nouns (**See p.19**).

Peculiarities of Adjective Use

Italian and French have similar grammatical rules of adjective use.

- As it has been mentioned before, adjectives, as a rule, are placed after a noun. However, some adjectives can be placed before a noun. Here are the most common adjectives:

Italian	French	English
bello	beau, joli	*beautiful*
giovane	jeune	*young*
vecchio	vieux	*old*
piccolo	petit	*small, little*
ricco	riche	*rich*

Study the following:

It. Una **bella** casa;

Fr. Une **belle** maison.

- A **beautiful** house

CHAPTER 2: ADJECTIVES

- Some adjectives have different lexical meanings depending on their position to the noun (before/after). Let us consider the most common of them:

It. **grande**, Fr. **grand**:

(It. *grande*, Fr. *grand*) + noun = *great*;

noun + (It. *grande*, Fr. *grand*) = *big*

Did you know?

France uses the most time zones in the world. Including all the territories and areas it stretches over 12 different time zones. These areas include Martinique, Guadeloupe, French Polynesia, French Guyana, Reunion and New Caledonia.

It. **buono**, Fr. **bon**:

(It. *buono*, Fr. *bon*) + noun = *kind*;

noun + (It. *buono*, Fr. *bon*) = *good*

It. **malo, cattivo**, Fr. **mauvais**:

(It. *malo, cattivo*, Fr. *mauvais*) + noun = *wrong*;

noun + (It. *malo, cattivo*, Fr. *mauvais*) = *bad*

It. **nuovo**, Fr. **nouveau**:

(It. *nuovo*, Fr. *nouveau*) + noun = *recently got*;

noun. + (It. *nuovo*, Fr. *nouveau*) = *brand-new*

It. **povero**, Fr. **pauvre**:

(It. *povero*, Fr. *pauvre*) + noun = *unfortunate, miserable*;

noun + (It. *povero*, Fr. *pauvre*) = *poor*

It. **vero**, Fr. **honnête, vrai**:

CHAPTER 2: ADJECTIVES

(It. *vero*, Fr. *honnête*, *vrai*) + noun = *real*;

noun + (It. *vero*, Fr. *honnête*, *vrai*) = *true*.

- There are patterns that substitute relative adjectives in Italian and French languages and consist of preposition Fr. *de*, *à*; It. *di*, *a* + **noun** (prepositions It. *in* and Fr. *en* are also used in this way) and which designate material, phenomenon and etc. They are used without an article:

It. una casa **di legno**,

Fr. une maison **en bois**

– **wooden** house,

It. una moneta **d'oro**,

Fr. une pièce **d'or**

– **golden** coin.

It is also possible to combine the preposition Fr. **de** and It. **di** with other parts of speech meaning relative adjective:

Did you know?

The capital city of Italy - Rome is over 3000 years old.

It. il giornale **di ieri**,

Fr. le journal **d'hier**

– **yesterday's** newspaper.

- In Italian there are adjectives with shortened forms.

In Italian the adjectives **bello** (*beautiful, handsome*), **grande** (*big*), **buono** (*good*) and **nessuno** (*no, not one*) get shortened forms before a noun.

Italian **Bello**

Gender (before nouns beginning with)	Singular	Plural
Masc. consonant	**bel** (il bel ragazzo)	**bei** (i bei ragazzi)
Masc. z, s plus consonant	**bello** (il bello zio)	**begli** (i begli zii)
Masc. vowel	**bell'** (il bell'uomo)	**begli** (i begli uomini)
Fem. consonant	**bella** (la bella zia)	**belle** (le belle zie)
Fem. vowel	**bell'** (la bell'estate)	**belle** (le belle amiche)

NOTE:
Remember that the word **belli** should be used when the adjective follows the noun:

It. gli zii **belli**,

gli uomini **belli**

Italian **Grande**

In Italian the adjective *grande* can be shortened to *gran* before *masculine* and *feminine* nouns beginning with a **consonant** other than **z**, **s** plus a **consonant** and **ps**. With those that begin with **z**, **s** plus a **consonant**, **ps** or a **vowel**, *grande* is used.

Masculine	Feminine
un **gran** signore – *a great gentleman*	una **gran** signora – *a great lady*
un **grande** zio – *a great uncle*	una **grande** zia – *a great aunt*
un **grande** studente – *a great student*	una *grande* studentessa – *a great student*

un *grande* psichiatra – *a great psychiatrist*	una *grande* psichiatra – *a great psychiatrist*
un *grande* artista – *a great artist*	una *grande* artista – *a great artist*

However, the adjective **grande** becomes **grand'** before a masculine noun that begin with **u**: **un grand'uomo** – *a great man*.

Italian **Buono** and **Nessuno**

Buono and *nessuno* are usually shortened to *buon* and *nessun* before all *masculine* nouns except those that begin with **z**, **s** plus a **consonant** or **ps**. *Buona* and *nessuna* which are feminine forms are used with all *feminine* nouns that begin with a **consonant**. Forms **buon'** and **nessun'** are used before *feminine* nouns starting with a vowel. **Nessuno** has no plural forms. **Buono** and **buona** have the following plural forms: **buoni, buone**.

Masculine	Feminine
un **buono** zio - *a kind uncle*	una **buona** zia - *a kind aunt*
un **buon** ragazzo - *a kind boy*	una **buona** ragazza - *a kind girl*
un **buon** amico - *a good friend*	una **buon'**amica - *a good friend*

CHAPTER 3: ADVERBS

An adverb is a word that can be used with verbs, adjectives or other adverbs giving more information about where, when, how, or in what circumstances something happens, for instance, there, yesterday, suddenly, excellently.

Use of Adverbs

Generally speaking, adverbs are used with:

- verbs (run quickly, speak loudly, laugh happily),
- adjectives (rather boring, gravely ill, immensely glad),
- other adverbs (too slowly, very well, really fast)

Forming Adverbs from Adjectives. Adverbs Ending in -mente (-ment)

Did you know?

Among the many inventions that have changed the world some notable ones are French. They are the hot air balloon, pasteurizer, stethoscope, and the parachute.

In English adverbs are usually formed by adding –*ly* to the end of the adjective (happy – happily). In Romance languages many adverbs of manner are formed with the suffix –*mente* (in Italian) and –*ment* (in French). This suffix originated from the Latin suffix of the feminine gender *mens* (-*mente* in instrumental case). Thus, the modern suffix –*mente* (–*ment*) inherited its compatibility with the feminine adjectives. Also, unlike adjectives, adverbs are invariable which means that they do not vary according to the gender, number or person of the word that they are modifying.

Therefore, in Italian many adverbs end in –*mente* (in French – *ment*). This is usually added to the end of the feminine singular form of the adjective.

Below is the table demonstrating the examples of adverb forming from the adjectives.

Italian	French	English
lento(-*a*) = lent**a**mente	lent(-*e*) = lent**e**ment	slow = slow**ly**
rapido(-*a*) = rapid**a**mente	rapide = rapid**e**ment	quick = quick**ly**

Peculiarities of Adverb Use

It is also worth mentioning the peculiarities of adverb formation.

Did you know?

Italian is considered the universal language of classic music, with numerous loanwords such as a capella, maestro, orchestra and soprano.

French

French adjectives ending in a vowel rather than **−e**, drop the feminine ending **−e** and add **−ment** while forming the adverb: ***vrai*** (masc.) − ***vraie*** (fem.) − *true* = ***vraiment*** (*truly*).

French adjectives, which end in **−ant** and **−ent** (except lent and present), change **nt** to **m** and add **−ment** to the adverb: **constant − constamment** (*constant − constantly*); **récent − récemment** (*recent − recently*).

Italian

In Italian language adjectives ending in **−le** or **−re** before a **vowel**, drop the vowel **−e** and add **−ment**: *facile − facilmente* (*easy − easily*).

Other Adverbs

Adverbs of manner

There are some common adverbs of manner which tell us how something is done.

Italian	French	English
bene	bien	*well*
male	mal	*badly/poorly*
così	ainsi	*thus*
presto	vite	*quickly*
adagio	lentement	*slowly*
meglio	mieux	*better*
peggio	pire	*worse*

Adverbs of place

Italian	French	English
qui	ici, là	*here*
là, lì; ci, vi, colà	là, là-bas	*there*
vicino, appresso	près	*near*
lontano	loin	*far*
di fronte	en face de	*in front of*
(di)dietro, indietro	en arrière, par derrière	*behind*
in alto, (di) sopra	en haut, au-dessus	*above*
in alto, (di) sopra	en haut	*on*
sopra	par-dessus, par en haut	*over*

Italian	French	English
sotto, (in) giù, verso il basso	en bas	*below*
giu, (di) sotto, in basso	en dessous	*under*
(al di) dentro, all'interno	dedans, à l'intérieur	*in, inside*
fuori, all'esterno	dehors, à l'extérieur	*out, outside*
dove	où	*where*
da qualche parte	quelque part	*somewhere*

Adverbs of time

Italian	French	English
oggi	aujourd'hui	*today*
ieri	hier	*yesterday*
domani	demain	*tomorrow*
ora, adesso	maintenant	*now*
prima	avant	*before*
dopo, poi	puis, après, ensuite	*after, later*
presto	tôt	*early*
tardi	tard	*late*
allora	alors	*then*
già	déjà	*already*

Italian	French	English
ancora	encore	*yet, still*
infine	enfin; à la fin	*at last*
sempre	toujours	*always, still*
mai	jamais	*never*
qualche volta, a volte, di tanto in tanto	parfois, de temps en temps	*sometimes, once in a while*

Adverbs of intensity

Italian	French	English
poco, un poco, un po'	un peu	*a little*
molto	très	*very*
più	plus	*more*
meno	moins	*less*
troppo	trop	*too much*
tanto	autant	*as much*
così, tanto	tellement, tant	*so much/many*
abbastanza	assez	*enough*
quasi	presque	*almost*
quanto	combien	*how much*

Adverbs of doubt

Italian	French	English
forse	peut être	*perhaps, maybe*
per caso	par hasard	*by chance*
possibilmente	possiblement	*possibly*
probabilmente	probablement	*probably*

Adverbs expressing affirmation

Italian	French	English
certamente	certainement	*certainly*
realmente, effettivamente	réellement, effectivement	*really*
esattamente	exactement	*exactly*

Adverbs expressing exclusion

Italian	French	English
solo, solamente	seulement	*only*
unicamente	uniquement	*merely*
semplicemente	simplement	*simply*
appena	à peine	*hardly, just*

Adverbs composed of several words

Adverbs can also consist of more than one word, for example:

It. *senza dubbio*,

Fr. *sans aucun doute*

– *without a doubt.*

Adverbial phrases

There are some fixed phrases which have an adverbial function. Below are some common ones:

Italian	French	English
alla cieca	à l'aveuglette	*blindly/in the dark*
sul serio	au sérieux	*take seriously*
a piedi	à pied	*on foot*
a mano	à la main	*by/at hand*
in segreto	en secret	*in secret*

It is also possible to build such phrases by using the following constructions:

Italian	French
con + abstract noun	**avec** + abstract noun
di\in maniera + adjective	**de manière** + adjective
di modo + adjective	**de mode** + adjective
di forma + adjective	**de forme** + adjective

Italian	French
di carattere + adjective	**de caractère** + adjective

Examples:

It. Lo fa **con** gioia,

Fr. Il le fait ***avec*** joie.

- *He does it with joy.*

It. Lei parla ***in maniera*** formale,

Fr. Elle parle ***de manière*** formelle.

- *She speaks in a formal manner.*

Position of Adverbs

In English adverbs can be put in different places in a sentence. In Romance languages adverbs follow verbs or are placed before the adjective.

Did you know?

French is taught in every country of the world, with around 100 million students.

It. Lui lavora **molto**;

Fr. Il travaille **beaucoup**.

- *He works **a lot**.*

It. Lei mangia **poco**;

Fr. Elle mange **peu**.

- *She eats **a little**.*

However, in French such short and common adverbs as **bien**, **assez**, **beaucoup**, **déjà**, **encore**, **enfin**, **jamais**, **mieux**, **toujours**,

***trop*, *vite*,** etc., are placed between auxiliary verb and past participle (Fr. Elle a **bien** chanté – *She sang well*).

Comparison of Adjectives and Adverbs

Did you know?

The first violin appeared in Italy in the 1500s in Cremona. The city later became the home of Antonio Stradivari (1644-1737), the most famous of violin-makers.

Comparative constructions are mainly used to convey inequality or equality. Comparison of adjectives and adverbs in English usually uses the *–er* form, where it is added to the end of the adverb or adjective, or *more* or *less* in front of them, for instance shorter, longer, more/less intelligent.

The superlative degree of comparison of adverbs and adjectives in English has *–est* attached to the end of them or *most* or *least* in front of them, for instance the shortest, the longest, the most/the least intelligent.

Like in English, in Romance languages there are also different degrees of comparison which are comparative and superlative. In Italian there also exists absolute superlative degree of comparison.

Below is the table that demonstrates comparative constructions of Romance languages:

Italian	French	English
The Comparative		
così/tanto...come/ quanto (È **così** intelligente **come** me.)	**aussi...que** (Il est **aussi** intelligent **que** moi.)	*as...as* (*He is as intelligent as I am.*)
più... di/che (Questo libro è **più** interessante **di** quello)	**plus...que** (Ce livre est **plus** intéressant **que** celui-là.)	*more...than* (*This book is more interesting than that one*)

CHAPTER 3: ADVERBS

Italian	French	English
meno...di/che	**moins...que**	*less...than*
(Questo vestito è **meno** bello **di** quello)	(Cette robe est **moins** belle **que** celle-là)	*(This dress is less beautiful than that one.)*

The superlative of an adjective and adverb is usually formed by adding the definite article to the comparative form. In such construction the preposition (It. *di*, Fr. *de*) is used and follows the superlative when it means *in*.

Italian	French	English
The Superlative		
il/la/i/le più...(di)	**le/la/les plus...(de)**	*the most*
(Questo ragazzo è **il più** intelligente **della** classe)	(Ce garçon est **le plus** intelligent **de** la classe)	*(This boy is the most intelligent in the class)*
il/la/i/le meno...(di)	**le/la/les moins...(de)**	*the least*
(Questo ragazzo è **il meno** intelligente **della** classe)	(Ce garçon est **le moins** intelligent **de** la classe)	*(This boy is the least intelligent in the class)*

As mentioned before, Italian also have the absolute superlative degree of comparison. The absolute superlative is usually formed by adding the suffix It. *–issimo* to an adjective or an adverb after dropping the last vowel. This conveys the meaning of *most*, *very* and *extremely*.

Italian	English
bello – bell**issimo**	*handsome – most handsome*
intelligente – intelligent**issimo**	*intelligent – extremely intelligent*
bene – ben**issimo**	*well – very well*
male – mal**issimo**	*badly – very badly*

However, in Italian, there are some spelling changes while adding the suffix *–issimo*.

Italian:

1. the endings *–co*, *–go*, and *–ga* must add **h** to the adjective before adding *–issimo* in order to preserve the hard sound:

    stan**co** – stanch**issimo** - *tired - the most tired*;

    lar**go** – largh**issimo** - *large - the largest.*

    However, superlatives can also be made by placing an appropriate adverb before the adjective:

    It. Peter è **molto** gentile

    – Peter is **very** polite.

Very (It. **molto**, Fr. **très**) is one of the most common adverbs used in sentences, but below is the list of other adverbs which can definitely help you enrich your language.

Italian	French	English
abbastanza	assez	*enough*
eccezionalmente	exceptionnellement	*exceptionally*
eccessivamente	excessivement	*excessively*
straordinariamente	extraordinairement	*extraordinarily*
estremamente	extrêmement	*extremely*
grandemente	grandement	*greatly*
immensamente	immensément	*immensely*
terribilmente	terriblement	terribly

Irregular Comparatives and Superlatives

There are some adjectives and adverbs which have irregular forms for the comparative and superlative. Below is the table presenting the most common of them:

Forms	Italian	French	English
Adjectives			
positive	buono	bon	*good*
comparative	migliore	meilleur	*better*
superlative	il migliore	le meilleur	*the best*
absolute	ottimo	N\A	*very good*
positive	cattivo	mauvais	*bad*
comparative	peggiore	pire	*worse*
superlative	il peggiore	le pire	*the worst*
absolute	pessimo	N\A	*very bad*
positive	grande	grand	*big*
comparative	maggiore	plus grand	*bigger*
superlative	il maggiore	le plus grand	*the biggest*
absolute	massimo	maximum	*very big*
positive	piccolo	petit	*small*
comparative	minore	plus petit	*smaller*

CHAPTER 3: ADVERBS

Forms	Italian	French	English
superlative	il minore	le plus petit	*the smallest*
absolute	minimo	minimum	*very small*
Adverbs			
positive	bene	bien	*well*
comparative	meglio	mieux	*better*
superlative	il meglio	le mieux	*the best*
absolute	benissimo	N\A	*very well*
positive	male	mal	*badly*
comparative	peggio	pire	*worse*
superlative	il peggio	le pire	*the worst*
absolute	malissimo	N\A	*very badly*
positive	molto	beaucoup	*many/much*
comparative	più	plus	*more*
superlative	il più	le plus	*the most*
absolute	moltissimo	N\A	N\A
positive	poco	peu	*little*
comparative	meno	moins	*less*
superlative	il meno	le moins	*the least*

CHAPTER 3: ADVERBS

Forms	Italian	French	English
absolute	pochissimo	N\A	N\A

NOTE:

*In French adjectives such as **petit** and **grand** have regular forms of comparatives and superlatives. However **petit** can also be used as **moindre** (comparative) and **le moindre** (superlative).*

CHAPTER 4: ARTICLES

An article is a word (the, a and an) which is placed in front of a noun.

Types of Article in English

1. The definite article **the** is normally used to identify a certain person or thing: *I'm going to **the** cinema.*
2. The indefinite article **a** or **an** is usually used to indicate something unfamiliar or unspecific: *He has **a** car.*
3. The partitive articles **some** or **any** (or no word) are used while talking about quantities or amounts: *We have **some** milk.*

Origin of Articles in Romance Languages. Definite and Indefinite Articles. Gender.

The definite article came into use in the period of transition from vulgar Latin to the Romance languages themselves, indicating connections of a noun in the context. For languages that do not have articles, such connections are understood from the particular situation. The Definite article in Romance languages as well as the personal pronoun of the 3rd person go back to the demonstrative pronouns Lat. **ille** > Sp. **el**, It. **il**, Fr. **le** and Lat. **illus** > It. **lo**.

Being a non-autonomous word, the article has a distinct position. Like in English, in Italian and French the article is placed in front of a noun.

The indefinite article goes back to Latin numeral **unus, una** – *one* which was used as indefinite pronoun while taking into consideration an object in archaic and classical Latin. The use of **unus** which accompanied a noun transforms it now into the indefinite article.

Thus, in Romance languages the article can be one of two types: definite and indefinite. Articles also have masculine and feminine forms. Looking at the common source of origin of the article, it is possible to state that in the Italian and French languages, the system of articles has common grammatical and lexical similarity.

Below is the table demonstrating the similarity of definite and indefinite articles of masculine and feminine gender in Romance languages.

Forms of article	Italian		French	
	singular masc./fem.	plural masc./fem.	singular masc./fem.	plural masc./fem.
Definite	il, lo, l'/ la, l'	i, gli, gl'/ le, l'	le, l'/ la, l'	les/ les
Indefinite	un, uno/ una, un'	dei, degli/ delle	un/une	des/ des

The article is placed before the noun and, like adjectives, agrees with it in number and gender:

Did you know?

The name "France" comes from a Germanic tribe called the Franks. The word "Frank" means free in Frankish.

It. *il* ragazzo > *la* ragazza > *i* ragazzi > *le* ragazze;

Fr. *le* garçon > *la* fille > *les* garçons > *les* filles.

- *the* boy > *the* girl > *the* boys > *the* girls.

French

In French the article of the singular *le* and *la* becomes *l'* before a noun that begins with a *vowel* or mute *h*: (l'enfant – *the child*, l'homme – *the man*).

Italian

In Italian the article of the masculine singular is *il* and plural *i*, but before all *masculine singular* nouns beginning with *z*, *s* plus a **consonant**, *y*, *ps* or *gn* the article *lo* is placed: (**lo st**udente – *the student*, **lo** **z**io – *the uncle*, **lo gn**omo - *the gnome*, **lo ps**icologo – *the psychologist* and etc.).

The definite article **lo** becomes **l'** before any **vowel**: (**l'**amico – *the friend*, **l'**italiano – *the Italian*, **l'**istituto – *the institute*), whereas the definite plural article **gli** transforms into **gl'** only before **i** (**gl'**italiani), however recently there is a tendency towards the preservation of the vowel sound: (**gli i**taliani).

The article of the feminine singular **la** becomes **l'** before <u>feminine singular</u> nouns beginning with a **vowel**: (**l'**amica – *the friend*, **l'**estate – *the summer*)

The indefinite plural article **dei** becomes **degli** before **a, u, i, o** (***dei*** libri - books; ***degli a***mici - friends).

Use of the Article

In general terms, the article in Romance languages has common ways of use.

General Use of the Indefinite Article

- It is used as numeral "*one*" to express only one thing a person has:

It. ho **un** figlio,

Fr. j'ai **un** fils

– *I have* **one** *son.*

- It is used to refer to someone or something not yet known or not specifically identified:

It. mia madre parla con **una** donna,

Fr. ma mère parle avec **une** femme

– *my mother is talking to* ***a*** *woman.*

CHAPTER 4: ARTICLES

> **Did you know?**
>
> *When Italy became one nation in 1861, only 2.5% of Italians could speak the standardized language.*

It. questo è **un** libro,

Fr. c'est **un** livre

– this is **a** book.

- The plural forms of the article in Romance languages are used with plural nouns in a similar way (meaning "*some*" in English):

It. sul tavolo ci sono ***dei*** fiori,

Fr. sur la table il y a ***des*** fleurs

– there are **some** flowers on the table.

General use of the Definite Article

- Generally speaking, the definite article is used to refer to someone or something specific in a particular situation:

It. Chiudi ***la*** finestra!

Fr. Fermez ***la*** fenêtre!

– *Close* **the** *window!*

- It is used to refer to the object which is unique in its category:

> **Did you know?**
>
> *French is second only to English when it comes to the number of countries where it is an official or co-official language. French is officially spoken in 32 countries.*

It. ***il*** sole,

Fr. ***le*** soleil

– **the** sun

CHAPTER 4: ARTICLES

- The definite article is put before a noun which is used to refer to an entire category of people or things in general:

    It. *Il* leone è un animale molto veloce,

    Fr. *Le* lion est un animal très rapide.

    - *Lions are very fast animals.*

- It is used with abstract nouns when they have a general use:

    It. Dobbiamo ridurre *la* povertà nel nostro paese.

    Fr. Nous devons réduire *la* pauvreté dans notre pays.

    - *We must reduce **the** poverty in our country.*

- It is used to refer to an object that became certain as it had been mentioned earlier:

    It. Lui ha una macchina. *La* macchina è nuova;

    Fr. Il a une voiture. *La* voiture est neuve

    – He *has a car.* ***The*** *car is new.*

- It is used before a noun that has a definition specifying the object being discussed:

    It. Prendete *il* giornale che sta sul tavolo,

    Fr. Prenez *le* journal qui est sur la table.

    - *Take **the** newspaper that is on the table.*

CHAPTER 4: ARTICLES

- It is used for any noun that refers to a general idea, practice or phenomenon. This includes colours, diseases, fields of activity and meals:

It. Non mi piace *il* verde come colore;

Fr. Je n'aime pas *le* vert comme couleur.

- I don't like the color green.

Below is a table presenting objects, concepts and phenomena which are to be used with the definite article in one or another Romance language. As a rule, nouns that have the masculine or feminine forms of the article designating the categories below:

the masculine definite article	**Italian**	**French**	*English*
- months	(**Il** mese di) gennaio	(**Le** mois de) janvier	*January*
	(**Il** mese di) febbraio	(**Le** mois de) février	*February*
	(**Il** mese di) marzo	(**Le** mois de) mars	*March*
	(**Il** mese di) aprile	(**Le** mois de) avril	*April*
- days of week	But: (**La**) domenica	(**Le**) dimanche	*Sunday*
	(**Il**) lunedì	(**Le**) lundi	*Monday*
	(**Il**) martedì	(**Le**) mardi	*Tuesday*
	(**Il**) mercoledì	(**Le**) mercredi	*Wednesday*
- seasons	(**L'**) inverno	(**L'**) hiver	*Winter*
	(**L'**) estate	(**L'**) été	*Summer*
	(**L'**) autunno	(**L'**) automne	*Autumn/Fall*

CHAPTER 4: ARTICLES

the masculine definite article	Italian	French	English
	But: (**La**) primavera	(**Le**) printemps	*Spring*
- corners of the earth	(**Il**) nord	(**Le**) nord	*North*
	(**Il**) sud	(**Le**) sud	*South*
	(**L'**) est	(**L'**) est	*East*
	(**L'**) ovest	(**L'**) ouest	*West*
- languages	(**Il**) giapponese	(**Le**) japonais	*Japanese*
	(**Il**) portoghese	(**Le**) portugais	*Portuguese*
	(**Il**) coreano	(**Le**) coréen	*Korean*
	(**Il**) francese	(**Le**) français	*French*
- trees	(**Il**) pino	(**Le**) pin	*Pine tree*
	(**La**) betulla	(**Le**) bouleau	*Birch*
	(**La**) quercia	(**Le**) chêne	*Oak*
	But: (**La**) palma	(**Le**) palmier	*Palm tree*
- metals	(**L'**) oro	(**L'**) or	*Gold*
	(**Il**) ferro	(**Le**) fer	*Iron*
	(**Il**) rame	(**Le**) cuivre	*Copper*
	(**L'**) argento	(**L'**) argent	*Silver*
- chemical substances	(**L'**) acido	(**L'**) acide	*Acid*
	(**L'**) alcali	(**L'**) alcali	*Alkali*
	(**Il**) cloruro	(**Le**) chlorure	*Chloride*

CHAPTER 4: ARTICLES

the masculine definite article	Italian	French	English
	But: (**La**) tossina	*But:* (**La**) toxine	*Toxin*
- transport	(**Il**) bus	(**Le**) bus	*Bus*
	(**L'**) aereo	(**L'**) avion	*Plane*
	(**Il**) treno	(**Le**) train	*Train*
	(**L'**) auto	*But:* (**La**) voiture	*Car*

the feminine definite article	Italian	French	English
- countries, cities, continents, islands	(**L'**) Italia	(**L'**) Italie	*Italy*
	(**La**) città di Parigi	(**La**) ville de Paris	*Paris*
	(**L'**) Europa	(**L'**) Europe	*Europe*
	(**Le**) isole hawaiane	(**Les**) îles hawaïennes	*Hawaiian islands*
- rivers, lakes	*But:* (**Il**) Rio delle Amazzoni	*But:* (**L'**) Amazone	*The Amazon*
	(**Il**) Mississippi	(**Le**) Mississippi	*The Mississippi River*
	(**L'**) Eufrate	(**L'**) Eufrate	*The Euphrates*
	(**Il**) lago Huron	(**Le**) lac Huron	*Lake Huron*
- sciences	(**La**) chimica	(**La**) chimie	*Chemistry*
	(**La**) biologia	(**La**) biologie	*Biology*
	(**La**) filosofia	(**La**) philosophie	*Philosophy*
	(**La**) letteratura	(**La**) littérature	*Literature*

CHAPTER 4: ARTICLES

NOTE:

The table demonstrates the general rule, however there are some exceptions for you to memorize.

Remember that rivers and lakes are used with the masculine definite article in Italian and French.

In Italian, the following words are used with the feminine definite article: **la domenica, la primavera, la palma, la tossina**.

In French, **la toxine** and **la voiture** have the feminine definite article.

Omission of the Definite Article

1. The definite article in Romance languages is usually omitted before names of cities and towns:

Did you know?

Parmesan cheese originated in Parma, Italy. Italians also created many other cheeses, including gorgonzola, mozzarella, provolone, and ricotta.

It. Parigi è la capitale della Francia,

Fr. Paris est la capitale de la France.

- Paris is the capital of France.

Exceptions

In <u>French</u> the definite article is usually omitted when the name of the region, country or continent is preceded by the preposition *en*.

However, the article may be placed if an adverb separates the verb from the language name, and this is common across all Romance languages:

It. Io parlo correttamente **il** francese,

Fr. Je parle correctement **le** français.

- I speak French correctly.

CHAPTER 4: ARTICLES

Omission of the Article

1. The article is omitted if there is a numeral or pronoun placed before a noun.

2. The article is omitted before nouns denoting quantity and used with a preposition:

It. *di*, Fr. *de*.

3. The indefinite article is usually omitted before prepositions:

It. **senza**, Fr. **sans** – *without*;

It. **con**, Fr. **avec** – *with*;

It. **come**, Fr. **comme** – *as, like*.

Did you know?

The two oldest cities in France are Marseille and Beziers, both were built by the Greeks in the 6th century BC.

It. Lui è uscito **senza** soldi,

Fr. Il est sorti **sans** argent.

- *He left **without** money.*

4. In <u>Italian</u> and <u>French</u> the indefinite article is omitted after the verb It. **essere**, Fr. **être** (*to be*) when it precedes unmodified nouns denoting nationality, profession or religion:

It. Lui è medico,

Fr. Il est médecin.

- *He is a doctor.*

However, the indefinite article is used when the noun put after the verb **to be** is modified:

It. Lui è **un** medico molto famoso,

Fr. Il est **un** médecin très célèbre.

- *He is a very **famous** doctor.*

CHAPTER 4: ARTICLES

The Partitive

Along with the definite article, in <u>French</u> and <u>Italian</u> (as early as the 14th century) there came into existence the partitive article that dates back to the combination **de + ille**, which represents the equivalent of the partitive non-autonomous pronoun It. **ne**, Fr. **en**, Lat. **inde**.

In English we usually use words such as *some* or *any* or no article at all with nouns that are not counted, for instance milk and tea. In Italian and French the partitive also designates undetermined quantity and is also used with uncounted nouns.

The partitive is formed as a result of liaison of the preposition: It. **di**, Fr. **de** with the definite article:

Italian	French
di + il = del;	**de + le = du;**
di + lo = dello / di + l'= dell';	**de + la = de la;**
di + la = della / di + gli = degli;	**de + les = des.**
di + i = dei / di + le = delle.	

1. In Italian and French the partitive is used with uncounted nouns:

It.: Ha comprato **del** pane, **dello** zucchero e **della** carne; Hanno bevuto **del** latte.

Fr.: Il a acheté **du** pain, **du** sucre et **de la** viande; Ils ont bu **du** lait.

- *He bought **some** bread, **some** sugar and **some** meat; They drank **some** milk.*

2. It is used with abstract nouns, designating an abstract idea:

Did you know?

There are 2 independent states within Italy: the Republic of San Marino (23.6 square miles) and the Vatican City (0.17 square miles).

It. Hai **del** talento.

Fr. Tu as **du** talent.

- *You are talented.*

CHAPTER 4: ARTICLES

3. It is used after nouns, designating quantity:

> *Did you know?*
>
> Belgium has 3 official languages: French, Dutch and German. Many Belgians are bilingual or trilingual.

It.: una bottiglia **di** vino

Fr.: une bouteille **de** vin

- a bottle **of** wine

There are such expressions of quantity as:

Italian	French	English
una scatola di	*une boîte de*	a box of
una bottiglia di	*une bouteille de*	a bottle of
un bicchiere di	*un verre de*	a glass of
una tazza di	*une tasse de*	a cup of
un chilo di	*un kilo de*	a kilogram of
un litro di	*un litre de*	a liter of
una dozzina di	*une douzaine de*	a dozen (of)
un pezzo di	*un morceau de*	a piece of
una fetta di	*une tranche de*	a slice of
un po' di	*un peu de*	a little

NOTE:

In French in negative sentences, the partitive article is replaced by **de**.

<u>Affirmative</u>: J'ai **du** pain.

<u>Negative</u>: Je n'ai pas **de** pain.

Also, when an adjective is placed before a noun in the plural, the partitive becomes **de**:

CHAPTER 4: ARTICLES

Singular: J'ai un bon ami.
Plural: j'ai **de** bons amis.

Contraction of the Article

When next to the definite article in Italian and French, the most frequently used prepositions become contracted forms. This phenomenon can be considered a declination of the article. The most common contracted forms are **ad + ille** and **de + ille**, which correspond to genitive and dative cases.

In Romance languages the article can be contracted as follow:

Latin	Italian	French
ad + ille	**a+il/lo=al/allo**	à+le= au
ad + illa	**a+la= alla**	à la
de +ille	**di+il/lo=del/dello**	de+le= du
de + illa	**di+la= della**	de la
in + ille	**in+il=nel, nello**	*el, eu, au*
in + illa	**in+la= nella**	*en la*
sub + ille	**su+il=sul,sullo**	-
sub + illa	**su+la= sulla**	-
per + ille	*pel*	-
per + illa	*pella*	-
cum + ille	**con+il=col**, *collo*	-
cum + illa	*colla*	-

NOTE:
In italics are archaic and dialect forms.

CHAPTER 4: ARTICLES

It. Lui va **al** cinema oggi;

Fr. Il va **au** cinéma aujourd'hui.

- *He goes to the cinema.*

Did you know?

Ballet originated in Italy during the 15th century and it was Catherine de Medici who introduced it to France later on.

It. Questa città è la migliore **del** mondo;

Fr. Cette ville est la meilleure **du** monde.

- *This city is the best in the world.*

From the table above it is clear that Romance languages have lexical similarity and common grammatical system of contraction the article with prepositions, which date back to their predecessor – Latin.

CHAPTER 5: PRONOUNS

A pronoun is a word we use and which serves as a noun when we do not want or need to name something or someone directly, for instance, I, you, it, him, her.

Personal Pronouns

There are five types of personal pronouns in Romance languages:
- subject pronoun;
- direct object pronoun;
- indirect object pronoun;
- prepositional (disjunctive) pronouns;
- reflexive pronouns.

Also, there are several pronouns in Italian and French (It. *ne, ci*; Fr. *en, y*), which are used in certain constructions.

Below is the table presenting all the types of personal pronouns:

	Italian	French	English
Subject	*io*	*je, j'*	I
	tu	*tu*	you (sing.inf)
	lui/lei/Lei/ egli/ella/ esso/essa	*il, elle, on*	he, it/she,it/you (sing.f.)
	noi	*nous*	we
	voi	*vous*	you (pl. inf.)
	loro/Loro/ essi/esse	*ils/elles*	they (m. fem)/ you (pl. f)

CHAPTER 5: PRONOUNS

	Italian	French	English
Direct object	mi	me/m'	me
	ti	te/t`	you (sing.inf)
	lo/la/l'	le/l` la/l'	him, it/her, it
	ci	nous	us
	vi	vous	you (pl.)
	li/ le	les	them (m, fem)
Indirect object	mi	me	me
	ti	te	you (sing.inf)
	gli /le	lui	him, it/her
	ci	nous	us
	vi	vous	you (pl. inf.)
	loro/Loro	leur	them
Prepositional pronouns	me	moi	me
	te	toi	you (sing.inf)
	lui/lei/Lei	lui/elle	him, it/her/you (sing.f.)
	noi	nous	us
	voi	vous	you (pl. inf.)
	loro/Loro	eux/elles	them (m. fem)/ you (pl. f)
Reflexive pronouns	mi	me/m'	myself
	ti	te/t'	yourself

CHAPTER 5: PRONOUNS

Italian	French	English
si	se/s'	himself/herself/itself
ci	nous	ourselves
vi	vous	yourselves
si	se	themselves

Subject Pronouns

Overview

Did you know?

France has the highest number of Nobel Prize in literature winners of any country, with 15 (followed by the United States with 11, and the UK with 10).

A subject pronoun, such as I, he, we, they, is used to perform the action, which is presented by the verb. Generally subject or personal pronouns replace a subject noun or name, and they can be classified in several different ways: person (1st, 2nd or 3rd), number (singular or plural), gender (male or female) and formality (formal or informal) in the Romance languages.

Below is the table showing all the forms of subject pronouns in Italian and French:

Italian	French	English
io	je, j'	I
tu	tu	you (sing.inf)
lui/lei/Lei/ egli/ella/esso/essa	il,elle,on	he, it/she,it/you (sing.f)
noi	nous	we

CHAPTER 5: PRONOUNS

Italian	French	English
voi	*vous*	you (pl. inf.)
loro/Loro/ essi/esse	ils/elles	they (m. fem)/you (pl. f)

Use of Subject Pronouns

Pronouns are used instead of nouns when it is clear who we talk about (e.g. His father is at work. He will return by 7 p.m.).

1st person singular in the Romance languages corresponds with that of English language. For example:

It. *Io* sono uno studente;

Fr. *Je* suis un étudiant;

- *I am a student.*

NOTE:

In <u>French</u> the pronoun of the 1st person *Je* changes to *J'* when it is placed before words which begin with a **vowel**, **h** or **y**. For example: J'aime – I love;

J'habite à Paris – I live in Paris;

J'y vais bientôt – I am going there soon.

In Romance languages there are several ways to express *you*.

Familiar way of addressing people:

It. **tu** (s.), **voi** (pl.);

Fr. **tu** (s.), **vous** (pl.)

The examples above are basically used to address people one knows very well: friends, relatives. Observe the following:

It. ***Tu*** sei molto gentile;

Fr. ***Tu*** es très gentil;

- ***You*** are very nice.

Formal way of addressing people:

It. ***Lei*** (*s.*), ***Loro*** (*pl.*)

Fr. ***vous*** (both *s.* and *pl.*)

These pronouns are used to address superiors, strangers, people who one does not know very well or has never met before, or show a relationship that is polite and respectful. For instance:

Did you know?

When Italy became one nation in 1861 and officially chose Tuscan Italian as the national tongue, only 2.5% Italians were able to speak the standardized language.

It. ***Lei*** è molto gentile;

Fr. ***Vous*** êtes très gentil.

- ***You*** are very nice.

In Italian it is important to notice the distinction between the capitalized ***Lei*** and ***Loro***, which are formal "you", and *lei* and *loro* which mean *she* and *they*. Also, Italian third person singular subject pronouns *lui* becomes ***egli*** or ***esso*** and *lei* becomes ***ella*** or ***essa*** in the formal way of addressing. Finally, the third person plural subject pronoun *loro* (they) becomes ***essi*** (masc.) and esse (fem.) in the formal form of address.

In French, as you can see, there is only one form: ***vous***. It is used to address people whatever their relation to each other.

CHAPTER 5: PRONOUNS

It is extremely important to note that Italian ***Lei***, ***Loro*** always take the 3rd person forms of the verb, singular and plural, respectively, which is why they are placed in the 3rd person in the table above. For instance:

It. ***Lei*** sa parlare inglese.

- ***You, sir***, *can speak English.*

Since nouns in Romance languages have two genders, masculine and feminine, the 3rd person singular and plural, as you can see from the table, also has masculine and feminine forms of the pronoun, which are used to talk about things, as well as about people or animals. Look at the following example:

It. Mi piace il cane del mio amico. ***Lui*** è molto intelligente;

Fr. J'aime le chien de mon ami. ***Il*** est très intelligent.

- *I like my friend's dog.* ***He/It*** *is very smart.*

NOTE:

In <u>French</u> *the pronoun* ***on*** *is used in the 3rd person form of the verb and means* ***one, people, they, you****. Example:*

Fr. Si ***on*** aime, on est heureux.

– *If* ***people (one, they, you)*** *love(s),* ***people (one, they, you)*** *are (is) happy.*

Also, in informal everyday French the pronoun ***on*** *can mean* ***we****, replacing the pronoun nous. Example:*

Fr. ***On*** va au cinema ce soir.

– ***We're*** *going to the cinema tonight.*

Finally, using the pronoun ***on****, we can avoid a passive construction. Example:*

Fr. ***On*** m'a donné un cadeau.

– *I was given a gift.*

Omission of Subject Pronouns

In Italian, subject pronouns are usually omitted, since the verb ending indicates the subject, which is not true for French where the ending of the verb is not pronounced and therefore the use of subject pronouns is necessary in order to indicate the subject.

Did you know?

Due to the Norman conquest, French was the official language of England for over 300 years from the 11th until the 15th century.

It. Oggi andiamo nel centro della città;

Fr. Aujourd'hui <u>nous</u> allons au centre ville.

- Today <u>we</u> are going to the city centre.

However, subject pronouns in Italian should be used in the following cases:

- It is used for emphasis:

It. ***Io*** lo faccio!

- ***I*** do it!

- It is used for contrast:

It. ***Io*** parlo e ***tu*** ascolti.

- ***I*** speak and ***you*** listen.

NOTE:

When we talk about the time and the weather in Italian, subject pronouns are also omitted. However, in French the pronoun **il** is used, which is often in the same way as we use some phrases with <u>it</u> in English. Example:

It. Piove;
Fr. ***Il*** pleut;
- ***It*** is raining.

- In Italian the subject pronoun is also used on its own without verb, for example:

It. Chi l'ha comprato? ***Io***.
- Who bought it? ***Me***.

NOTE:
However, in French when we want to emphasize something or show a contrast or use a pronoun on its own without a verb, we should use the disjunctive pronoun (**See the Disjunctive Pronouns p.89**) in this case:

Fr. ***Toi***, tu m'as dit que tu étais chez toi.
- ***You***, you told me that you were at home.

Fr. Qui a acheté ça? ***Moi***.
- Who bought it? ***Me***.

Direct Object

Direct objects are nouns which receive the action of a verb in sentences. The direct object pronouns (me, him, us and them) are used to replace that noun.

Below is the table that shows all the forms of direct object pronouns in Italian and French:

CHAPTER 5: PRONOUNS

Italian	French	English
mi	*me/m'*	me
ti	*te/t`*	you (sing.inf)
lo/la/l'	*le/l` la/l'*	him, it/her, it
ci	*nous*	us
vi	*vous*	you (pl.)
li/le	*les*	them (m. fem)

Just like personal subject pronouns are used instead of subject nouns in sentences, direct object pronouns replace the direct object noun in a sentence, which is a thing or a person:

It. Leggiamo libri.

Fr. Nous lisons des livres.

– We read books.

Italian "*libri*" and French "*livres*" receive the action of It. *leggiamo*, Fr. *lison*. In this sentence It. "*libri*", Fr. "*livres*" are the direct object. They are plural and masculine and, as it represents an inanimate object, they are the 3rd person, and therefore, we can replace it with the direct object pronoun It. *li*, Fr. *les*:

It. *Li* leggiamo,

Fr. Nous *les* lisons

– We read **them**.

As we said, the direct object of a sentence can be a person as well:

73

> **Did you know?**
>
> Many of the most influential scientists and mathematicians were born Italy, including Galileo Galilei and Alessandro Volta.

It. Loro **mi** amano,

Fr. Ils **m**'aiment.

– They love **me**.

In French the direct object pronouns **me**, **le** and **la** and Italian **lo** and **la** become **m'** and **l'** before verbs that begin with a **vowel** or mute **h**:

It. **L'**apro.

– I open **it**.

Fr. Ils **m'**aiment.

– They love **me**.

Fr. Elle **l'**achète.

– She buys **it**.

Use of Direct Object Pronouns

1. We use them to substitute nouns when it is clear what or who is being discussed, and also to avoid the repetition of the noun. Note that direct object pronouns precede the conjugated form of the verb.

It. Mark legge il libro. Lui **lo** legge;

Fr. Mark lit le livre. Il **le** lit.

– Mark reads a book. He reads **it**.

CHAPTER 5: PRONOUNS

2. It, *lo*; Fr. *le* are sometimes used to replace the entire information or idea that has already been presented.

It. Ho comprato un vestito nuovo. - *Lo* so;

Fr. J'ai acheté une nouvelle robe. – Je *le* sais.

– I bought a new robe. - I know (*it*).

Word Order of Direct Object Pronouns

1. As it was said earlier the direct object is usually put before a verb:

It. *Ti* conosco;

Fr. Je *te* connais.

– I know *you*.

Did you know?

Until World War II, France was on the same time zone as London. After occupying the country in 1940, Germany forced France to conform with Berlin time, and this change has never been canceled.

2. In the perfect tense, which is formed with verbs *have* or *be* and the past participle, the direct object pronoun precedes *have* or *be* in the verb conjugation.

It. Lei *mi* ha visto;

Fr. Elle *m'*a vu.

– She has seen *me*.

3. In Italian, you attach the direct object pronouns to the end of affirmative commands (In French you do not attach it). In negative commands, you place it between *no* (or other negative word) and the verb (in Italian you attach it to the end of the verb).

It. Leggi*lo*;

CHAPTER 5: PRONOUNS

Fr. Lis **le**.

– *Read **it**.*

> **Did you know?**
>
> *Italy's San Marino is the world's oldest republic (301 A.D.), and holds the world's oldest continuous constitution.*

It. Non legger**lo**.

Fr. Ne **le** lis pas.

– *Do not read **it**.*

Divergent Aspects in Word Order

However, there are some divergent peculiarities in word order of direct object pronouns in the Romance languages that need to be remembered.

1. When a verb is followed by another verb in the infinitive (the "to" form), the direct pronoun is put before the infinitive in French, for example:

Fr. Il voudrait **la** voir.

– *He would like to see **her**.*

However, in Italian the direct pronoun can be placed whether before the first verb or after the infinitive attaching to it. Observe the following:

It. Mi piacerebbe veder**la**.

– *I would like to see **her**.*

Indirect Object

An indirect object pronoun tells us "*to whom*" or "*for whom*" something is done. Just like how direct object pronouns are used instead

CHAPTER 5: PRONOUNS

of direct objects, indirect object pronouns replace indirect objects, which are personal nouns.

Below is the table that shows all the forms of indirect object pronouns in Italian and French:

Italian	French	English
mi	*me*	me
ti	*te*	you (sing.inf)
gli /le	*lui*	him, it/her
ci	*nous*	us
vi	*vous*	you (pl. inf.)
gli/a loro	*leur*	them

Use of Indirect Object Pronouns

Like direct, indirect object pronouns in Romance languages can be used only in conjugation with verbs. It is important to see the difference between direct and indirect object, since they have different forms in English and Romance languages. In general, to indicate the indirect object phrase in a sentence, you should ask "*to whom?*", "*for whom?*" For example:

Did you know?

Over 95% of the population of Canada's Quebec is French speaking, with French as the only provincial official language.

It. Ha scritto una lettera *a Sandra*.

Fr. Il a écrit une lettre *à Sandra*.

– He wrote a letter **to Sandra**.

A Sandra is the indirect object, and therefore, we can replace it with the indirect object pronoun It. *le*, Fr. *lui*:

77

CHAPTER 5: PRONOUNS

> **Did you know?**
>
> From Cappelletti to Cavatelli, there are over 140 types of pastas in Italy. Some of these pastas are only native to specific regions.

It. lui **le** ha scritto.

Fr. Il **lui** a écrit.

– *He wrote **to her**.*

One more example:

It. Lui ha comprato un regalo **per me**.

Fr. Il a acheté un cadeau **pour moi**.

- *He bought a gift **for me**.*

He bought a gift for whom? *For me*. Therefore, we should use the indirect object pronoun *me*:

It. **Mi** ha comprato un regalo.

Fr. Il **m**'a acheté un cadeau.

- *He bought **me** a gift.*

It should be said that direct and indirect object pronouns are the same for Romance languages except in the 3rd person.

NOTE:

In French, the 3rd person indirect object pronoun is gender neutral.

However, Italian differentiates the 3rd person singular and plural indirect pronouns **gli** *(to him, to them)* and the 3rd person indirect pronoun **le** *(to her)* in the singular. Note, that **gli** and **le** put before the conjugated form of the verb, whereas **a loro** follows the conjugated *verb form. Also, as you noticed, there is no gender identification with **a loro**.*

***Gli** becomes **gl'** before forms of the verb that begin with **–i**, whereas **le** and **a loro** never contract in Italian. However, this rule is quite old and it's possible to use **gli** before **-i** without any contraction. For example:*

*Io scrivo a John – Io **gli** scrivo. – I write to John. I write to **him**.*

*Tu insegni a John – Tu **gl'insegni** (or Tu **gli** insegni).- You teach John. You teach **him**.*

*Parliamo a Sandra – **Le** parliamo. – We speak to Sandra. We speak to **her**.*

*Parla agli studenti – Parla **a loro**. – She speaks to the students. She speaks to **them**.*

Common Verbs Used with an Indirect Object in Romance Languages

Below is the list of words which usually take a person as the indirect object in Romance languages.

Italian	French	English
comprare qualcosa a **(gli/le)**	acheter quelque chose à **(lui)**	to buy smth for smb
raccontare qualcosa a **(gli/le)**	raconter quelque chose à **(lui)**	to tell smth to smb
dare qualcosa a **(gli/le)**	donner quelque chose à **(lui)**	to give smth to smb
dire qualcosa a **(gli/le)**	dire de quelque chose à **(lui)**	to say smth to smb
scrivere qualcosa a **(gli/le)**	écrire quelque chose à **(lui)**	to write smth to smb
inviare, mandare qualcosa a **(gli/le)**	envoyer quelque chose à **(lui)**	to send smth to smb

Italian	French	English
mostrare qualcosa a (**gli/le**)	montrer quelque chose à (**lui**)	to show smth to smb
chiedere qualcosa a (**gli/le**)	demander de quelque chose à (**lui**)	to ask smth of smb
servire qualcosa a (**gli/le**)	servir quelque chose à (**lui**)	to serve smth to smb
portare qualcosa a (**gli/le**)	apporter quelque chose à (**lui**)	to bring smth to smb

Word Order of Indirect Object Pronouns

Generally indirect object pronouns follow the same word order rules as direct object pronouns. (**See Word Order of Direct Object Pronouns p.75**)

Contraction.
Using Direct and Indirect Object Pronouns in the Same Sentence

Did you know?

With 11 million km², France has the second largest maritime surface area after the United States.

When direct and indirect object pronouns appear in the same sentence, they can be combined (contracted), which is a natural way to make our pronunciation simpler. Once we have both the direct and indirect object pronouns in the same sentence, the indirect object pronoun goes in front of the direct object pronoun.

Unlike the French language, the phenomenon of contraction exists only in Italian. Moreover, Italian has its own special cases of combining the indirect object pronoun with the direct object pronoun, which require particular consideration, as this phenomenon significantly distinguishes one from the other.

CHAPTER 5: PRONOUNS

Italian

When both the indirect object pronoun and the direct object pronoun appear in the same sentence in Italian, the indirect object pronoun also precedes the direct object pronoun.

It should be noted that *mi*, *ti*, *ci* and *vi* change to *me*, *te*, *ce* and *ve* when followed by the direct object pronoun. Also, when the indirect object pronouns *gli* (*to him*), *le* (*to her*), and *Le* (*to you*, formal) are followed by the direct object pronouns *lo*, *la*, *li*, *le* combine into one word: *glielo*, *gliela*, *glieli*, *gliele*) and formal *Le* retain its capital letter and starts with capital G after combining: *Le – Glielo* (-a, -i, -e).

Below is the table that shows the combination of the indirect object pronoun and the direct object pronoun in Italian.

Indirect	Direct					
+	lo	la	l'	li	le	ne
mi	= me lo	= me la	= me l'	= me li	= me le	= me ne
ti	= te lo	= te la	= te l'	= te li	= te le	= te ne
ci	= ce lo	= ce la	= ce l'	= ce li	= ce le	= ce ne
vi	= ve lo	= ve la	= ve l'	= ve li	= ve le	= ve ne
gli	= glielo	= gliela	= gliel'	= glieli	= gliele	= gliene
le	= glielo	= gliela	= gliel'	= glieli	= gliele	= gliene
Le	= glielo	= gliela	= gliel'	= glieli	= gliele	= gliene

Examples:

It. Lei *mi* dà un libro. Lei *me lo* dà.

– She gives *me* a book. She gives *it to me*.

It. Lui *ti* compra dei regali. Lui *te ne* compra.

– He buys *you* some gifts. He buys *you some* (*of it, of them*).

CHAPTER 5: PRONOUNS

Italian ci, ne and French y, en Special Pronouns

Italian *ci* and French *y* Pronouns

Ci and *y* pronouns are also called adverbial pronouns and are widely used in these Romance languages. Since Italian *ci* and French *y* pronouns have identical rules of use, they will be considered together, which will help to demonstrate areas of convergence of these pronouns.

Use of *ci* and *y*

Below are the rules of use for these pronouns:

1. Italian *ci* and French *y* usually replace a place and is used to say *"there"*. They replace a noun or a phrase (representing a place), which is introduced by a preposition of place, which can be Fr. *à, dans, en, chez, sur, sous*; It. *a, in, su, con*. For instance:

Did you know?

Sicily has the largest opera house in Italy. The Teatro Massimo was built in Palermo in 1897. Sicily is also the largest island in the Mediterranean Sea covering almost 10,000 square miles.

It. Vado *a* Madrid = *ci* vado;

Fr. Je vais *à* Madrid = j'*y* vais.

– *I go to Madrid = I go **there**.*

Let's take one more example:

It. Vai *in* Francia = *ci* vai;

Fr. Tu vas *en* France = tu *y* vas.

– *You go to France = you go **there**.*

CHAPTER 5: PRONOUNS

2. Italian **ci** and French **y** usually replace *a thing* which is also preceded by Fr. *à* (*au, aux, à l', à la*), It. *a* (sometimes *in, su, con*). For example:

It. Penso spesso *al* mio lavoro = **ci** penso spesso;

Fr. Je pense souvent *à* mon travail = j'**y** pense souvent.

– *I often think about my job = I often think **about it**.*

The prepositions, such as French **à** and Italian **a** are usually used with certain verbs. According to the grammar, particular verbs should always be followed by the particular preposition like Fr. **à** or It. **a** (ex. It. pensare **a**; Fr. penser **à** – *to think of/about*).

To know when to put the pronoun **ci** and **y**, it is advisable to learn the most common verbs followed by the preposition **à** in French and **a** in Italian.

Below is the list of the most common verbs followed by the preposition à in French and a in Italian after which the infinitive is used.

Italian Verbs with a + the infinitive	French Verbs with à + the infinitive	English
aiutare a fare qualcosa	aider à faire quelque chose	*to help to do smth.*
imparare a fare qualcosa	apprendre à faire quelque chose	*to learn how to do smth.*
arrivare a fare qualcosa	arriver à faire quelque chose	*to succeed in doing smth.*
avere <u>da</u> fare qualcosa	avoir à faire quelque chose	*to have to / be obliged to do smth.*
provare a fare qualcosa	chercher à faire quelque chose	*to attempt to do smth.*
cominciare (iniziare) a fare qualcosa	commencer à faire quelque chose	*to begin to do smth.*

Italian Verbs with a + the infinitive	French Verbs with à + the infinitive	English
continuare a fare qualcosa	continuer à faire quelque chose	*to continue to do smth.*
acconsentire a fare qualcosa	consentir à faire quelque chose	*to agree to do smth.*
decidersi a (di) fare qualcosa	se décider à faire quelque chose	*to make up one's mind to do smth.*
incoraggiare qualcuno a fare qualcosa	encourager quelqu'un à faire quelque chose	*to encourage someone to do smth.*
abituarsi a fare qualcosa	s'habituer à faire quelque chose	*to get used to doing smth.*
esitare a fare qualcosa	hésiter à faire quelque chose	*to hesitate to do smth.*
chiamare (qualcuno) a fare qualcosa	inviter (quelqu'un) à faire quelque chose	*to invite (someone) to do smth.*
mettersi a fare qualcosa	se mettre à faire quelque chose	*to start doing smth.*
forzare (qualcuno) a fare qualcosa	forcer (quelqu'un) à faire quelque chose	*to force (someone) to do smth.*
obbligare (qualcuno) a fare qualcosa	obliger (quelqu'un) à faire quelque chose	*to oblige (someone) to do smth.*
riuscire a fare qualcosa	parvenir à faire quelque chose	*to succeed in doing smth.*
passare (trascorrere) il tempo a fare qualcosa	passer du temps à faire quelque chose	*to spend time doing smth.*
pensare a fare qualcosa	penser à faire quelque chose	*to think of doing smth.*

Italian Verbs with a + the infinitive	French Verbs with à + the infinitive	English
perdere tempo a fare qualcosa	perdre du temps à faire quelque chose	*to waste time doing smth.*
persistere a fare qualcosa	persister à faire quelque chose	*to persist in doing smth.*
spingere (qualcuno) a fare qualcosa	pousser (quelqu'un) à faire quelque chose	*to push someone to do smth.*
prepararsi a fare qualcosa	se préparer à faire quelque chose	*to prepare oneself to do smth.*
ricominciare a fare qualcosa	recommencer à faire quelque chose	*to begin doing smth. again*
rinunciare a fare qualcosa	renoncer à faire quelque chose	*to give up doing smth.*
resistere a fare qualcosa	résister à faire quelque chose	*to resist doing smth.*
riuscire a fare qualcosa	réussir à faire quelque chose	*to succeed in doing smth.*
insistere a fare qualcosa	tenir à faire quelque chose	*to insist on doing smth.*
divertirsi a fare qualcosa	s'amuser à faire quelque chose	*to have fun doing smth.*
aspettarsi _di_ fare qualcosa	s'attendre à faire quelque chose	*to expect doing smth.*
autorizzare (qualcuno) a fare qualcosa	autoriser (quelqu'un) à faire quelque chose	*to allow someone to do smth.*
interessarsi a qualcosa	s'intéresser à quelque chose	*to show a special interest in smth.*

It is notable that these pronouns can replace only a thing and never a person because in this case the indirect object or the disjunctive pronoun should be used. For instance:

It. Hai parlato a Daniela? Sì **le** ho parlato.

Fr. Tu as parlé à Daniela? Oui je **lui** ai parlé.

- *Have you talked to Daniela? Yes, I have talked* ***to her***.

Example using disjunctive pronoun:

It. Penso a ***lui***;

Fr. Je pense à ***lui***.

- *I think of* ***him***.

3. ***Ci*** and ***y*** are also used in such expression as It. ***c'è*** (*singular*), ***ci sono*** (*plural*); Fr. ***il y a*** meaning the existence of something – *there is, there are*. For example:

Did you know?

Tunisia is one of North Africa's most tourist friendly countries. Hammamet city has been the biggest tourist resort since the 1960s, attracting tourists from all over Europe. Arabic, French and Berber are spoken in the country.

Fr. ***Il y a*** un livre sur la table;

It. ***C'è*** un libro sul tavolo.

– ***There is*** *a book on the table.*

Fr. ***Il y a*** des lettres sur la table;

It. ***Ci sono*** delle lettere sul tavolo.

– ***There are*** *letters on the table.*

Italian *ne* and French *en* Pronouns

Italian ***ne*** and French ***en*** pronouns are also called adverbial pronouns and are often used in these languages. Since ***ne*** and ***en*** pronouns also have identical rules of use, they will be considered together.

Use of *ne* and *en*

Below are the rules of use of these pronouns:

1. Italian **ne** and French **en** replace <u>a quantity</u> (direct object representing a quantity), which can be introduced by a partitive article (Fr. *de, du, de la, de l', des*), a number, a fraction (Fr. *un quart*), an adverb of quantity (Fr. *beaucoup de, un peu de*) or an expression of quantity (Fr. *un litre de, un kilo de, une bouteille de*). For example:

It. Ho ***due fratelli*** = ***Ne*** ho due;

Fr. J'ai ***deux frère*** = J'***en*** ai deux.

– *I have **two brothers** = I have two **of them**.*

Let's take one more example:

It. ***Quanti libri*** hai comprato? ***Ne*** ho comprati moltissimi;

Fr. ***Combien de livres*** as-tu acheté? J'***en*** ai acheté beaucoup.

– ***How many books*** *did you buy? I bought a lot.*

It should be remembered that the quantity and the adverb of quantity is always repeated (ex. It. Compro **una bottiglia di** latte = **ne** compro una bottiglia; Fr. J'achète **une bouteille de** lait = J'**en** achète une bouteille. – *I bought one bottle of milk = I bought one bottle **of it**.*)

2. Italian **ne** and French **en** usually replace <u>a thing</u> (a noun or sentence) which is introduced by the prepositions: It. *di, da*; Fr. *de, du, de la, de l', des*. - *of, about.*

For example:

CHAPTER 5: PRONOUNS

Did you know?

Historically Italians don't put meatballs in their pasta. In most Italian meals, the first course (Primo piatto) is pasta followed by the main course of meat or fish (the secondo piatto).

It. Parlo **del** mio lavoro = **Ne** parlo;

Fr. Je parle **de** mon travail – J'**en** parle.

– I speak **about** my job = I speak **about it**.

The prepositions, such as French **de, du, des** and Italian **di, da** are usually used with certain verbs, that is to say that according to the grammar, particular verbs should always be followed by the particular preposition like Fr. **de** or It. **di** (ex. It. **parlare di**; Fr. **parler de** – to speak about). And to better know when to put the pronoun **ne** and **en**, it is advisable to learn the most common verbs followed by the preposition **de** in French and **di** in Italian.

It is notable that these pronouns can replace only a thing and never a person because in this case the disjunctive pronoun should be used. Observe the following:

It. Hai parlato di Daniela? Sì, ho parlato di **lei**.

Fr. Tu as parlé de Daniela? Oui j'ai parlé d'**elle**.

- Did you speak about Daniela? Yes, I spoke about **her**

3. **ne** and **en** are also used in such expression as:

It. **Me ne vado**;

Fr. **Je m'en vais**.

– I am going away (I am leaving).

It should be noted that the pronouns It. **ci, ne** and Fr. **y, en** go before the conjugated verb.

> **NOTE:**
> If a sentence contain two verbs, in which one is conjugated verb and one infinitive, in Italian you should attach **ci** or **ne** to the infinitive. For example:
>
> Voglio anda**rci**. – I want to go **there**.
>
> Ha bisogno di compra**rne** tre. – He needs to buy three **of them**.
>
> But in French the pronouns **y** and **en** are placed in front of the infinitive. For example:
>
> Je veux **y** aller. – I want to go **there**.
>
> Il a besoin d'**en** acheter trois. – He needs to buy three **of them**.

Prepositional (Disjunctive) Pronouns

In Romance languages the prepositional or disjunctive pronouns follow a preposition or a verb or when you want to emphasize something.

Below is the table that shows all the forms of prepositional (disjunctive) pronouns in Italian and French:

Italian	French	English
me	moi	me
te	toi	you (sing.inf)
lui/lei/Lei	lui/elle	him, it/her/you (sing.f.)
noi	nous	us
voi	vous	you (pl. inf.)
loro/Loro	eux/elles	they (m. fem)/you (pl. f)

Use of prepositional (Disjunctive) Pronouns

1. In Romance languages prepositional (disjunctive) pronouns are used after prepositions:

    It. *a, di, in, per, su, senza di*;

Fr. *à*, *de*, *en*, *pour*, *sur*, *avec*, *sans*.

- to (at), from, in, for, on (about), with, without.

For example:

It. Questo è *per* te;

Fr. C'est *pour* toi.

– *This is for you.*

It. Suo padre parla *di* me;

Fr. Son père parle *de* moi.

– *His father is talking about me.*

Use of Prepositional (Disjunctive) Pronouns in French. Special Cases

Besides the cases listed above, in French, disjunctive pronouns are also called emphatic pronouns, which are also used to emphasize something. Therefore, emphatic pronouns are used in the following circumstances:

- for emphasis (ex. *Toi*, tu m'as dit que tu étais chez toi. – *You, you told me that you were at home.*)
- for contrast (ex. *Moi*, je parle maintenant. – *Me, I speak now.*)
- on its own without a verb (ex. Qui a acheté? *Moi*. *Who bought it? Me.*)
- after *c'est* and *ce sont*, which means *it is* (ex. *C'est moi*, Daniela. – *It's me, Daniela. Ce sont eux. – It is them.*)
- in comparison (true for Italian as well) (ex. Fr. Elle est plus jeune que *lui*. It. Lei è più giovane di *lui* – *She is younger than him.*)

In order to emphasize something in Romance languages you can add It. *stesso*, Fr. *même* to the subject pronouns in Italian and to the disjunctive pronouns in French. Study the following:

CHAPTER 5: PRONOUNS

Did you know?

Totalling around 29,000km, the French rail network is the second largest in Europe (after Germany) and the ninth biggest in the world.

It. L'ho fatto **io stesso**;

Fr. Je l'ai fait **moi-même**.

– I did it **myself**.

Reflexive Pronouns

Reflexive pronouns collaborate along with reflexive verbs in order to indicate that a person performs the action toward or for himself or herself. Reflexive pronouns and reflexive verbs are widely used in Romance language (**See Reflexive Verbs p.318**).

Below is the table that shows all the forms of reflexive pronouns in Italian and French:

Italian	French	English
mi	*me/m'*	myself
ti	*te/t'*	yourself
si	*se/s'*	himself/herself/itself
ci	*nous*	ourselves
vi	*vous*	yourselves
si	*se*	themselves

For example:

It. ***Mi*** vesto;

Fr. Je ***m***'habille.

– I get dressed.

As you can see from the French example, the reflexive pronouns *me*, *te* and *se* become *m'*, *t'* and *s'* before verbs that begin with a ***vowel*** or silent ***h***. It should also be mentioned that there is a liaison between *nous* or *vous* and a word that begins with a vowel or silent ***h*** (ex. Nous nou**s h**abillons - *We get dressed*).

Use of Reflexive Pronouns

Reflexive verbs require the use of reflexive pronouns in order to show that the direct object of the verb is also the subject, that is to say the subject is performing the action on himself or herself. Compare, for example, two sentences in two Romance languages where one sentence is reflexive and another is not:

It. ***Mi*** lavo. Lavo ***il mio cane***.

Fr. Je ***me*** lave. Je lave ***mon chien***.

– *I wash **myself**. I wash **my dog**.*

The given examples demonstrate that the verb to wash yourself (It. ***lavarsi***, Fr. ***se laver***) is reflexive (used with the reflexive pronoun) and another to wash (It. **lavare**, Fr. **laver**) is not reflexive.

We can also add reflexive pronouns to some other verbs, which are not initially reflexive to make them reflexive:

Did you know?

Italy's Sardinia is one of the most ancient civilizations in Europe, which has over 7000 prehistoric archaeological sites dating from before 1000 BC.

It. ***parlarsi***,

Fr. ***se parler***

– to talk to oneself (each other).

Word Order of Reflexive Pronouns

In Italian and French, reflexive pronouns are usually put right before the verb and after indirect and direct object pronouns. (**See**

Word Order of Direct Object Pronouns p. 75 and Reflexive Verbs p.318)

In the case of compound verbs such as perfect tenses or verb + the infinitive, present progressive etc., the reflexive pronoun should either be attached to the infinitive in Italian or be placed before the infinitive in French or go before the first conjugated verb (present progressive, perfect tenses) in Italian and French (**See Word Order of Direct Object Pronouns p. 75 and Reflexive Verbs p.318**).

Possessive Adjectives and Pronouns in Romance Languages

Possessive Adjectives

Possessive adjectives (English my, your, his, her, etc.) are used to indicate possession and ownership. For example, my car, his house. In Romance languages all possessive adjectives agree in gender and number with the noun that they modify. For example:

Did you know?

Guadeloupe is a French department (since 1946), and a group of islands located in the southern Caribbean Sea. It has incredible white sand beaches and the highest waterfall in the Caribbean.

It. ***la mia*** casa,

Fr. ***ma*** maison.

– ***My*** house.

The word *"house"* in Romance languages is feminine, so we need to use possessive pronoun which is also feminine. As we could also see from the previous example, in Italian the possessive adjectives are preceded by the appropriate definite article and in French no definite articles are used with the possessive pronouns.

Below is a table presenting all the types of possessive adjectives in Romance languages:

CHAPTER 5: PRONOUNS

Italian	French	English
masc./pl.masc. *fem/pl.fem*	*masc./pl.masc.* *fem/pl.fem*	
il mio/i miei **la mia/le mie**	**mon/mes** **ma**	*my*
il tuo/i tuoi **la tua/le tue**	**ton/tes** **ta**	*your*
il suo/i suoi **la sua/le sue**	**son/ses** **sa**	*his, her, its*
il nostro/i nostri **la nostra/le nostre**	**notre/nos**	*our*
il vostro/i vostri **la vostra/le vostre**	**votre/vos**	*your*
il loro/i loro **la loro/le loro**	**leur/leurs**	*their*

    Below will be demonstrated how the possessive adjectives agree in gender and number and with a noun and how they are used in sentences. We will take words *book* (It. **libro**, Fr. **livre**), which is masculine in Romance languages and *house* (It. **casa**, Fr. **maison**), which is feminine to demonstrate it.

	Italian			
	singular		**plural**	
	masculine	**feminine**	**masculine**	**feminine**
1st person	il mio libro i miei libri	la mia casa le mie case	il nostro libro i nostri libri	la nostra casa le nostre case
2nd person	il tuo libro i tuoi libri	la tua casa le tue case	il vostro libro i vostri libri	la vostra casa le vostre case
3rd person	il suo libro i suoi libri	la sua casa le sue case	il loro libro i loro libri	la loro casa le loro case

CHAPTER 5: PRONOUNS

	singular		plural	
	masculine	**feminine**	**masculine**	**feminine**
1st person	mon livre mes livres	ma maison mes maisons	notre livre nos livres	notre maison nos maisons
2nd person	ton livre tes livres	ta maison tes maisons	votre livre vos livres	votre maison vos maisons
3rd person	son livre ses livres	sa maison ses maisons	leur livre leurs livres	leur maison leurs maisons

It is notable that in French the possessive adjectives **mon, ton** and **son** should be used before *feminine* nouns or adjectives that begin with a **vowel** or silent **h**. For example:

Elle est **mon a**mie – *she is my friend.*

C'est **mon h**istoire favorite. – *This is my favourite story.*

NOTE:

In Italian the possessive adjectives do not usually use the definite article when followed by singular nouns relating to family members or relatives (e.g. **mio** fratello – **my** brother), except with **loro** (e.g. **il loro** padre – **their** father; **i nostri** zii - *our uncles;* **i vostri** zii - *your uncles*).

Possession with *de* (French) and *di* (Italian)

In Romance languages it is possible to form the possession with the prepositions It. *di*, Fr. *de*, which are used with the name of a person or the appropriate noun in order to avoid the variety of meanings and ambiguity the use of the possessive pronouns (his, her, its), which are similar in Romance languages. Study the following:

It. la casa ***di*** John,

Fr. la maison ***de*** John.

– *John's house.*

It. la casa ***di*** un ragazzo,

Fr. la maison ***d'***un garçon.

– ***His*** house (Fr. *boy's house*).

NOTE:

In French the possession can be expressed in the following ways:

- *by **a demonstrative pronoun** + **de** + **a noun** (Ma maison est **celle de** mon **père** - My house is that of my father).*
- *by using **être à** + **the disjunctive pronoun** (Cette voiture **est à moi**. C'est ma propre voiture - This is my own car).*

Omission of Possessive Adjectives

Unlike in English, in Romance languages possessive adjectives are not used when relating to parts of the body, clothing or personal possessions when the possessor is clear, in this case, the definite article is used. For example:

It. Ha messo ***le*** mani ***nelle*** tasche,

Fr. Il a mis ***les*** mains dans ***les*** poches.

– *He put his hands in his pockets.*

But when the possessor is not clear, the possessive pronoun should be used.

Possessive Pronouns

In Romance languages possessive pronouns are used to replace a noun accompanied by a possessive adjective. They can be used to shorten a phrase (*my car – mine*). The possessive pronouns must agree with the noun it replaces in gender (masculine and feminine) and number (singular and plural) and are used with the appropriate definite article.

For instance:

Did you know?

Italian is one of Switzerland's four national languages. Over 350 thousand people (8.1%) speak it natively in Ticino and Grisons (Grigioni) cantons.

It. La tua casa è più grande **della mia**;

Fr. Ta maison est plus grande que **la mienne**.

– *Your house is bigger than* **mine**.

It. Il mio computer è rotto. Posso usare **il tuo**?;

Fr. Mon ordinateur est en panne. Puis-je utiliser **le tien**?

– *My computer is broken. Can I use* **yours**?

The possessive pronouns can also be used with contracted forms of the definite article. (**See Contraction of the Article p.63**). For example:

It. Ho inviato una lettera al mio amico. L'hai mandato **al** tuo?;

Fr. J'ai envoyé une lettre à mon ami. En as-tu envoyé **au** tien?

– *I sent a letter to my friend. Did you send one* **to** *yours?*

NOTE:

In Italian the definite article is usually omitted after the verb **essere**: Questo libro **è mio** - *This* book **is mine**.

Below is the table presenting all the types of possessive pronouns in Romance languages:

Italian	French	English
masc./pl.masc. *fem/pl.fem*	*masc./pl.masc.* *fem/pl.fem*	
il mio/i miei **la mia/le mie**	**le mien/les miens** **la mienne/les miennes**	*mine*
il tuo/i tuoi **la tua/le tue**	**le tien/les tiens** **la tienne/les tiennes**	*yours*
il suo/i suoi **la sua/le sue**	**le sien/les siens** **la sienne/les siennes**	*his, hers, its*
il nostro/i nostri **la nostra/le nostre**	**le nôtre/les nôtres** **la nôtre/les nôtres**	*ours*
il vostro/i vostri **la vostra/le vostre**	**le vôtre/les vôtres** **la vôtre/les vôtres**	*yours*
il loro/i loro **la loro/le loro**	**le leur/les leurs** **la leur/les leurs**	*theirs*

Look at the following examples:

It. E'questo il cellulare di Maria? Sì, questo è ***il suo***.

Fr. Est-ce le téléphone portable de Maria? Oui, c'est ***le sien***.

– *Is this Maria's cellphone. Yes, it is* **hers**.

Demonstrative Adjectives and Pronouns in Italian and French

Demonstrative Adjectives

Demonstrative adjectives (English this/that and these/those) are used with nouns which they modify and point out the location of a particular thing or person. They are basically used to say "*which*" noun or to emphasize a noun, for example, ***this*** man, ***that*** car.

In Romance languages all demonstrative adjectives agree in gender and number with the noun that they modify. For example:

Did you know?

Luxembourg has 3 official languages: French, German and Luxembourgish. Children are taught in Luxembourgish in nursery schools, and French and German at primary schools.

It. **quest'**uomo,

Fr. **cet** homme.

– ***This*** man.

It. **questa** donna,

Fr. **cette** femme.

– ***This*** woman.

The word "*man*" in Romance languages is masculine, so we need to use a demonstrative adjective which is also masculine, whereas the word "*woman*" is feminine and thus, the masculine demonstrative adjective should be used. As we could also see from the previous examples, the definite article is not used with demonstrative adjectives in Italian and French.

It should be mentioned that Italian has two sets of demonstrative adjectives like English and French has only one.

Forms of Demonstrative Adjectives

Below is a table presenting all the sets of demonstrative adjectives in Romance languages:

Demonstrative adjectives	Italian	French
this (*singular masc. and fem.*)	*questo/questa*	*ce (cet)/cette*
these (*plural masc. and fem.*)	*questi/queste*	**ces**

CHAPTER 5: PRONOUNS

Demonstrative adjectives	Italian	French
that *(singular masc. and fem.)*	quello (quel')/ quella	—
those *(plural masc. and fem.)*	quei (quegli)/ quelle	—
that over there *(singular masc. and fem.)*	—	—
those over there *(plural masc. and fem.)*	—	—

NOTE:

In Italian the forms of the demonstrative adjective **quello** are similar to the forms of the definite article (e.g. <u>masculine</u>: **quello** studente – **quell'**amico – **quel** libro – **quegli** studenti – **quei** libri; <u>feminine</u>: **quella** studentessa – **quell'**amica – **quella** rivista – **quelle** studentesse – **quelle** riviste.) **(See the Definite Article p.51)**. Also, **quello** has the same forms as **bello** (beautiful) **(See Bello p.35)**

In French, the demonstrative adjective **ce** becomes **cet** in front of masculine singular nouns which begin with a vowel and most words beginning with **h**.

Demonstrative Adjectives *this* and *these* in Romance Languages

As it is seen from the table demonstrative adjectives:

It. **questo/quella/questi/queste**; Fr. **ce (cet)/cette/ces** - *this,these* are used to indicate nouns which are physically near the speaker and the person to whom he or she is speaking. It is within reaching distance. For example:

It. **Questo** libro è il mio preferito;

Fr. **Ce** livre est mon favori

CHAPTER 5: PRONOUNS

Did you know?

If you're looking for "latte" in Italy, you will probably be served a glass of milk. Instead, you should ask for "latte macchiato" which is milk with espresso.

– **This** book is my favourite.

It. **Questa** casa è molto bella;

Fr. **Cette** maison est très belle

– **This** house is very beautiful.

These demonstrative adjectives also signify the time and proximity:

It. Vado all'università **questo pomeriggio**;

Fr. Je vais à l'université **cet après-midi**.

– I go to the university **this afternoon**.

Demonstrative Adjectives *that* and *those* in Romance Languages

It. **quello/quella/quei (quegli)/quelle** - that, those are used indicate nouns which are farther from the speaker and not within the reach or rather the noun can be nearer to the listener, not the speaker.

NOTE:

As is obvious from the table, demonstrative adjectives such as <u>that</u> and <u>those</u> do not exist in French, but in order to make a clear distinction between <u>this</u> and <u>that</u>, the suffixes **–ci** (this) or – **là** (that) are added to the noun (e.g. ce livre-**ci** – ce livre-**là** – this book – that book). However, it is possible to use **ce (cet)/cette/ces** to say <u>that</u> or <u>those</u>.

Below are the examples that demonstrate the use of *that* and *those* in Romance languages:

It. Quanto costa **quel** cappello?

CHAPTER 5: PRONOUNS

Fr. Combien coûte ce chapeau-*là*?

– *How much does **that** hat cost?*

> **Did you know?**
>
> Paris Gare du Nord is Europe's busiest railway station with over 195 million passengers passing through each year.

It. **Quella** maglietta è molto costosa;

Fr. Cette chemise-***là*** est très chère.

– ***That** shirt is very expensive.*

Word Order of Demonstrative Adjectives

Demonstrative adjectives in Romance languages are placed right before the noun they modify. If there is one or more than one noun in the sentence, the demonstrative adjective should be placed before each noun, for example:

It. **Quei** libri e ***quei*** giornali sono sul tavolo;

Fr. **Ces** livres et **ces** journaux sont sur la table.

– ***Those** books and **those** newspapers are on the table.*

Demonstrative Pronouns

Demonstrative pronouns demonstrate or indicate the location of the noun they replace. You can use demonstrative pronouns when you have several options to choose and while choosing you can say "*this one*" (the one close to you) or "*that one*" (the one far from you). So, the words "*this one*" and "*that one*" are both demonstrative pronouns.

Demonstrative pronouns in Romance languages replace a noun in a phrase instead of modifying it like an adjective would. Observe the following:

It. **Quello** che lavora qui è mio fratello.

CHAPTER 5: PRONOUNS

Fr. ***Celui*** qui travaille ici est mon frère.

– ***This one*** who works here is my brother.

Forms of Demonstrative Pronouns

Below is a table presenting all the sets of demonstrative pronouns in Romance languages:

Demonstrative pronouns	Italian	French
this *(singular masc. and fem.)*	*questo/questa*	*celui/celle*
these *(plural masc. and fem.)*	*questi/queste*	*ceux/celles*
that *(singular masc. and fem.)*	*quello/quella*	—
those *(plural masc. and fem.)*	*quelli/quelle*	—
that over there *(singular masc. and fem.)*	—	—
those over there *(plural masc. and fem.)*	—	—

Like demonstrative adjectives, demonstrative pronouns of Romance languages have similar set, demonstrating the location of a noun (object) and how far from the speaker it is. All demonstrative pronouns agree in gender and number with the noun that they substitute.

NOTE:

In French in order to distinguish between this one and that one and between these and those, the suffixes **–ci** (this) or **–là** (that) are added to demonstrative pronoun (e.g. J'aime celui-**ci** – J'aime celle-**là** – I like **this one** – I like **that one**).

In Italian in order to emphasize the forms of **questo** and **quello**, the words **qui** (here) and **là/lì** (there) may be used (e.g. Mi piace **questo** *qui* – *Mi piace **quello lì** – I like **this one here** – I like **that one there***).

Below is an example that demonstrates the use of demonstrating pronouns in Romance languages:

It. La mia casa è più grande di ***quella***;

Fr. Ma maison est plus grande que ***celle-là***.

– *My house is bigger than **that one***.

Possession with the Demonstrative Pronoun and *de* (*di*)

In Romance languages the demonstrative pronoun followed by the preposition **de** in French and **di** in Italian can indicate possession. For example:

It. L'automobile di Peter e ***quella di*** Maria;

Fr. La voiture de Peter et ***celle de*** Maria.

– *Peter's car and Maria's*.

Did you know?

Naples is the 3rd largest city in Italy after Rome and Milan. It has a population of about 1 million people. It is also one of the oldest continuously inhabited cities in the world (over 2800 years).

Interrogative Pronouns and Adjectives

In Romance languages direct and indirect questions, other than "yes or no" questions, contain interrogative words at the beginning of the phrase. Such interrogative words can be pronouns, adjectives or adverbs as they answer the questions: *Who? What? Where? How? When? Why?*. For example:

CHAPTER 5: PRONOUNS

It. ***Cos'***è questo?

Fr. ***Qu'est-ce que*** c'est?

- ***What*** is this?

Below is the table showing all the interrogative words in Romance languages:

Interrogative words	Italian	French
	s.masc./s.fem./ pl.masc./pl.fem.	s.masc./s.fem./ pl.masc./pl.fem.
what/which?	***cosa (cos')/che cosa/che?***	***que (qu')?***
about what?	***di che?***	***de quoi?***
who/whom?	***chi?***	***qui?***
whose?	***di chi?***	***à qui (de qui)?***
which one(-s)?	***quale/ quali?***	***quel/quelle/ quels/quelles?***
		lequel/laquelle/ lesquels/lesquelles
how much/how many?	***quanto/quanta/ quanti/quante?***	***combien?***
how?	***come?***	***comment?***
when?	***quando?***	***quand?***
where?	***dove?***	***où?***
from where?	***di (da) dove?***	***d'où?***
why?	***perché?***	***pourquoi?***

NOTE:

In French:

- **que** becomes **qu'** before a word that begins with a vowel (**qui** never combines with a word beginning with a vowel), for example: **qui** as-tu vu?; **qu'**as-tu vu?- Whom did you see?; What did you see?.
- Also it should be noted that French **que** cannot be used after a preposition, in this case, **quoi** should be used, for example: **à quoi** pense-tu? – What are you thinking about?
- **Quoi** can be used without a verb in certain idiomatic expressions, for example: **Quoi** de neuf? **Quoi** de nouveau? – What's new?
- **Quoi** can also be used alone, for example: **Quoi**? Vous me parlez? – What? Are you speaking with me?
- in French interrogative words are widely used with **est-ce que** or **est-ce qu'** (before a vowel) constructions, which are placed right after the interrogative word, and in this case, the word order is direct, for example: **qu'est-ce que** tu fais (**que** fais-tu?) - What do you do?

What
It. Cosa (Che, Che cosa), Fr. Que (Qu')/Quoi

The interrogative pronouns It. **cosa** (**che, che cosa**), Fr. **que** (**qu'**)/**quoi** - *what* can be used as subjects, direct objects, or objects of a preposition. For example:

Did you know?

The Republic of Madagascar is the 4th largest island in the world. It has 2 official languages - French and Malagasy. Madagascar was under French rule from 1895-1957.

As a subject:

It. **Cos'**è quello?

Fr. **Qu'est-ce que** c'est?

– **What** is that?

As an object:

It. ***Cosa*** (***Che, Che cosa***) vuoi?

Fr. ***Que*** veux-tu?

– ***What*** do you want?

These interrogative pronouns can also be used after prepositions such as (It. ***a, di, in, su***; Fr. ***à, de, en***) **(See Verbs with Prepositions and Prepositions p.370)**.

For instance, they are used with the preposition It. ***di*** and Fr. ***de*** meaning *about, from*: It. ***di che?*** Fr. ***de quoi?*** – *about what?*. In this case the interrogative pronouns are used:

As objects of a preposition:

It. ***Di che*** parlano?

Fr. ***De quoi*** parlent-ils?

– ***What*** do they talk about?

NOTE:
In Italian **che, che cosa** and **cosa** are equally used depending on a region *(e.g. **Che** fai? – **Che cosa** fai? – **Cosa** fai? – **What** are you doing?)*

Who
It. *Chi*, Fr. *Qui*

The interrogative pronouns It. ***chi***, Fr. ***qui*** can be used as subjects, direct objects, or objects of a preposition in the sentences as well.

As a subject:

It. ***Chi*** è lei?

Fr. ***Qui*** est-elle?
– ***Who*** is she?

As an object:

It. ***Chi*** vuoi vedere?
Fr. ***Qui*** voulez-vous voir?
– ***Who*** do you want to see?

As object of a preposition:

It. ***Di chi*** parlano?
Fr. ***De qui*** parlent-ils?
– ***Who*** are they talking about?

Whose
de (di or à) + It. ***Chi****, Fr.* ***Qui***

These interrogative pronouns can also be used with the preposition It. **di** and Fr. **à** meaning *whose*, denoting ownership for people: It. ***di chi?*** Fr. ***à qui?*** – *whose?* For instance:

It. ***Di chi*** è questa casa?
Fr. ***À qui*** est cette maison?
– ***Whose*** house is this?

NOTE:

In French ***De qui*** *is used to denote relationship to someone. For example:* ***De qui*** *est-il le frère?*
– ***Whose*** *brother is he?*

Which or Which one/ones
It. *Quale*, Fr. *Quel (Lequel)*

NOTE:

In Italian **quale** drops the final *–e* before *è* or *era*, and an apostrophe is not used: **Qual** era il film che guardavi? – **What** was the film that you watched?

In Italian these interrogative pronouns agree in number with what it is referred to, whereas in French they agree in gender and number. Normally the interrogative pronouns It. **quale/quali**, Fr. **quel/quelle/quels/quelles** can be used with reference both to people or things. For example:

It. **Qual** è il nome di questa via?

Fr. **Quel** est le nom de cette rue?

– **What** is the name of this street?

It should be remembered that It. **quale**, Fr. **quel** are also used, instead of It. **che**, Fr. **que (qu')**, with the verb It. **essere**; Fr. **être** followed by an abstract noun, unless a mere definition is being requested, for instance:

It. **Qual** è la ragione per la quale è partito?

Fr. **Quelle** est la raison pour laquelle il est parti?

– **What** is the reason for which he left?

It. **Cos'**è il buddismo?

Fr. **Qu'est-ce que** le bouddhisme?

– **What** is Buddhism?

Difference between
It. *Quale*, Fr. *Quel (Lequel)* and
It. *Che*, Fr. *Que (Qu')*

It should be noted that It. *quale*, Fr. *quel* (*lequel*) express more clearly the idea of choice from a limited number of things than It. *chi*, Fr. *qui*. The principal difference between these two types of interrogative pronouns is that It. *che*, Fr. *que* (*qu'*) is usually followed by <u>a noun</u> but It. *quale*, Fr. *quel* (*lequel*) <u>never</u> is. For example:

It. *Che musica* preferisci? *Qual è* la tua musica preferita?

Fr. *Quelle musique* préfères-tu? *Quelle est* votre musique favorite?

– **What music** do you prefer? **Which is** your favourite music?

French *lequel*

The interrogative word ***lequel*** which means *which one* agrees with the noun to which it refers (***lequel/laquelle/lesquels/lesquelles***). The main difference between French ***quel*** and ***lequel*** is that

- ***lequel*** is used with more limited number of things to choose from (2 or 3 things):

Lesquels de ces livres veux-tu?

– **Which ones** of these books do you want?

(***lequel*** means *which one* only, whereas ***quel*** can also stand for *which*).

- ***lequel*** is used after prepositions such as ***à*** or ***de*** (except in feminine singular), while ***quel*** never is (**See Verbs with Prepositions p.370**). For example:

Auquel de ces hommes parles-tu?

– ***To which*** one of these men are you speaking?

Desquelles parles-tu?

– **Of which ones** do you speak?

Below is the table with contracted forms of *lequel* with *à* and *de*:

French	
à	*de*
à + lequel = auquel	de + lequel = duquel
à + laquelle = à laquelle (not combined)	de + laquelle = de laquelle (not combined)
à + lesquels = auxquels	de + lesquels = desquels
à + lesquelles = auxquelles	de + lesquelles = desquelles

How much/How many
It. Quanto, Fr. Combien

In Italian the interrogative pronouns It. **quanto/quanta/quanti/quante** (*how much/how many*) must also agree in number and gender with the noun it modifies, while in French the interrogative pronoun Fr. **combien** does not.

It. **Quanto** costa questa camicia?

Fr. **Combien** coûte cette chemise?

– **How much** does this shirt cost?

It. **Quante** mele hai?

Fr. **Combien de** pommes as-tu?

– **How many** apples do you have?

NOTE:

In French the preposition **de** is used with

CHAPTER 5: PRONOUNS

combien *before a noun:*
Combien de *tables? - How many tables?*

How
It. Come, Fr. Comment

Along with all listed above interrogative pronouns, some adverbs are also used to ask questions. For example:

It. ***Come*** stai?

Fr. ***Comment*** vas-tu?

– ***How*** *are you?*

It. ***Come*** ti chiami?

Fr. ***Comment*** t'appelles-tu?

– ***What*** *is your name?*

When
It. Quando, Fr. Quand

It. ***Quando*** vieni?

Fr. ***Quand*** viens-tu?

– ***When*** *are you coming?*

Where
It. Dove, Fr. Où

It. ***Dove*** si trova il bagno?

Fr. ***Où*** se trouvent les toilettes?

– ***Where*** *is the restroom?*

It. **Dov'è** la banca?

Fr. **Où** est la banque?

– *Where* is the bank?

From where
It. Di (Da) dove, Fr. D'où

It. **Di dov'è** Lei?

Fr. **D'où** êtes-vous?

– *Where* are you from?

Why
It. Perché, Fr. Pourquoi

Did you know?

Breakfast in Italy is a simple affair. If you want to eat like the locals, you'll have to be satisfied with just a cappuccino and a croissant (such as brioche).

It. **Perché** dici questo?

Fr. **Pourquoi** dis-tu cela?

– *Why* do you say that?

Exclamations with Interrogative Pronouns

Exclamations are used in order to convey a strong feeling or opinion about something. Exclamatory words make a phrase into a statement of surprise or amazement. They are very similar to interrogative words, but instead of asking something, they declare an idea or opinion, for example:

CHAPTER 5: PRONOUNS

It. **Che** bello!

Fr. **Quel** beauté!

– **How** nice!

> **NOTE:**
> In French, a noun should be used with **Quel/Quelle/Quels/Quelles** to convey an exclamation.

Below are the exclamatory words used in Romance languages:

Exclamatory words	Italian	French
	s.masc./s.fem./pl.masc./pl.fem.	s.masc./s.fem./pl.masc./pl.fem.
What a! (How!)	Che!	Quel!/Quelle!/Quels!/Quelles!
How much/how many!	Quanto! Quanta! Quanti! Quante!	Combien!
How!	Come!	Comme! Que!

> **NOTE:**
> In French in order to say **What a...!** the exclamatory word **Quel/Quelle/Quels/Quelles...!** is used. It is used with a noun.
>
> It is also possible to use **Comme** or **Que**, since they are utterly interchangeable.

What a! (How!)
It. *Che!* Fr. *Quel!*

In Romance languages these exclamatory words are used in front of nouns, adjectives and adverbs and mean *How* or *What a...!*:

CHAPTER 5: PRONOUNS

It. *Che* macchina!

Fr. *Quelle* voiture!

– *What a* car!

It. *Che* buono!

Fr. *Quel* délice!

– *How* delicious!

NOTE:

In Romance languages a qualifying adjective after the noun is usually preceded by either It. *più, tanto;* Fr. *plus, tant - the most, so.*

How much/how many!
It. Quanto! Fr. Combien!

These exclamatory words are used in front of nouns in order to express surprise at an amount and in front of a verb to stress the intensity or extent of the action *How many* (*much*):

It. *Quanti* amici hai!

Fr. *Combien d'*amis qu'as-tu!

– You have *so many* friends!

It. *Quanto* abbiamo corso questa mattina!

Fr. *Combien* nous avons couru ce matin!

– We ran *so much* this morning!

How!
It. Come! Fr. Comment!

These exclamatory words are only used in front of verbs to express surprise at how a verb was done:

It. **Come** balla quell'uomo!

Fr. **Comment** danse cet homme!

– **Oh how** that man dances!

Relative Pronouns

Relative pronouns (*who, whom, which, that, where, whose* in English) are used to introduce a clause that modifies a noun in order to make it clear which person or thing is being talked about. For example: The man *who* you see is my brother. In the example "*who you see*" is the relative clause introduced by the relative pronoun *who*.

Relative pronouns are also used to introduce further information about someone or something. For example: My brother, *who* is an outstanding singer, released a new album.

The clause which is introduced by the relative pronouns designates *the subordinate clause*. The clause containing the component modified by the relative clause is called *the main clause*. The noun, pronoun or phrase which is modified by the relative pronoun is called an *antecedent*.

It should be mentioned that, in English, the relative pronouns can be omitted (e.g. the book *that* you bought is interesting = the book you bought is interesting), but in Romance languages *that* is always required. Observe the following:

Did you know?

Marcel Proust's masterpiece A la recherche du temps perdu (Remembrance of things past) holds the record as the world's longest novel. It has 13 volumes and over 3,000 pages.

It. il libro **che** hai comprato è interessante;

Fr. le livre **que** tu as acheté est intéressant.

– The book (**that**) you bought is interesting.

Generally speaking the relative pronouns are used to connect two short sentences, for example:

It. Peter vive in una città. La città si chiama Sydney. = Peter vive in una città **che** si chiama Sydney.

Fr. Peter vit dans une ville. La ville s'appelle Sydney. = Peter vit dans une ville **qui** s'appelle Sydney.

Peter lives in a city. The city is called Sydney. = Peter lives in a city (**that is**) called Sydney.

Below is a table demonstrating the relative pronouns in Romance languages:

Relative pronouns	**Italian**	**French**
	s.masc./s.fem./ pl.masc./pl.fem.	s.masc./s.fem./ pl.masc./pl.fem.
that/who/which	***che***	***que (qu')***
who/whom/which	***cui***	***lequel/laquelle lesquels/lesquelles***
who/ whom	***chi***	***qui***
	colui che/colei che coloro che	
who/whom/which	***il quale/ la quale i quali/le quali***	—
what/which (neuter)	***quello che/ quel che/ciò che***	***ce qui/ ce que***
as much/ many	***quanto/quanta/ quanti/quante***	***combien***
whose	***il cui/la cui i cui/le cui***	***dont***

Relative pronouns	Italian	French
where	*dove*	*où*
when	*quando*	*quand*

That/Who/Which
It. Che, Fr. Que

This relative pronoun is one of the most frequently used in Romance languages. It can refer to either people or things. In Italian it can be used as the subject or object of a clause, whereas in French the relative pronoun **que** functions only as the direct object of a clause (**qui** is used as a subject of a clause). It is notable that in French **que** becomes **qu'** before a vowel. For example:

As the subject:

    It. La donna **che vive** là è mia sorella.

    Fr. La femme **qui vit** là est ma sœur.

    – The woman **who lives** there is my sister.

As the object:

    It. La donna **che abbiamo visto** ieri è mia sorella.

    Fr. La femme **que nous avons vu** hier est ma sœur.

    – The woman **who we saw** yesterday is my sister.

Que (Fr.) and **che** (It.) are used after nouns denoting periods of time (e.g. It. **volta, giorno, anno**; Fr. **fois, jour, an** - time, day, year.

For example:

    It. La prima **volta che** lo vidi era la settimana scorsa;

    Fr. La première **fois que** je l'ai vu c'était la semaine dernière.

– *The first time (that) I saw him was last week.*

Who/Whom/Which
It. *Cui*; Fr. *Lequel*

In Italian and French the relative pronouns It. *cui*; Fr. *lequel/laquel/lesquels/lesquelles* (*who/whom/which*) are used instead of It. *che*, Fr. *que* when it is preceded by a preposition.

These relative pronouns can be used with the following prepositions:

It. *a, con, di, da, in, per, su, tra/fra*;

Fr. *à, avec, de, dans, pour, sur*.

Also, these relative pronouns can refer to things or persons and agree with antecedent, except Italian:

It. La casa **in cui** vivo è grande.

Fr. La maison **dans laquelle** j'habite est grande.

– *The house **in which** I live is big.*

It. Il motivo **per cui** lo fa è chiaro.

Fr. La raison **pour laquelle** elle le fait est claire.

– *The reason **why/for which** she does it is clear.*

NOTE:

In French the relative pronoun Fr. **qui** is used with the preposition when it refers to person, whereas in Italian it is always **cui** that is used with prepositions. (**See the Relative Pronoun Qui p.120**), for instance:

It. Il ragazzo **a cui** parlo è intelligente.

Fr. Le garçon **à qui** je parle est intelligent.

– The boy **with whom** I speak is smart.

It should be noted that, in English, in informal speech a preposition can be placed at the end of the relative clause, but in Romance languages it should be placed immediately before the associated relative pronoun (ex. The boy *whom* I speak *with* is smart).

Combination of French **Lequel** with Prepositions

French **lequel/lesquelles/lesquels** (*which*) is combined with the prepositions **à** and **de** and the definite article (**laquelle** doesn't change).

Below is the table with all combined forms:

French	
à	**de**
à + lequel = auquel	de + lequel = duquel
à + laquelle = à laquelle	de + laquelle = de laquelle
à + lesquels = auxquels	de + lesquels = desquels
à + lesquelles = auxquelles	de + lesquelles = desquelles

Who/Whom/The one who
It. Che, Fr. Qui

This relative pronoun is also one of the most frequently used in Romance languages.

NOTE:

It should be remembered that in French **qui** can be used only as the subject of the clause and may refer to either a person or a thing.

In Italian **che** is used in this case.

This relative pronoun can be used in the constructions "*it is/was (you/Peter/him and etc.) who (the one/those who/that)*", when the verb It. **essere**, Fr. **être** – *to be* introduces the subordinate clause:

It. È stato lui **che** l'ha fatto.

Fr. C'était lui **qui** l'avait fait.

– *It was he **who** did it.*

It. È lei **che** non vuole venire.

Fr. C'est elle **qui** ne veut pas venir.

– *It is her **who** does not want to come.*

In French the relative pronouns Fr. **qui** are used to refer to a person and follow a preposition such as:

*Fr. **avec, à, contre, entre, pour, sauf (excepté), sur;***

Study the following example:

Fr. La femme **avec qui** je parlais est ma professeure.

– *The woman **with whom** I spoke is my professor.*

(or *The woman **whom** I spoke **with** is my professor*).

NOTE:

In Italian, it is always **cui** that is used with prepositions:

It. La donna **con cui** ho parlato è la mia professoressa.

– *The woman **with whom** I spoke is my professor.*

(or *The woman **whom** I spoke **with** is my professor*).

Who/Whom
Italian ***Colui che/Colei che/Coloro che***

In Italian **chi** is always followed by *a singular verb* (**Chi** studia, impara – *He who studies, learns*). Alternate forms of **chi** are **colui che**, **colei che**, **coloro che**. **Coloro che** is followed by *a plural verb*:

Colui che studia, impara; = ***Colei che*** studia, impara; = ***Coloro che*** studiano, imparano.

- *He who studies, learns = She who studies, learns = They who study, learn.*

Who/Whom/Which
It. *Il quale*

In Italian this relative pronoun can be used instead of It. **che** (**cui**). Therefore they are similar in terms of their grammatical function; however they are not very common in speech and are primarily used in written language and official documents.

It. Gli amici con ***i quali*** ho studiato, hanno trovato un lavoro.

– *My friends with **whom** I studied found a job.*

In colloquial Italian the sentence would be:

It. Gli amici con **cui** ho studiato, hanno trovato un lavoro.

What/Which
Neuter Relative Pronoun It. ***quello che/quel che/ ciò che****; Fr.* ***ce qui/ce que***

In Romance languages the neuter relative pronouns It. **quello che/quel che/ciò che**; Fr. **ce qui/ce que** are used to replace a general or abstract idea when there is no antecedent:

CHAPTER 5: PRONOUNS

It. ***Quello che (Quel che)*** dici è vero.

Fr. ***Ce que*** tu dis est vrai.

– ***What*** you say is true.

It. Non capisco ***ciò che*** dici.

Fr. Je ne comprends pas ***ce que*** tu dis.

– I don't understand ***what*** you say.

NOTE:

It should be mentioned that in French the neuter relative pronoun ***ce qui*** is used as the subject of the clause and ***ce que*** – as the object of a verb in a relative clause. For example:

<u>As the subject</u>:

Fr. ***Ce qui*** est intéressant est sa manière de chanter.

– ***What*** is interesting is his manner of singing.

<u>As the object</u>:

Fr. Je ne comprends pas ***ce que*** vous dites

– I do not understand ***what*** you say.

In Romance languages the neuter relative pronoun can be combined with It. ***tutto***; Fr. ***tout*** – *everything*:

It. ***Tutto ciò che*** fa è buono.

Fr. ***Tout ce qu'***il fait est bon.

– ***Everything*** he does is good.

Whose
It. *il cui*; Fr. *dont*

The relative pronouns It. ***il cui*** (***la cui, i cui, le cui***), Fr. ***dont*** denote <u>ownership</u>. They can refer to people or things and are immediately followed by a noun with which they agree in gender and number (except in French). Observe the following:

It. Ho un amico *il cui* padre è un medico.

Fr. J'ai un ami *dont* le père est un médecin.

– *I have a friend whose father is a doctor.*

It. Sandra, *la cui* sorella ha una boutique, studia con me.

Fr. Sandra, *dont* la sœur a une boutique, étudie avec moi.

– *Sandra, whose sister has a boutique, studies with me.*

NOTE:
In French *dont* can also mean *of (about) which, of (about) whom*:

Fr. L'homme *dont* vous parlez est mon patron.
– *The man of whom you speak is my boss.*

Fr. Le plat *dont* nous parlons est bon.
– *The dish of which we speak is tasty.*

Dont cannot be followed by a possessive adjective (e.g. C'est le garçon *dont* je connais les parents. – *This is the boy whose parents I know*).

Where
It. *dove*, Fr. *où*

In Romance languages It. *dove*, Fr. *où* introduce a relative clause that refers to a place or time in order to avoid using a preposition and a form of It. *cui*, Fr. *lequel*:

CHAPTER 5: PRONOUNS

It. Questa è la casa dove vive l'attore. (Questa è la casa in cui vive l'attore);

Fr. Ceci est la maison où vit l'acteur (Ceci est la maison dans laquelle vit l'acteur).

– This is the house where the actor lives (This is the house in which the actor lives).

NOTE:

In Romance languages they may have some variations:

It. **dove** (does not change)/**di (da) dove**, Fr. **où** (does not change)/ **d'où** – to where/from where:

It. Il museo **dove (in cui)** vai è bello;
Fr. Le musée **où** tu vas est beau.
– The museum you are going to is beautiful.

It. **Di dove** sei? (but **Da dove** vieni?)
Fr. **D'où** es-tu?
- Where are you from?

When
It. *quando*, Fr. *quand*

Example:

Did you know?

Milan is the second biggest Italian city (over 1.3 million people) after Rome (over 2.8 million people). Milan is considered to be the financial and economic capital of Italy.

It. Ho un esame la prossima settimana **quando** arrivano i tuoi genitori.

Fr. J'ai un examen la semaine prochaine **quand** tes parents arrivent.

– I have an exam next week **when** your parents arrive.

Indefinite Adjectives and Pronouns

Indefinite adjectives and pronouns are groups of words which are used to quantify inexactly things or people (e.g. *some, several, a few, many*), distinguish one thing from another (e.g. *other, a certain*), or relate one thing to another (e.g. *each, both*). In general, indefinite adjectives and pronouns refer to an unspecified third person or thing.

Below are the most common indefinite adjectives and pronouns in Romance languages:

Italian	French	English
s.masc./s.fem. pl.masc./pl.fem.	s.masc./s.fem. pl.masc./pl.fem.	
qualcosa	quelque chose	*something*
qualcuno	quelqu'un	*someone*
alcuno/alcuna alcuni/alcune	quelque/ quelques	*some*
certo/certa/ certi/certe	certain/certaine certains	*certain*
tale/tali	tel/telle tels/telles	*such*
ogni	chaque	*each, every*
ognuno/ognuna	chacun/chacune	
vario/varie vari/varie; diverso/diversa diversi/diverse	divers/ diverses	*various, several*
differente/differenti	différent/différente/ differents/différentes	*different*
solo/sola soli/sole	seul/seule seuls/seules	*alone*
sufficiente/-i (*adj.*)	suffisant/suffisante suffisants/suffisantes (*adj.*)	*enough, sufficient*

Italian	French	English
abbastanza (*adv.*)	assez (*adv.*)	
molto/molta molti/molte	beaucoup/ beaucoup de; plusieurs	*many, much, a lot*
poco/poca pochi/poche	peu	*few*
troppo/ troppa troppi/ troppe	trop de	*too many/ much*
	trop (*adv.*)	
tutto/tutta tutti/tutte	tout/toute tous/toutes	*all*
tutto	tout	*everything*
il resto	le reste	*the rest (the others)*
nessuno/nessuna nessuni/nessune	aucun/aucune aucuns/aucunes	*none*
nessuno	personne	*nobody/no one*
niente	rien	*nothing*
entrambi/ambedue (tutti e due)	les deux (tous les deux)	*both*

Something
It. ***qualcosa****, Fr.* ***quelque chose***

It is invariable and can be used as a pronoun (when referring only to things) meaning "*something*" or "*anything*":

It. Ho **qualcosa** per te;

Fr. J'ai **quelque chose** pour toi.

– *I have* **something** *for you.*

It. Vuoi **qualcosa**?

Fr. Veux-tu **quelque chose**?

– *Do you want **anything**?*

Someone
*It. **qualcuno**; Fr. **quelqu'un***

It is a pronoun that refers only to people meaning "*someone*" or "*somebody*". When it is used in questions it means "*anyone*" or "*anybody*":

It. C'è **qualcuno** in casa;

Fr. Il y a **quelqu'un** dans la maison.

– *There is **someone** in the house.*

It. **Qualcuno** ha visto John?

Fr. **Quelqu'un** a vu John?

– *Has **anyone** seen John?*

Some
*It. **alcuno**; Fr. **quelque***

Italian **alcuno** and French **quelque** can be used as an adjective or as a pronoun that refers to things, places or people meaning "*some*" and "*any*". They agree in number and gender:

It. (*s.masc.*) **alcuno**; (*s.fem.*) **alcuna**; (*pl.masc.*) **alcuni**; (*pl.fem.*) **alcune**.

Unlike other Romance languages, in French **quelque** agrees only in number:

Fr. (*singular*) **quelque**; (*plural*) **quelques**.

CHAPTER 5: PRONOUNS

In the plural Italian **alcuni** and French **quelques** mean *"some"* or *'a few"*. When they are used in questions they mean *"any"*. When they are used as pronouns they mean *"one/some of them"*:

It. Ci sono **alcune** città dove non ci sono teatri;

Fr. Il y a **quelques** villes où il n'y a pas de théâtres.

– *In **some** cities there are no theatres.*

It. Ho visto **alcune** persone nella strada;

Fr. J'ai vu **quelques** personnes dans la rue

– *I saw **some** people in the street.*

Certain
It. certo, Fr. certain

It. **certo**, Fr. **certain** are adjectives which agree in number and gender and are placed before the noun meaning *"certain"*:

It. **Certe** macchine sono molto care.

Fr. **Certaines** voitures sont très chères.

– ***Certain** cars are very expensive.*

It is notable once It. **certo**, Fr. **certain** put after the noun, they mean reliable, definite, certain:

It. Non è **certo**;

Fr. Ce n'est pas **certain**.

– *It is not **certain**.*

Such
It. tale; Fr. tel

Italian **tale** can only vary in number (Plural It. **tali**), except in French where **tel** can agree in number and gender respectively: (*s.masc.*) **tel**, (*s.fem.*) **telle**, (*pl.masc.*) **tels**, (*pl.fem.*) **telles**. They can only come before a noun in Romance languages.

It. **Tale** professione è prestigiosa;

Fr. **Telle** profession est prestigieuse

– **Such** *a profession is prestigious.*

It. Non mi piacciono **tali** cose;

Fr. Je n'aime pas de **telles** choses.

– *I don't like* **such** *things.*

It should be remembered that It. **tale**; Fr. **tel** cannot be followed by an indefinite article, like it can in English.

Every
It. ogni; Fr. chaque

It. **ogni**; Fr. **chaque** – "*every/each*" are unchangeable and are used as an adjective:

It. Vado in Spagna **ogni** anno;

Fr. Je vais en Espagne **chaque** année.

– *I go to Spain* **every** *year.*

Each one, Everyone
Italian ognuno and French chacun

It. (*s.masc*) ***ognuno*** / (*s.fem.*) ***ognuna*** and Fr. (*s.masc.*) ***chacun*** / (*s.fem.*) ***chacune*** are used as nouns and mean "*each one*" or "*everyone*":

It. ***Ognuno*** ha i propri gusti;

Fr. ***Chacun*** a son propre goût.

– ***Everyone*** *has its own taste.*

Several, Varied
It. vario (diverso); Fr. divers

These are used as an indefinite adjective as well as a pronoun meaning "*several*". In French it is only used in the plural with the masculine and feminine forms (Fr. ***divers/diverses***, whereas in Italian ***vario*** and ***diverso*** also has the singular: (*s.masc.*) ***vario/diverso***, (*s.fem.*) ***varia/diversa***, (*pl.masc.*) ***vari/diversi***, (*pl.fem.*) ***varie/diverse***.

It. ***Vari (Diversi)*** scrittori sono noti in questo paese;

Fr. ***Divers*** écrivains sont connus dans ce pays.

– ***Several*** *writers are well known in this country.*

It. ***vari (diversi)***; Fr. ***divers*** can also mean "*varied*" or "*different*":

It. Ha un vestito di ***vari (diversi)*** colori;

Fr. Elle a une robe de ***diverses*** couleurs.

– *She has a dress of **various** colors.*

Different
It. differente; Fr. different

These adjectives can be placed after the noun and agree in number, except French where it agrees in number and gender:

It. Ha un vestito di colori **differenti**;

Fr. Elle a une robe de couleurs **différentes**.

– *She has a dress of **different** colours.*

Alone, Only
It. solo; Fr. seul

When It. **solo**; Fr. **seul** can be used as an adjective and agree in number and gender in Italian and French meaning "*alone*":

It. Sono andato **solo** al cinema;

Fr. Je suis allé **seul** au cinéma.

– *I went **alone** to the cinema.*

It should be said that in Italian these adjectives cannot be used to convey English "*the only*". In this case, the word It. **unico** – *the only* is used. In French **seul** can be used to say *the only*. For example:

It. L'**unico** cinema che proietta questo film è nel centro della città;

Fr. Le **seul** cinéma qui montre ce film est dans le centre de la ville.

– *The **only** cinema that shows this film is in the centre of the city.*

It. **solo**; Fr. **seul** can also be used as an adverb meaning "*only*", which is equivalent to It. **solamente**; Fr. **seulement**.

However unlike in Italian, in French the adverb **seulement** is used to say "*only*".

It. Ho **solo** due ore per lavorare;

Fr. J'ai **seulement** deux heures pour travailler.

– *I have **only** two hours to work.*

CHAPTER 5: PRONOUNS

Enough (Sufficient)
It. sufficiente; Fr. suffisant (assez)

When It. ***sufficiente***; Fr. ***suffisant*** (***assez***) – "*enough*", "sufficient" are used as adjectives or pronouns, they agree in number in Italian. In French it agrees in number and gender:

It. Questo è sufficiente per me;
Fr. Cela est suffisant pour moi.
– This is enough for me.

When they are used as *an adverb*, they take the form of ***abbastanza*** in Italian and ***assez*** in French.

As an adverb: It. ***abbastanza***; Fr. ***assez*** are invariable. As an adverb they are generally used to indicate quantity or extent. When it comes to the quantity, French ***assez*** is used with the preposition ***de***. Study the following:

It. Abbiamo abbastanza tempo per andare lì;
Fr. Nous avons assez de temps pour y aller.
– We have enough time to go there.

It. La sua casa è abbastanza grande;
Fr. Sa maison est assez grande.
– Her house is quite big.

Much/Many/A lot of, Few/Little
It. molto, poco; Fr. beaucoup (de), peu

- As an *adjective or pronoun* It. ***molto/a/i/e***; Fr. ***beaucoup de*** means "*much*", "*many*", "*a lot of*" and agree in number and gender (except in French):

CHAPTER 5: PRONOUNS

It. Ha **molto** lavoro;

Fr. Elle a **beaucoup de** travail.

– *She has **a lot of** work.*

- As *adjectives* or *pronouns* It. **poco/a/pochi/poche**; Fr. **peu de** mean *"few"*, *"little"* and also agree in number and gender (except in French):

It. Hanno **pochi** amici;

Fr. Ils ont **peu d'**amis.

– *They have **few** friends.*

NOTE:
When used as an adjective **beaucoup** and **peu** are used with the preposition **de** in French.

- It. **molto/a**; Fr. **beaucoup** can also be used as unchangeable *neuter pronouns*:

It. Abbiamo **molto** da fare;

Fr. Nous avons **beaucoup** à faire.

– *We have **a lot** to do.*

- As *adverbs* It. **molto**; Fr. **beaucoup** mean *"much"*, *"a lot"*.

It. Lei lavora **molto**;

Fr. Elle travaille **beaucoup**.

– *She works **a lot**.*

- As *adverbs* It. **poco**; Fr. **peu** mean "*little*", "*few*", but are also used to negate an adjective (in English it is the prefix *un-*):

>It. Lui sorride **poco**;
>
>Fr. Il sourit **peu**.
>
>– He smiles **a little**.

>It. È **poco** probabile
>
>Fr. C'est **peu** probable.
>
>– It is unlikely.

It is notable that when It. **poco**; Fr. **peu** are preceded by the indefinite article, they mean "*a little*":

>It. È '**un po**' strano;
>
>Fr. Il est **un peu** étrange.
>
>– It is **a little** strange.

NOTE: *Italian **poco** becomes **un po'**.*

When it comes to the quantity of something It. **un po'**; Fr. **un peu** are used with the preposition **de** in French and **di** in Italian, and the noun that follows doesn't have any article at all (**See the Partitive p.61 and Expressions of Quantity p.62**):

>It. Vuoi **un po' di** succo?
>
>Fr. Veux-tu **un peu de** jus?
>
>– Do you want **a little** juice?

Too much, Too many
It. *troppo*; Fr. *trop*

It. ***troppo*** are adjectives or pronouns that mean *"too much"*, *"too many"*. In Italian it changes in gender and number:

- It. (*s.masc.*) ***troppo***, (*s.fem.*) ***troppa***, (*pl.masc.*) ***troppi***, (*pl.fem.*) ***troppe***;

It. C'è ***troppa*** gente in strada.

– *There are **too many** people in the street.*

NOTE:
*Unlike in Italian, in French **trop** is an adverb and when is preceded by a noun, it is used with the preposition **de**:*

Fr. Il y a ***trop de*** gens dans la rue.

– *There are too many people in the street.*

Also, Italian ***troppo*** can also be used as adverbs meaning *"too (much)"* and, in this case, it does not change neither in gender nor in number. However, as an adverb in French ***trop*** is used:

It. Ho lavorato ***troppo*** ieri;

Fr. J'ai ***trop*** travaillé hier.

– *I worked **too much** yesterday.*

NOTE:
*In French **trop** should be put before past participle in a sentence.*

As an unchangeable neuter pronoun It. ***troppo***; Fr. ***trop*** mean *"too"*:

It. La luce è ***troppo*** forte;

Fr. La lumière est ***trop*** forte.

*- The light is **too** strong.*

All
*It. **tutto**; Fr. **tout***

It. ***tutto***; Fr. ***tout*** as an adjective or pronoun changes in gender and number. As an adverb it is unchangeable.

- As adjectives, they mean *"all (of)"*, *"the whole"*, *"the entire"*. In this case It. ***tutto***; Fr. ***tout*** can be used with a noun preceded by the definite article, possessive or demonstrative adjectives:

It. ***Tutta la strada*** è coperta di neve;

Fr. ***Toute la rue*** est couverte de neige.

– ***The whole street*** *is covered with snow.*

It. ***Tutti i nostri amici*** sono gentili;

Fr. ***Tous nos amis*** sont gentils.

– ***All of our friends*** *are nice.*

- It. ***tutto***; can be used before a pronoun or place name, except in French:

It. ***Tutti loro*** vogliono parlare spagnolo;

Fr. ***Tous*** veulent parler espagnol.

– ***All of them*** *want to speak Spanish.*

CHAPTER 5: PRONOUNS

- It. ***tutto***; Fr. ***tout*** in previous examples were put before the word they modified, but they can also be placed in other positions in the sentence, still agreeing with the associated noun:

> It. Gli studenti sono ***tutti*** molto intelligenti;
>
> Fr. Les élèves sont ***tous*** très intelligents.
>
> – *The students are **all** very smart.*

- When It. ***tutto/i***; Fr. ***tout/s*** are used with nouns preceded by <u>the definite article</u> that refer to periods of time, they mean "*every*":

> It. ***Tutte le*** settimane, ***Tutti i*** giorni;
>
> Fr. ***Toutes les*** semaines, ***Tous les*** jours.
>
> – ***Every*** *week*, ***Every*** *day.*

  - It. ***tutto***; Fr. ***tout*** with <u>the indefinite article</u>.

NOTE:
*In order to express "**a whole/an entire**" in Romance languages, it is better to use the adjective It. **intero/a/i/e**; Fr. **entier/ère/s/ères** which goes with the indefinite article and agrees in number and gender with the noun it defines:*
> It. una giornata ***intera*** (un giorno ***intero***);
>
> Fr. une journée ***entière*** (un jour ***entier***)
>
> – *A **whole** day.*

- It. ***tutto***; Fr. ***tout*** can also be used with <u>relative pronouns</u> making common relative constructions, such as:

1. It. ***tutto quello que***; Fr. ***tout ce que*** – *all/everything that*. For example:

It. Voglio sapere **tutto quello che** sai;

Fr. Je veux savoir **tout ce que** tu sais.

– *I want to know **everything that** you know.*

2. It. ***tutti quelli che/ tutte quelle che***; Fr. ***tous ceux qui/ touttes celles qui***. – *all (those)/everyone who.* For instance:

It. Abbiamo parlato con **tutti quelli che** sono venuti;

Fr. Nous avons parlé à **tous ceux qui** sont venus.

– *We talked to **all those who** came.*

- There are also fixed expressions with It. ***tutto***; Fr. ***tout*** that should be remembered. However, in some cases It. ***ogni*** "*every*" is more common than It. ***tutto*** in some sentences:

Italian	French	English
in tutti i casi, in ogni caso	en tout cas, dans tous les cas	*in any case*
in ogni momento	à tout moment	*at any time*
a tutte le ore	à toutes heures	*at all hours*
tutti i tipi di	tous types de, toutes sortes de	*all kinds of*
a tutti i costi, ad ogni costo	à tout prix	*at all costs*
in ogni luogo	en tout lieu, partout	*everywhere*

- As a pronoun It. ***tutto***; Fr. ***tout*** mean "*all*" or "*everyone*":

It. dal punto di vista di ***tutti***;

Fr. du point de vue de ***tous***.

– *From **everyone's** point of view.*

CHAPTER 5: PRONOUNS

It. Questo è quello che dice a **tutti**;

Fr. Voilà ce qu'elle dit à **tous**.

– *That's what she says to **everyone**.*

NOTE:

*In French **tout le monde** is the equivalent to the pronoun "<u>everyone</u>". In Italian **tutti** is more common in this case. For example:*

It. **Tutti** lo sanno;
Fr. **Tout le monde** le sait.
– ***Everyone** knows it.*

Everything
It. tutto; Fr. tout (as an invariable pronoun)

As an invariable pronoun It. **tutto**; Fr. **tout** refer to "*all*", "*everything*" in general:

It. Ho comprato **tutto**;

Fr. J'ai **tout** acheté.

– *I bought **everything**.*

NOTE:

*In French **tout** should be put before past participle in a sentence.*

The rest, The others
It. il resto; Fr. le reste

It. **il resto**, Fr. **le reste** mean "*the rest*", "*the others*", which are completely unchangeable.

It. ***Il resto*** dei visitatori non può venire;

Fr. ***Le reste*** des visiteurs ne peut pas venir.

– ***The rest*** *of the visitors cannot come.*

It. ***il resto***, Fr. ***le reste*** can also be used to mean *"everything else"*, *"the rest"*, for example::

It. Lei mi ha telefonato, ***il resto*** non importa;

Fr. Elle m'a téléphoné, ***le reste*** n'a pas d'importance.

– *She phoned me,* ***the rest*** *does not matter.*

Anyone, None
It. nessuno; Fr. aucun

The indefinite pronoun It. ***nessuno/a***; Fr. ***aucun/e*** agree in gender in Romance languages and mean *"anyone"*, *"none"*:

It. ***Nessuno*** di loro è venuto;

Fr. ***Aucun*** d'eux n'est venu.

– ***None*** *of them came.*

It. Hai regali per loro? – ***Nessuno***;

Fr. As-tu des cadeaux pour eux? – ***Aucun***.

– *Do you have any gifts for them?* – ***None***.

NOTE:
In French the negative sentence requires the negative particle **ne** *after* **aucun** *(See the* ***Negation p.209 and Present Tense p.147***).

No one, Nobody
It. *nessuno;* Fr. *personne*

The indefinite pronouns It. **nessuno**; Fr. **personne** mean "*no one*", "*nobody*". Note that French **personne** also requires the negative particle **ne**, which can become n' before <u>a vowel</u>:

It. **Nessuno** è venuto;

Fr. **Personne n'**est venu.

– **No one** came.

It. Non vedo **nessuno**;

Fr. Je ne vois **personne**.

– I see **no one**./I **don't** see **anyone**.

The previous example shows that unlike in English, in Romance languages a negative sentence has double negation, which contains a negative particle and an indefinite pronoun: It. **non...nessuno**; Fr. **ne...personne** (See the Negation p.209 and Present Simple p.147).

Nothing
It. *niente;* Fr. *rien*

The indefinite pronoun It. **niente**; Fr. **rien** mean "*nothing*". In French **rien** is also used with the negative particle **ne**.

It. Non vedo **niente**;

Fr. Je ne vois **rien**.

– I see **nothing**./I **don't** see **anything**.

Both
It. entrambi/ambedue (tutti e due); Fr. les deux (tous les deux)

It. ***ambedue*** (***tutti e due***); Fr. ***les deux*** (***tous les deux***) are always used in the plural as an adjective or pronoun and refer to two people, things or places and mean "*both*" in English. They change in gender, except Italian where ***ambedue*** is invariable.

In Italian ***entrambi*** and ***ambedue*** and ***tutti e due*** are interchangeable as well as ***les deux*** and ***tous les deux*** in French. Observe the following:

It. ***Entrambi*** sono venuti;

Fr. ***Les deux*** sont venus.

– ***Both*** *of them came.*

It. Ho parlato con tutti ***e due***;

Fr. J'ai parlé à tous ***les deux***.

– *I spoke to* ***both*** *of them.*

NOTE:

It is notable that English speakers should not use It. ***ambedue/entrambi***; Fr. ***les deux*** as an equivalent to "both" in sentences like: both sister and brother. In Romance languages both is used for emphasis and cannot be translated literally. For example:

It. Ho parlato con il fratello e la sorella;
Fr. J'ai parlé avec le frère et la sœur.
– I spoke to both brother and sister.

CHAPTER 6: VERBS

A verb is a word that indicates an action or a state of being, for example: go, live, be.

Overview

Verbs in Romance languages have categories of mood, tense, person, number, gender and voice. Also, there are personal and impersonal forms of the verb in Romance languages. Personal forms of the verb have the mood and person; impersonal - the category of gender for participles; and both personal and impersonal forms - the category of tense and number. Personal forms of the verb are: the indicative, the subjunctive, the conditional and the imperative. Impersonal forms of the verb are: the participle, the gerund and the infinitive.

Italian and French verbs have different tenses in three moods: indicative, subjunctive and conditional mood.

> **Did you know?**
>
> Abidjan is the economical capital and chief port of the Ivory Coast (Côte d'Ivoire) with the 3rd largest French speaking population in the world. It is also the 4th most populous city in Africa (over 4.3 million people).

In Italian and French the indicative mood consists of eight tense forms. They are divided into simple (only one single word) and compound (made up of an auxiliary verb and a past participle) tense forms. The simple tenses include the present, imperfect, simple perfect, and future simple. The compound tenses include a present perfect, recent past, past perfect, pluperfect and the future prefect. Compound tenses in all Romance languages are formed using the auxiliary verbs "to be" and "to have".

Subjunctive in Italian and French has four tenses, which are present subjunctive, past subjunctive, imperfect subjunctive and pluperfect subjunctive.

In the conditional mood the whole number of tense forms across Romance languages is two.

There is also the imperative mood of the verb that does not have different tenses. The imperative mood expresses commands, orders or instructions.

Now, all the categories of the verb will be considered in more detail for Italian and French.

The following demonstrates all the moods and tenses of the 1st person singular of the regular verb It. ***lavorare***; Fr. ***travailler*** - to work.

	Italian	**French**
	Indicative mood	
	Present tenses	
Present tense	lavoro	je travaille
Present Perfect	ho lavorato	j'ai travaillé
	Past tenses	
Preterite	lavorai	je travaillai
Imperfect	lavoravo	je travaillais
Past Perfect	ebbi lavorato	j'eus travaillé
Pluperfect	avevo lavorato	j'avais travaillé
	Future tense	
Future	lavorerò	je travaillerai
Future Perfect	avrò lavorato	j'aurai travaillé
	Conditionals	
Conditional present	lavorerei	je travaillerais
Conditional Perfect (Past)	avrei lavorato	j'aurais travaillé
	Subjunctive mood	
	Present tenses	
Present tense	lavori	je travaille

CHAPTER 6: VERBS

	Italian	**French**
Present Perfect	*abbia lavorato*	*j'aie travaillé*
	Past tenses	
Past tense	*lavorassi*	*je travaillasse*
Past Perfect	*avessi lavorato*	*j'eusse travaillé*
	Future tenses	
Future tense	—	—
Future Perfect	—	—
	Imperative mood	
	lavora (tu) *lavori (lei)* *lavoriamo (noi)* *lavorate (voi)* *lavorino (loro)*	*travaille (tu)* *travaillez (vous)* *travaillons (nous)* *travaillez (vous)* *travaillez (vous)*
	Infinitive	
	lavorare	*travailler*
	Compound infinitive	
	avere lavorato	*avoir travaillé*
	Participle	
Present Participle (gerund)	(gerund) *lavorando* (part.pres) *lavorante*	*travaillant*
Compound Present Participle	—	—
Past Participle	*lavorato*	*travaillé*

CHAPTER 6: VERBS

The Indicative Mood

The Present Tense

In Indo-European languages there is a division of verbs into groups. Thus, all the Latin verbs were divided into four conjugations:

1st conj.: *-a-*

2nd conj.: *-e-*

3rd conj.: – ***zero conjugation*** or *-u-*

4th conj.: *-i-*.

The conjugation type defined the positional change of morphemes. In Vulgar Latin and, later, in the Romance languages, we observe fewer types of Latin verb formations. Key changes in this field that occurred by the time of the emergence of the first Romance languages are:

1. The disappearance of the third type of conjugation, which was distributed between the 2nd and 4th types of conjugation.

2. The emergence of a group of verbs containing the suffix *-sc-*, which lost its characteristic meaning of "inceptiveness" in Latin and received its productivity in the verbs of the 2nd and 4th conjugations in all the Romance languages.

3. The past participle in Romance languages reduced the number of modifications. For example, the suffix *–itus* (***perditus***) disappeared; in Italian and French the Vulgar Latin suffix *–utus* for the verbs of 2nd and 3rd conjugation spread widely replacing non-standard forms.

Thus, Spanish, Portuguese, Italian and French verbs are divided into 3 groups (conjugations) that are conjugated according to the endings of the infinitive forms.

Below is a table illustrating the endings of all 3 groups (conjugations) of the verbs:

CHAPTER 6: VERBS

Italian	French
1st group	
-are	-er
2nd group	
-ere	-re
3rd group	
-ire	-ir

NOTE:

In French, verbs ending in **–ir** really belong to the 2nd group. It was deliberately put into the 3rd group by the author for the sake comparison of the verbs.

Verbs are conjugated by removing the infinitive ending and adding necessary endings to the stem of the verb, which indicate the mood, tense, person, voice and number.

This table shows the formation of the present tense of regular verbs:

	Italian	French
	1st group	
	-ARE	-ER
Singular	-o, -i, -a,	-e, -es, -e,
Plural	-iamo, -ate, -ano	-ons, -ez, -ent
	2nd group	

CHAPTER 6: VERBS

	Italian	French
	-ERE	**-RE**
Singular	-o, -i, -e,	-s, -s, -NA,
Plural	-iamo, -ete, -ono	-ons, -ez, -ent
	3rd group	
	-IRE	**-IR**
Singular	-o, -i, -e, (-isco, - isci, - isce,)	-s, -s, -t, (-is, - is, - it)
Plural	-iamo, -ite, -ono (-iamo, -ite, -iscono)	-ons, -ez, -ent (-issons, -issez, -issent)

Below is a table displaying an example of conjugation of all three groups in the present tense:

Italian	French
1 group	
It.: <u>parl**are**</u>	Fr.: <u>parl**er**</u>
io parl**o** tu parl**i** lui\lei parl**a** noi parl**iamo** voi parl**ate** loro parl**ano**	je parl**e** tu parl**es** il\elle parl**e** nous parl**ons** vous parl**ez** ils\elles parl**ent**

CHAPTER 6: VERBS

Italian	French
2 group	
It.: <u>vend**ere**</u>	Fr.: <u>vend**re**</u>
vend**o** vend**i** vend**e** vend**iamo** vend**ete** vend**ono**	je vend**s** tu vend**s** il/elle vend nous vend**ons** vous vend**ez** ils/elles vend**ent**
3 group	
It.: <u>part**ire**</u>	Fr.: <u>part**ir**</u>
part**o** part**i** part**e** part**iamo** part**ite** part**ono**	je par**s** tu par**s** il/elle par**t** nous part**ons** vous part**ez** ils/elles part**ent**

It should be noted that in Italian and French some verbs in the 3rd group in the present tense add the suffix *–isc–* (in Italian) and *–iss–* (in French).

Did you know?

The Vatican has its own Post office and issues its own stamps. The Vatican mail system is widely used by people of Rome as in most cases is a lot quicker than Italian mail.

In Italian *–isc–* precedes the conjugated ending, except the 1st and 2nd person plural of the verb. In French the suffix *–iss–* also precedes the ending, but only in the plural:

CHAPTER 6: VERBS

Italian	French
finire	*finir*
fin**isc**o	je finis
fin**isc**i	tu finis
fin**isc**e	il finit
finiamo	nous fin**iss**ons
finite	vous fin**iss**ez
fin**isc**ono	ils fin**iss**ent

NOTE:

In Italian and French, the majority of verbs of the 3rd group are conjugated as It. ***finire*** and Fr. ***finir***, rather than as the It. ***partire*** and Fr. ***partir*** type of verbs. French verbs that are not conjugated as ***finir*** are considered to be irregular. However, the number of verbs ending in −**ir** are still conjugated in accordance with the conjugation paradigm of the verb **partir**. According to this pattern of conjugation, the verbs having two consonants at the end of their stems (partir: part-) drop the last consonant of the stem in the singular of the present tense and change it to the **-s**, **-s**, **-t** endings.

The most common verbs of the 1st group

Many of the most frequently used verbs in the Romance languages belong to this 1st group conjugation. Below is the list of some of them:

Italian	French	English
abitare	**habiter**	*to live*
affittare	**louer**	*to rent*

CHAPTER 6: VERBS

Italian	French	English
alzare	lever	to lift
sollevare	soulever	to pick up
elevare	élever	to raise
amare	aimer	to love
arrivare	arriver	to arrive
ascoltare	écouter	to listen
ballare, danzare	danser	to dance
brillare	briller	to shine
cambiare	changer	to change
cammin-are	marcher	to walk
cantare	chanter	to sing
cercare	chercher	to look for
cenare	diner	to dine
chiamare	appeler	to call
comandare	commander	to order
comprare	acheter	to buy
contare	compter	to count
cucinare	cuisinier	to cook

CHAPTER 6: VERBS

Italian	French	English
desiderare	**désirer**	*to desire*
disegnare	**dessiner**	*to draw*
domandare	**demander**	*to ask*
firmare	**signer**	*to sign*
formare	**former**	*to form*
frequentare	**fréquenter**	*to frequent*
guadagnare	**gagner**	*to win, to earn*
giocare	**jouer**	*to play*
guardare	**regarder**	*to look at*
guidare	**conduire**	*to drive*
guidare	**guider**	*to guide*
gustare, assaggiare	**goûter**	*to taste*
informare	**informer**	*to inform*
insegnare	**enseigner**	*to teach*
invitare	**inviter**	*to invite*
lasciare	**laisser**	*to leave*
lavare	**laver**	*to wash*
lavorare	**travailler**	*to work*

CHAPTER 6: VERBS

Italian	French	English
mandare, inviare	envoyer	to send
nuotare	nager	to swim
parlare	parler	to speak
pensare	penser	to think
passare	passer	to pass, to spend
presentare	présenter	to present
preparare	préparer	to prepare
raccontare	raconter	to narrate
salutare	saluer	to greet
saltare	sauter	to jump
sposare	marier	to marry
studiare	étudier	to study
suonare	sonner	to ring / to play
telefonare	téléphoner	to telephone
toccare	toucher	to touch
attravers-are	traverser	to cross
ingannare	tromper	to deceive
visitare	visiter	to visit

CHAPTER 6: VERBS

The most common verbs of the 2nd group

Below is a list of some common verbs of the second conjugation:

Italian	French	English
apprendere	**apprendre**	*to learn*
battere	**battre**	*to beat*
conoscere	**connaître**	*to know*
credere	**croire**	*to believe*
descrivere	**décrire**	*to describe*
difendere	**défendre**	*to defend*
eleggere	**élire**	*to elect*
leggere	**lire**	*to read*
mettere	**mettre**	*to put*
mordere	**mordre**	*to bite*
nascere	**naître**	*to be born*
offendere	<u>*offenser*</u>	*to offend*
perdere	**perdre**	*to lose*
prendere	**prendre**	*to take*
promettere	**promettre**	*to promise*
rispondere	**répondre**	*to answer*
scrivere	**écrire**	*to write*
vendere	**vendre**	*to sell*

Italian	French	English
vivere	vivre	to live

The most common verbs of the 3rd group

Below is a list of the most common verbs of the third-conjugation:

Italian	French	English
aprire	ouvrir	to open
applaudire	applaudir	to applaud
bollire	bouillir	to boil
costruire	construire, bâtir	to build, to construct
coprire	couvrir	to cover
dormire	dormir	to sleep
fuggire	*fuir*	to flee
offrire	offrir	to offer
partire	partir	to leave
riaprire	réouvrir	to reopen
scoprire	découvrir	to discover
seguire	*suivre*	to follow

Italian	French	English
sentire	sentir	to feel, to smell
servire	servir	to serve
soffrire	souffrir	to suffer
vestire	vêtir	to dress, to wear

> **NOTE:**
> Underlined verbs belong to different groups and are to be memorized.

Irregular Verbs in the Present Tense

It is important to note that the set of irregular verbs, in whole, are common for all considered Romance languages. Below is the list of the most frequently used irregular verbs in Italian and French:

Italian	French	English
avere (ho, hai, ha, abbiamo, avete, hanno)	**avoir** (ai, as, a, avons, avez, ont)	to have
tenere (tengo, tieni, tiene, tengono)	**tenir** (tiens, tiens, tient, tiennent)	to hold, to keep
essere (sono, sei, è, siamo, siete, sono)	**être** (suis, es, est, sommes, êtes, sont)	to be
stare (stai, stanno)	―	to be

CHAPTER 6: VERBS

Italian	French	English
andare (vado, vai, va, vanno)	**aller** (vais, vas, va, allons, allez, vont)	*to go*
dare (dai, dà, danno)	***donner*** (regular)	*to give*
fare (faccio, fai, facciamo, fanno)	**faire** (faisons, faites, font)	*to do*
dire (dico, dici, dice, diciamo, dicono)	**dire** (disons, dites, disent)	*to say*
potere (posso, puoi, può, possiamo, possono)	**pouvoir** (peux, peux, peut, peuvent)	*can*
volere (voglio, vuoi, vuole, vogliamo, vogliono)	**vouloir** (veux, veux, veut, veulent)	*to want*
sapere (so, sai, sa, sappiamo, sanno)	**savoir** (sais, sais, sait)	*to know*
porre (pongo, poni, pone, poniamo, ponete, pongono)	**mettre** (mets, mets, met)	*to put*
conoscere (regular)	**connaître** (connais, connais, connaît, connaissons, connaissez, connaissent)	*to get to know*
venire (vengo, vieni, viene, vengono)	**venir** (viens, viens, vient, viennent)	*to come*
dormire (regular)	**dormir** (dors, dors, dort)	*to sleep*

Italian	French	English
sentire (regular)	sentir (sens, sens, sent)	*to feel*
morire (muoio, muori, muore, muoiono)	**mourir** (meurs, meurs, meurt, meurent)	*to die*

Verb Spelling and Vowel Changes

Did you know?

The word "spa", that's being used to talk about places to relax and get wellness treatments, comes from the Belgian city Spa.

However, despite the majority of similar irregular verbs, each of the considered Romance languages has its own number of irregular verbs with specific models of conjugation, which means that some verbs have specific spelling changes in order to preserve the pronunciation (sound) presented in the infinitive and others change their vowel within the stem. Therefore, it is highly important to regard the special rules for when the spelling or vowels change in a verb conjugation. Since the rules are very divergent and particular for each language, it makes it difficult to somehow combine these changes occurring in a verb conjugation of the Romance languages. So, it is necessary to consider them separately in Italian and French.

Italian

‣ Verbs ending in **–*ciare*, –*giare*, –*chiare*** and **–*ghiare***

Verbs that end in **–*ciare*, –*giare*, –*chiare*** and **–*ghiare*** drop the **–*i*** in *the 2nd person singular and plural* (tu, noi) before the regular endings (**–*i*** and **–*iamo***) are added.

For example: Cominciare: comincio – cominc*i* – comincia – cominc*iamo* – cominciate – cominciano.

Below are some common verbs ending in *–ciare*, *–giare*, *–chiare* and *–ghiare*:

cominciare	to start
marciare	to march
racconciare	to fix, to mend
assaggiare	to taste
noleggiare	to rent
parcheggiare	to park
viaggiare	to travel
rischiare	to risk
invecchiare	to grow old
avvinghiare	to grip, to clunch

- Verbs ending in *–care*, *–gare*

All verbs ending in *–care*, *–gare* add an *–h–* to the root in *the 2nd person singular and plural* (tu, noi) in order to preserve the hard sound of the *c* or *g* of the infinitive.

For example: Cercare: cerco – cer*ch*i – cerca – cer*ch*iamo – cercate – cercano.

Below are some common verbs ending in *–care*, *–gare*:

allargare	to widen
allungare	to lengthen
attaccare	to attack, to glue
divagare	to amuse
frugare	to rummage
impaccare	to pack
indagare	to investigate

sbarcare	to disembark
toccare	to touch
troncare	to break, to cut off

- Verbs ending in *–cere*.

It is notable that the spelling changes in *the 1st person singular and 2nd and 3rd person plural* (io, noi, loro) when the verbs of *–cere* group are conjugated.

For example: Pia**cere**: pia**cci**o – pia**ci** – pia**ce** – pia**cci**amo (*piaciamo*) – piacete – pia**cci**ono.

Below are some common verbs ending in *–cere*:

compiacere	to gratify, to please
dispiacere	to displease, to dislike
giacere	to lie down
piacere	to like
tacere	to keep silent

- Verbs with *–isc–*

Many *–ire* or 3rd group verbs add *–isc–* to the root in all forms of the present tense, *except the 1st and 2nd person plural* of the verb (noi and voi).

For example: Capire: cap**isc**o – cap**isc**i – cap**isc**e – capiamo – capite – cap**isc**ono.

The following is a list of some Italian verbs gaining the suffix *–isc–*:

apparire	to appear, to seem
capire	to understand

comparire	to appear
costruire	to build, to construct
differire	to differ
dimagrire	to lose weight
finire	to end, to finish
impedire	to prevent
ingrandire	to enlarge
preferire	to prefer
pulire	to clean
riferire	to relate
ubbidire	to obey

It is notable that the verbs ***apparire*** (*to appear*), ***comparire*** (*to appear*), and ***scomparire*** (*to disappear*) have two different ways of conjugation in the present tense, *except the 2nd and 3rd person plural* (noi and voi), which have regular endings. They can be conjugated either using *–isc–* suffix or using alternate endings. These verbs drop the *–rire* and add *–i–* to the root in *the 1st person singular and 3rd person plural* (io and loro). To illustrate:

Apparire: appaio (appar***isc***o) – appari (appar***isc***i) – appare (appar***isc***e) – appariamo – apparite – appaiono (appar***isc***ono);

Comparire: compaio (compar***isc***o) - compari (compar***isc***i) - compare (compar***isc***e) - compariamo - comparite - compaiono (compar***isc***ono);

Scomparire: scompaio (scompar***isc***o) - scompari (scompar***isc***i) - scompare (scompar***isc***e) - scompariamo - scomparite - scompaiono (scompar***isc***ono).

▸ Verbs ending in *–durre*

Some Italian verbs ending in *–durre* are considered to be irregular whose roots for the present tense come from the original Latin infinitives (e.g. it. condurre - lat. conducere - to drive; it. produrre - lat. producer - to produce). When conjugated such verbs add **-c-** to stem before the regular conjugating endings. It is notable that endings are the same as the endings of regular *-ere* verbs.

For instance: Con***durre***: condu**c**o - condu**c**i - condu**c**e - condu**c**iamo - condu**c**ete - condu**c**ono.

Below are some common verbs ending in *-durre*:

condurre	to to lead, to drive
introdurre	to introduce
produrre	to produce
ridurre	to reduce
tradurre	to translate

▸ Verbs ending in *–dire*

Some Italian verbs ending in *–dire* are also considered to be irregular. One verb having this ending was already presented previously in the table of irregular verbs, which is ***dire*** - *to say*. Such verbs come from its original Latin infinitive ***dicere*** and when conjugated they also add *–c–* to stem before the regular conjugating endings. It is notable that endings are the same as the endings of regular *–ere* verbs, but the 2nd person plural has the form *dite*.

For example: Contrad***dire***: contraddi**c**o - contraddi**c**i - contraddi**c**e - contraddi**c**iamo - contrad***dite*** - contraddi**c**ono.

Below are some common verbs ending in *–dire*:

contraddire	to contradict
disdire	to cancel
indire	to announce, to declare
interdire	to prohibit
maledire	to curse

▸ Verbs ending in *–porre*

CHAPTER 6: VERBS

Like the ending -dire, there are some Italian verbs ending in **–porre** are also regarded as irregular. One verb that has this ending was presented previously in the table of irregular verbs, which is **porre** - *to put*. Such verbs come from its original Latin infinitive **ponere** Therefore, it should be noted that there is a **-g-** added in *the 1st person singular and 3rd person plural* (io and loro) forms.

For example: Com**porre**: compon**g**o - componi - compone - componiamo - componete - compon**g**ono.

Below are some common verbs ending in *–porre*:

comporre	to compose
disporre	to dispose, to provide
esporre	to expose, to show
imporre	to impose
opporre	to oppose
posporre	to postpone
proporre	to propose
riporre	to put back
supporre	to suppose

NOTE:

The verbs **rimanere** *(to stay),* **valere** *(to be worth) and* **salire** *(to climb) also have a* **-g-** *in the 1st person singular and 3rd person plural (io and loro) forms of the present tense. All other forms are regular and are conjugated as either as -ere or -ire verbs depending on the conjugation to which they belong.*

For example: **Rimanere**: *rimang*o - *rimani - rimane - rimaniamo - rimanete - rimang*ono.

‣ Verbs ending in **–trarre**

The verb **trarre** (*to pull, to extract, to draw*) as well as all verbs that have the suffix **–trarre** gain a **double g** in *the 1st person singular and 3rd person plural* (io and loro) forms. They come from Latin *trahere*.

For example: **Trarre**: tra**gg**o - trai - trae - traiamo - traete - tra**gg**ono.

Below are some common verbs ending in *–trarre*:

attrarre	to attract
distrarre	to distract
contrarre	to contract
sottrarre	to subtract

- Verbs ending in **–gliere**

All verbs that end in **–gliere**, like the verb **cogliere** (*to pick, to gather*) become **–olgo** and **–olgono** in *the 1st person singular and 3rd person plural* (io and loro) forms respectively.

For example: **Cogliere**: c**olgo** - cogli - coglie - cogliamo - cogliete - c**olgono**.

Below are some common verbs ending in *–gliere*:

accogliere	to welcome, to receive
cogliere	to pick, to gather
raccogliere	to collect, to pick up
togliere	to remove, to take away

- Verbs conjugated as **tenere** and **venire**

You are already familiar with the Italian irregular verbs like **tenere** (*to have, to keep*) and **venire** (*to come*) and with the way they are conjugated. Note that all verbs that have a prefix plus **-tenere** or **–venire** gain a **g** in *the 1st person singular and the 3rd person plural* (io and loro) forms. Also, the vowel of the root changes to **-ie-** in *the 2nd and 3rd person singular* which are tu and lui/lei forms.

CHAPTER 6: VERBS

For example: ***Appartenere***: - appart*e*n*go* - appart*i*eni - appart*i*ene - apparteniamo - appartenete - apparten*go*no.

Below are some commonly used verbs with a prefix plus *–tenere* or *–venire*:

appartenere	to belong
contenere	to contain
intrattenere	to entertain
mantenere	to maintain
ottenere	to obtain
ritenere	to retain
sostenere	to sustain, to support
trattenere	to withhold, to detain
avvenire	to happen, to occur
contravvenire	to contravene
convenire	to convene
divenire	to become
intervenire	to intervene
provenire	to come from, to proceed
sovvenire	to help, to remember
svenire	to faint

- Verbs with *–io*

Such verb as ***parere*** (*to seem*) gains *i* in *the 1st person singular and the 3rd person plural* (io and loro) forms, and has the alternate 2nd person plural (noi) form.

For instance: ***Parere***: pa*i*o - pari - pare - pa*i*amo (pariamo) - parete - pa*i*ono.

CHAPTER 6: VERBS

- **Other verbs with a vowel change of the root**

Sedere

Such verb as *sedere* (*to sit down*) changes the vowel *e* to *ie* in all forms except *the 1st and 2nd person plural* (noi and voi). There is also an alternate form is used for *the 1st person singular and the 3rd person plural* (io and loro).

Sedere: si*e*do (*seggo*) - si*e*di - si*e*de - sediamo - sedete - si*e*dono (*seggono*)

Udire

The vowel *u* in the verb *udire* (*to hear*) changes to *o* in all forms except *the 1st and 2nd person plural* (noi and voi).

Udire: *o*do - *o*di - *o*de - udiamo - udite - *o*dono.

Uscire

The vowel *u* in the verb *uscire* (*to go out*) changes to *e* in all forms of the present tense except *the 1st and 2nd person plural* (noi and voi). It should be said that the verb *riuscire* (*to succeed*) is conjugated like *uscire*.

Uscire: *e*sco - *e*sci - *e*sce - usciamo - uscite - *e*scono.

Dovere

Dovere (*to have to, must*) is considered to be irregular and has specific conjugation in all forms except *the 2nd person plural* (voi). It is notable that *the 1st person singular and 3rd person plural* (io and loro) have two forms of conjugation.

Dovere: ***devo*** (***debbo***) - ***devi*** - ***deve*** - ***dobbiamo*** - dovete - ***devono*** (***debbono***).

French

- **Verbs starting with a vowel**

There are many verbs that begin with a vowel or silent *h* belong to *–er* group of verbs. Therefore, while interacting with such verbs, the pronoun *je* becomes *j'*, which is called elision. In spoken French in the 1st, 2nd and 3rd person plural (nous, vous, ils/elles) forms, a /z/ sound is pronounced between the pronoun and a following verb. This

CHAPTER 6: VERBS

phenomenon is called liaison. The **n** of **on** is also pronounced before words that begin with a vowel. For example:

Aimer: j'aime - tu aimes - il, elle aime - on_**a**ime - nou**s**_**a**imons - vou**s**_**a**imez - ils/elle**s**_**a**iment.

Below are some common –*er* verbs beginning with a vowel:

abandonner	to bandon
accrocher	to hang
admirer	to admire
aider	to help
aimer	to love
allumer	to light
amuser	to amuse
apporter	to bring
arriver	to arrive
attacher	to attach
attirer	to attract

Spelling changes

- Verbs ending in –*cer* and –*ger*

Verbs that end in –*cer* add a cedilla to the c before the letters *a* or *o* in order to keep the soft *c* sound. For example:

Avancer (*to advance*): nous avançons

Commencer (*to start*): nous commençons

Lancer (*to throw, to launch*): nous lançons

Verbs ending in –*ger* gain *e* after *g* before the letters *a* and *o* to keep the soft *g* sound. For example:

Changer (*to change*): nous changeons

Manger (*to eat*): nous mangeons

Nager (*to swim*): nous nageons

- Verbs with **-é-** in the infinitive

Verbs that have **-é-** in the next to the last syllable of the infinitive change its **-é-** to **-è-** in all forms except *the 1st and 2nd person plural* (nous and vous) forms.

For example: ***Espérer***: j'espère - tu espères - il, elle, on espère - nous espérons - vous espérez - ils, elles espèrent.

Below are some some of verbs following this rule:

céder	to yield, to cede
célébrer	to celebrate
compléter	to complete
considérer	to consider
espérer	to hope
interpréter	to interpret
posséder	to possess
précéder	to precede
préférer	to prefer
protéger	to protect
répéter	to repeat

- Verbs with **-e-** in the infinitive

Some verbs containing **-e-** in the next to the last syllable of the infinitive, change the **-e-** to **-è-** in all forms except *the 1st and 2nd person plural* (nous and vous) forms.

For instance: ***Acheter***: J'achète - tu achètes - il, elle, on achète - nous achetons - vous achetez - ils, elles achètent.

CHAPTER 6: VERBS

Some of the commonly used verbs that follow this rule are:

acheter	to buy
mener	to lead
amener	to bring, to lead toward
emmener	to take away, to lead away
promener	to take a walk
lever	to lift
élever	to raise
enlever	to remove, to take off
geler	to freeze
peser	to weigh

NOTE:

*Other verbs that have -e- in the infinitive, **double** the final consonant in all except the 1st and 2nd person plural (nous and vous) forms.*

*For example: **Appeler**: j'appelle - tu appelles - il, elle, on appelle - nous appelons - vous appelez - ils, elles appellent.*

There are two common verbs that belong to this group:

appeler	to call
jeter	to throw away

‣ Verbs with *–yer* in the infinitive

Verbs ending in *–oyer*, *–uyer* and *–ayer* change *–y–* to *–i–* in all but *the 1st and 2nd person plural* (nous and vous) forms.

To illustrate: ***Payer***: je paie - tu paies - il, elles, on paie - nous payons - vous payez - ils, elles paient.

CHAPTER 6: VERBS

Some commonly used verbs with *–yer* ending are:

balayer	to sweep
employer	to use
ennuyer	to bore
envoyer	to send
essayer	to try
essuyer	to wipe
nettoyer	to clean
payer	to pay

NOTE:

*Verbs **payer** and **essayer** can also be conjugated regularly without changing -y- to -i- (e.g. je paye; j'essaye)*

- **Other irregular verbs**

Verbs like *ouvrir*

There some verbs that end in *–ir* but are conjugated like regular *–er* verbs.

To illustrate: ***Ouvrir***: j'ouvr**e** - tu ouvr**es** - il, elle, on ouvr**e** - nous ouvr**ons** - vous ouvr**ez** - ils, elles ouvr**ent**

Some of the most common verbs of this group are:

ouvrir	to open
couvrir	to cover
recouvrir	to cover again
découvrir	to discover
offrir	to offer

souffrir (de)	to suffer
cueillir	to pick, to gather
accueillir	to welcome
recueillir	to collect, to gather

Verbs like *courir*

Some verbs ending in *–ir* or *–re* can be conjugated like regular *–re* verbs except in *the 3rd person singular* (il, elle, on) form where t is added to the stem.

For example: ***Courir***: je cours - tu cours - il, elle, on cour**t** - nous courons - vous courez - ils, elles courent.

Some of the most common verbs conjugated like *courir* are:

courir	to run
parcourir	to pass through, to pass over, to travel
secourir	to help, to assist
rire	to laugh
sourire	to smile
conclure	to conclude
rompre	to break
corrompre	to corrupt, to spoil
interrompre	to interrupt

Verbs like battre and *mettre*

CHAPTER 6: VERBS

French verbs like ***battre*** and ***mettre*** and their derivatives are conjugated like regular *—re* verbs of the second-conjugation except that the ***double t*** becomes a ***single t*** in the singular forms. For example:

Battre: je ba**t**s - tu ba**t**s - il, elle, on ba**t** - nous ba**tt**ons - vous ba**tt**ez - ils, elles ba**tt**ent.

Mettre: je me**t**s - tu me**t**s - il, elle, on me**t** - nous me**tt**ons - vous me**tt**ez - ils, elles me**tt**ent.

Battre, mettre and their derivatives:

battre	to to beat, to hit, to win, to fight, to combat
se battre	to fight
combattre	to combat
mettre	to put, to wear, to put on
admettre	to admit
permettre	to permit
promettre	to promise
remettre	to put back
soumettre	to overcome, to submit, to subjugate, to subject
se mettre à	to begin
transmettre	to transmit

Verbs like *partir*

Verbs like ***partir*** are usually conjugated like regular *—re* verbs (2nd group) in the plural. But in the 1st and 2nd person singular forms (je, tu) the final consonant is dropped when the regular endings of the *—re* group are added to the stem. In the 3rd person singular form (il, elle, on) the final consonant is also dropped when **-t-** is added. Study the following:

173

Partir: je **pars** - tu **pars** - il, elle, on **part** - nous partons - vous partez - ils, elles partent.

Below are some common verbs conjugated like *partir*:

partir	to leave
dormir	to sleep
s'endormir	to fall asleep
mentir	to tell a lie
servir	to serve
sentir	to feel, to smell
sortir	to leave, to go out

NOTE:

*In the plural the consonant sounds **t** in **partir**, **mentir** and **sortir**; and **m** in **dormir** and **v** in **servir**.*

Verbs like *vaincre*

Verbs **vaincre** (*to conquer*) and **convaincre** (*to convince*) are conjugated like regular second-conjugation group **–re** of the verbs except that the **c** changes to **qu** in the plural.

For instance: **Vaincre**: je vaincs - tu vaincs - il, elle, on vainc - nous vain**qu**ons - vous vain**qu**ez - ils, elles vain**qu**ent.

Verbs like *connaître*

The verb **connaître** as well as similar verbs are conjugated in the way that the **circumflex** is put over the **i** in the 3rd person singular.

For example: **Connaître**: je connais - tu connais - il, elle, on connaît - nous connaissons - vous connaissez - ils, elles connaissent.

Below are some common verbs of this group including *connaître*:

CHAPTER 6: VERBS

connaître	to know someone, to be acquainted	**paraître**	to seem, to appear
apparaître	to appear, to seem	**reconnaître**	to recognize
disparaître	to disappear	**naître**	to be born

NOTE:

The verb **haïr** *(to hate) is also conjugated like* **connaître** *in the singular, except that there is no circumflex put above the i in the 3rd person singular. It is noticeable that the diaeresis is placed on the i in the plural. To illustrate:*

Haïr*: je hais - tu hais - il, elle, on hait - nous haïssons - vous haïssez - ils, elles haïssent.*

The verbs **plaire** *(to be pleasing),* **déplaire** *(to displease) and se* **taire** *(to be quiet) are also conjugated like* **connaître** *but there is only one s in the plural. There is no circumflex on the i in the 3rd person singular of* **se taire***. For example:*

Plaire*: je plais - tu plais - il, elle, on plaît - nous plaisons - vous plaisez - ils, elles plaisent.*

Se taire*: je me tais - tu te tais - il, elle, on se tait - nous nous taisons - vous vous taisez - ils, elles se taisent.*

Verbs ending in *–ire*

Many verbs ending in *–ire* add the endings *–s, –s,–t, –sons, –sez, –sent* to the stem.

For example: **Lire**: je li**s** - tu li**s** - il, elle, on li**t** - nous li**sons** - vous li**sez** - ils, elles li**sent**.

The most common verbs belonging to this group are:

lire	to read
élire	to elect

dire	to say
interdire	to forbid
suffire	to be sufficient
conduire	to drive, to conduct
produire	to produce
traduire	to translate
construire	to build
reconstruire	to rebuild, to reconstruct
détruire	to destroy
cuire	to cook
nuire	to do harm

NOTE:
The 2nd person plural of **dire** *(vous* **dites***) is an exception.*

Verbs like *écrire, vivre, suivre*

French verbs such as *écrire, vivre, suivre* are conjugated similarly and add *v* in the plural. For instance:

Écrire: j'écris - tu écris - il, elle, on écrit - nous écri*v*ons - vous écri*v*ez - ils, elles écri*v*ent.

Below are some common verbs of this group including *écrire, vivre, suivre*:

écrire	to write
décrire	to describe
vivre	to live
survivre	to survive

suivre	to follow, to take a class
poursuivre	to pursue, to follow up
s'ensuivre	to come after, to follow

Verbs like *croire* and *voir*

Like *–yer* verbs, **croire** (*to believe*), **voir** (*to see*), **prévoir** (*foresee*) and **revoir** (*to see again*) experience an internal vowel change. The *i* changes to *y* in *the 1st and 2nd person plural forms* (nous, vous). Other forms are conjugated like regular second-conjugation group (*–re*) of verbs except in *the 3rd person singular*, where *t* is added to the stem. For example:

Croire: je crois - tu crois - il, elle, on croi*t* - nous cro*y*ons - vous cro*y*ez - ils, elles, croient.

Voir: je vois - tu vois - il, elle, on voi*t* - nous vo*y*ons - vous vo*y*ez - ils, elles voient.

> *NOTE:*
>
> *The verbs **fuir** (to flee) and **s'enfuir** (to flee, to run away) have absolutely the same vowel change in the 1st and 2nd person plural:*
>
> ***Fuir**: je fuis - tu fuis - il, elle, on fuit - nous fuyons - vous fuyez - ils, elles fuient.*

Verbs like *craindre, peindre, joindre*

The verbs in this group undergo an internal change from *n* to *gn* in the plural. For instance:

Craindre: je crains - tu crains - il, elle, on craint - nous crai*gn*ons - vous crai*gn*ez - ils, elles crai*gn*ent.

Peindre: je peins - tu peins - il, elle, on peint - nous pei*gn*ons - vous pei*gn*ez - ils, elles, on pei*gn*ent.

Joindre: je joins - tu joins - il, elle, on joint - nous joi*gn*ons - vous joi*gn*ez - ils, elles joi*gn*ent.

Below are some verbs of this group including *craindre, peindre, joindre*:

craindre	to fear
plaindre	to pity, to feel sorry for
se plaindre	to complain
atteindre	to reach
éteindre	to extinguish, to put out
peindre	to paint
joindre	to join
rejoindre	to rejoin, to reunite

Verbs like *prendre*

Verbs like ***prendre*** (*to take, to take food, to drink - beverage, to buy a ticket*) are conjugated like the **–re** group of verbs (2nd group) in the singular, but in the plural, the final **–d** is dropped from the stem and regular ending is added. Also, the consonant **n** is doubled in the 3rd person plural:

Prendre: je prends - tu prends - il, elle, on prend - nous pre***nons*** - vous pre***nez*** - ils, elles pre***nnent***.

Below are some other verbs which are conjugated like *prendre*:

apprendre	to learn
comprendre	to understand
reprendre	to take back
surprendre	to surprise

Verbs like *tenir* and *venir*

The verbs ***venir*** (*to come*), ***tenir*** (*to hold*) and its derivatives are conjugated similarly and change the vowel from **-e-** to **-ie-** in the singular forms and the 3rd person plural and double **nn** in the 3rd person plural:

Tenir: je t**ie**ns - tu t**ie**ns - il, elle, on t**ie**nt - nous tenons - vous tenez - ils, elles t**ienn**ent.

Venir: je v**ie**ns - tu v**ie**ns - il, elle, on v**ie**nt - nous venons - vous venez - ils, elles v**ienn**ent.

Below is a list of commonly used derivatives of the verbs *tenir* and *venir*:

Tenir		Venir	
appartenir	to belong to	**revenir**	to come back
contenir	to hold, to contain	**convenir**	to be convenient
maintenir	to maintain	**devenir**	to become
obtenir	to obtain	**redevenir**	to become again
retenir	to retain	**parvenir**	to reach, to attain
		se souvenir (de)	to remember

Verbs *acquérir* and *conquérir*

The verbs **acquérir** (*to acquire, to buy, to gain*) and **conquérir** (*to conquer, to win*) undergo an internal vowel change from **é** to **ie** in all the forms except the 1st and 2nd person plural (nous and vous). For instance:

Acquérir: j'acqu**ie**rs - tu acqu**ie**rs - il, elle, on acqu**ie**rt - nous acqu**é**rons - vous acqu**é**rez - ils, elles acqu**iè**rent.

Verbs like *boire, devoir, recevoir*

The verbs **boire** (*to drink*), **devoir** (*to owe, to have to*), **recevoir** (*to receive*), **apercevoir** (*to perceive*) and **décevoir** (*to disappoint, to deceive*) are conjugated alike and have the internal vowel change in the 1st and 2nd person plural forms and also the **v** is added in all plural forms. It is noticeable that the **cedilla** is placed on the **c** in the singular

CHAPTER 6: VERBS

and 3rd person plural forms of **recevoir** and its derivatives. Study the following:

Boire: je b**oi**s - tu b**oi**s - il, elle, on b**oi**t - nous b**uv**ons - vous b**uv**ez - ils, elles b**oiv**ent.

Devoir: je d**oi**s - tu d**oi**s - il, elle, on d**oi**t - nous d**ev**ons - vous d**ev**ez - ils, elles d**oiv**ent.

Recevoir: je re**çoi**s - tu re**çoi**s - il, elle, on re**çoi**t - nous re**cev**ons - vous re**cev**ez - ils, elles re**çoi**vent.

Valoir and *falloir*

The verbs ***valoir*** (*to be worth*) and ***falloir*** (*to be necessary*) are considered to be irregular and their conjugation should be remembered since they were not presented in the table of irregular verbs previously. Note that *falloir* has *only the 3rd person singular form.*

Valoir: je ***vaux*** - tu ***vaux*** - il, elle, on ***vaut*** - nous ***valons*** - vous ***valez*** - ils, elles ***valent***.

Falloir: il *faut*

Use of the Present Tense

The present tense in Romance languages is used:

Actions in the present

‣ To identify an action that takes place in the present or at the moment of speech:

It. Che *fai*?

Fr. Que *fais*-tu? (tu *fais* quoi?)

- *What **are** you **doing**?*

It. ***Lavoro*** ora;

Fr. Je ***travaille*** maintenant.

CHAPTER 6: VERBS

*- I'm **working** now.*

NOTE:

Like in English, in Romance languages the present continuous is usually used in this case, however it is also possible to use the present tense here.

Habitual actions

▸ To indicate the regular repetitive action or things that one does as a habit:

Did you know?

The modern Italian language was created by Dante Alighieri (14th century). In his poem Divine Comedy (Divina Commedia) he used several south Italian dialects with his mother tongue - The Tuscan language. The result became the base for the standardized Italian language.

It. Lui ***viaggia*** molto;

Fr. Il ***voyage*** beaucoup.

*- He **travels** a lot.*

It. ***Studio*** le lingue straniere all'università.

Fr. J'***étudie*** les langues étrangères à l'université.

*- I **study** foreign languages in college.*

Universal truths

▸ To indicate the action that is not referred to a certain moment, but refers to general statements, scientific definitions, proverbs and etc.:

It. L'uomo ***ha bisogno*** d'amore;

Fr. L'homme ***a besoin*** d'amour.

*- Men **need** love.*

> **Did you know?**
>
> The Republic of Mali is the largest country in West Africa (1,240,000 square kilometres) and the 24th biggest country in the world. It is about twice the size of Texas. Its capital, Bamako, is the fastest growing city in Africa.

It. L'Everest **è** la montagna più alta della Terra;

Fr. L'Everest **est** la montagne la plus haute de la Terre.

- Everest **is** the tallest mountain on Earth.

Replacing the Future tense

- To refer to close or planned future:

It. **Vado** al cinema stasera;

Fr. Je **vais** au cinéma ce soir.

- I **am going** to the cinema tonight.

It. Il mio treno **arriva** alle nove;

Fr. Mon train **arrive** à neuf heures.

- My train **arrives** at nine.

Special Use of the Present Tense and Prepositions

In Romance languages the present tense, together with the prepositions of time It. **da, fa...che** (**sono...che**) Fr. **depuis, ça fait... que** are generally used to describe an action that started in the past and still continues in the present. In English the present perfect is used in this case.

> **NOTE:**
>
> There is a difference in use between those prepositions of time in Italian and French:
>
> It. **da**; Fr. **depuis** (since) are primarily used to indicate the definite moment (day, month, year)

in the past since when somebody has started to do something. Study the following:

It. Lavoro in banca **dal** 2013;
Fr. Je travaille dans la banque **depuis** 2013.
- I have been working in the bank **since** 2013.

It. **fa...che/ è da (sono...che)** Fr. **ça fait... que** (for/since) are used in general terms when there is no specific date from which somebody has been doing something. Observe the following:

It. **È da** due anni **che** lavoro in banca (**Sono** due anni **che** lavoro in banca);
Fr. **Ça fait** deux ans **que** je travaille dans la banque.
- I have worked in the bank **for** 2 years.

In order to ask the question *since when*, It. **da quando, da quanto**; Fr. **depuis quand, depuis combien de temps** are used. Study the following:

It. **Da quando** lavori in banca? (**Da quanto tempo** lavori in banca?)

Fr. **Depuis quand** travailles-tu dans la banque? (**Depuis combien de temps** travailles-tu dans la banque?)

- **Since when** have you been working in the bank? (**For how long** have you been working in the bank?)

The Past Participle

Overview

The past participle is a very useful form of a verb that can function as an adjective, a predicative, or as a verb in conjugation with It.

avere; Fr. *avoir* - *have* to form the perfect (compound) tenses, which is the most common use of the past participle.

Formation of Past Participle of Regular Verbs

In Romance languages the Past Participle of regular verbs is formed by dropping the infinitive ending and adding the appropriate past participle ending to the stem of the verb.

Below is a table presenting how the past participle of regular verbs is formed:

	1st conj.	2nd conj.	3rd conj.
Italian	-**are**; -**ato** (parl**are** – parl**ato**)	-**ere**; -**uto** (vend**ere** – vend**uto**)	-**ire**; -**ito** (part**ire** – part**ito**)
French	-**er**; -**é** (parl**er** – parl**é**)	-**re**; -**u** (vend**re** – vend**u**)	-**ir**; -**i** (part**ir** – part**i**)

Irregular Past Participles

Italian and French have also irregular forms of past participle, which need to be memorized.

Below is a list of verbs, the past participles of which are irregular in all or some of the Romance languages:

Italian	French	English
avere – avuto	avoir – eu	*have - had*
essere – stato	être – été	*be - been*
fare – fatto	faire – fait	*do - done*
dire – detto	dire – dit	*say - said*
capire – capito	comprendre – compris	*understand - understood*

CHAPTER 6: VERBS

Italian	French	English
imparare– imparato	apprendre– appris	learn - learned
prendere – preso	prendre – pris	take - taken
scrivere – scritto	écrire – écrit	write - written
porre – posto; mettere – messo	mettre – mis	put - put
tradurre – tradotto	traduire – traduit	translate - translated
venire – venuto	venir – venu	come - come
vedere – visto; veduto	voir – vu	see - seen
sapere – saputo	savoir – su	know - known (about); or can - been able to
conoscere– conosciuto	connaître – connu	know - known (someone, something); or be familiar with
aprire – aperto	ouvrir – ouvert	open - opened
morire – morto	mourir – mort	die - died
credere – creduto	croire – cru	believe - believed
leggere – letto	lire – lu	read - read
portare – portato	apporter - apporté	bring - brought

Use of Past Participle

▸ **As an adjective**

Past participles in Romance languages can be used as adjectives and must agree in gender and number with the nouns they modify. For example:

> *Did you know?*
>
> The Vatican City is the smallest country in the world with the smallest population. It measures 44 hectares (110 acres) and has a population of about 1000 people.

It. il portafoglio **perso**;

Fr. le portefeuille **perdu**.

- *The **lost** wallet.*

It. la porta **aperta**;

Fr. la porte **ouverte**.

- *The **open** door.*

➢ **As a Predicative adjective**

Past participles can also act as predicative adjectives when used in conjugation with a linking verb It. **essere, stare**; Fr. **être**. In this case, they must agree in gender and number with the nouns they modify, for example:

It. la porta **è chiusa**;

Fr. la porte **est fermée**.

- *The door **is closed**.*

➢ **The perfect tenses (*See The Perfect Tense p. 255*)**

The Present Perfect

Formation of the Present Perfect

In Romance languages the present perfect is formed by the combining present indicative of the auxiliary verb It. **avere**; Fr. **avoir** - *to have*, which is conjugated to the subject of the sentence, and the past participle.

CHAPTER 6: VERBS

Below is the present perfect formula in the Romance languages:

Present Perfect Formula

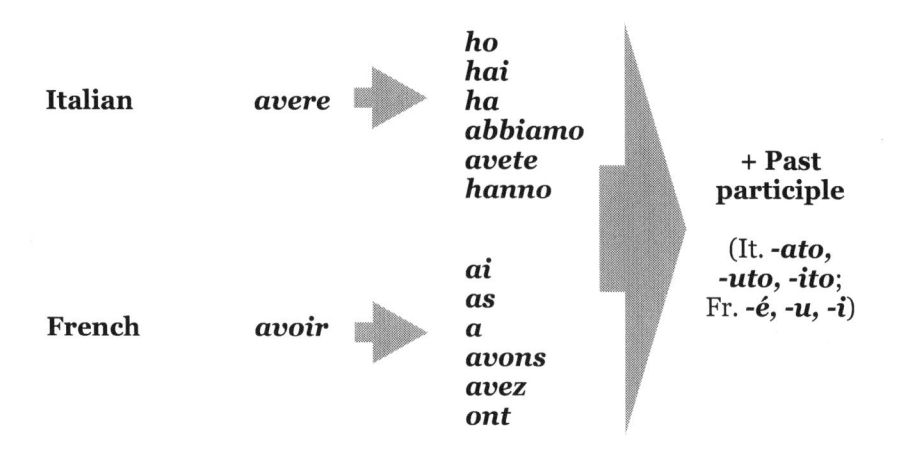

Italian	*avere*	→	ho hai ha abbiamo avete hanno	→	+ Past participle
French	*avoir*	→	ai as a avons avez ont		(It. *-ato, -uto, -ito*; Fr. *-é, -u, -i*)

For example:

Did you know?

The largest agricultural, forestry and agri-food fair in Europe, the Foire de Libramont, is held in Belgium.

It. **Hai cant*ato*** molto bene;

Fr. Tu **as** très bien **chant*é***.

- You **have sung** very well.

NOTE:

*The auxiliary verb It. **avere**; Fr. **avoir** never separate from the past participle. If there are object pronouns in the sentence, they are immediately placed before the auxiliary verb. Study the following:*

It. **L'**hai visto?

Fr. **L'**as-tu vu?

- Have you seen **her**?

CHAPTER 6: VERBS

Formation of the Present Perfect with the Verb *to be* in Italian and French

In Italian and French the auxiliary verb It. ***essere***; Fr. ***être*** - *to be* is used with reflexive and intransitive verbs (which are used to talk about movement or a change of some kind) in order to form the present perfect. For example:

Did you know?

Genoa (It. Genova), the capital of the Italian region of Liguria, is the birthplace of world famous explorer and navigator Christopher Columbus (born in 1451).

It. Lui **è arrivato**, Mi **sono alzato**;

Fr. Il **est arrivé**, je me **suis levé**.

- He **arrived**, I **got up**.

Italian and French have a similar group of intransitive verbs with which the auxiliary verb *to be* is used.

Below is a list of the most frequent intransitive verbs in Italian and French:

Italian		French	
andare	ritornare	aller	retourner
arrivare	rivenire	arriver	revenir
entrare	uscire	entrer	sortir
scendere	cadere	descendre	tomber
divenire,	venire	devenir	venir
diventare	restare,	monter	rester
salire	rimanere	mourir	
morire	**essere, stare***	naître	
nascere	**riuscire***	partir	
partire	**vivere***		

*In Italian the verbs like ***essere***, ***stare*** (*to be*), ***riuscire*** (*to succeed*), ***vivere*** (*to live*) are used with the verb <u>***essere***</u> (*to be*) in order to form the present perfect. However, in French above-listed verbs, which are ***être***, ***réussir***, ***vivre*** are used with <u>***avoir***</u> (*to have*) to form this tense.

CHAPTER 6: VERBS

Agreement of the Past Participle

In Italian and French the past participle used with *to be* (It. *essere*, Fr. *être*) always agrees in gender and number with the subject; that is, the endings change in the feminine and plural forms the way they change in adjectives: in French **-e** is added to agree with the feminine and **-s-** with the masculine; in Italian to agree with the feminine **-a** is used and **-i**, **-e** with the plural for masculine and feminine respectively.

It. Io sono arriv**ato** (*masc.s.*) – io sono arriv**ata** (*fem. s.*);

Lui è part**ito** – Lei è part**ita**;

Noi siamo part**iti** – Noi siamo part**ite**.

Fr. Je suis arriv**é** (*masc.s.*) – je suis arriv**ée** (*fem. s.*);

Il est part**i** – Elle est part**ie**;

Nous sommes part**is** – Nous sommes part**ies**.

I have arrived (*masc.s; fem.s.*)

He/she has arrived

We have arrived

Agreement of the Past Participle with *avoir* in French

The past participle of verbs that use *avoir* in the present perfect also agree in number and in gender with a preceding direct object in French. Study the following:

Fr. C'est **la lettre** que j'ai **écrite**;

C'est **les photos** que j'ai **vues**;

Ce sont **les livres** que j'ai **achetés**.

CHAPTER 6: VERBS

This is the letter I wrote;

This is the photos I took;

These are the book I bought.

Be attentive since most past participle sound similar in the masculine and feminine except for those ending in a consonant. Also, it should be noted that there is no oral or written change for the masculine singular and plural when the past participle ends in **s**. For example: le livre que j'ai **pris**; les livres que j'ai **pris** - *the books that I took*.

The past participle of verbs with ***avoir*** is unchangeable:

- when it is used an impersonal verb, for example: la neige qu'***il y a eu***
- when the past participle is followed by a complementary infinitive and when it is the infinitive that relates to the preceding direct object, for instance: les devoirs qu'il a ***dû compléter***.
- the past participle of some intransitively used verbs is invariable when accompanied by a unit of price, weight, distance, length and time, for example: l***es trois heures*** que j'ai ***marché***.

Use of the Present Perfect

The present perfect in Italian and French is used:

- To describe actions that happened in the past and continue into the present or actions that happened in the recent past, which usually refer to what someone has done:

Did you know?

The Republic of Benin (formerly Dahomey) is a French speaking West African country. Benin became independent from France on August 1, 1960. Cotonou Beaches are some of Benin's greatest beaches.

It. ***Ha scritto*** un libro;

Fr. Elle ***a écrit*** un livre.

- *She **has written** a book.*

Special Use of the Present Perfect in Italian and French

However, it is notable that in conversational French the present perfect (*passé composé*) is used as the preterite, which is the most common tense to talk about past events and actions. All above-listed examples of the present perfect should be translated or conveyed in the preterite tense in French.

Like in French, in conversational Italian the present perfect tense is used as the preterite tense.

Fr. *venir de* + The Infinitive

To express something that has just been done Fr. **venir de** is used. Note that in French the present tense of these verbs is used.

NOTE:

In Italian, in this case, the present perfect is used with the adverb **appena** which is put right after the auxiliary verb **avere** or **essere**. Study the following:

It. **Ho appena** letto questo libro;

Fr. Je **viens de** lire ce livre.

- I **(have) just** read this book.

The Preterite

Formation of the Preterite

The preterite (also called the simple past, the past definite and the past absolute) is formed by dropping the infinitive ending and adding the appropriate personal ending to the root of a verb.

Below is a table demonstrating the endings of the preterite tense:

CHAPTER 6: VERBS

	Italian	French
	1st group	
	-ARE	**-ER**
Singular	-ai, -asti, -ò,	-ai, -as, -a,
Plural	-iamo, -aste, -arono	-âmes, -âtes, -èrent
	2nd group	
	-ERE	**-RE**
Singular	-ei, -esti, -è,	-is, -is, -it,
Plural	-emmo, -este, -erono	-îmes, -îtes, -irent
	3rd group	
	-IRE	**-IR**
Singular	-i, -isti, -i,	-is, -is, -it,
Plural	-immo, -iste, -irono	-îmes, -îtes, -irent

Below is the table displaying the example of conjugation of regular verbs in the preterite tense:

Italian	French	English
1st group		
Parl*are*	**Parl*er***	*To speak*
io **parl*ai***	je **parl*ai***	*I spoke*
tu **parl*asti***	tu **parl*as***	*you spoke*
lui\lei\Lei **parl*ò***	il\elle\on **parl*a***	*he\she\it spoke*
noi **parl*ammo***	nous **parl*âmes***	*we spoke*
voi **parl*aste***	vous **parl*âtes***	*you spoke*
loro\Loro **parl*arono***	ils\elles **parl*èrent***	*they spoke*
2nd group		
Vend*ere*	**Vend*re***	*To sell*

Italian	French	English
io *vend__ei__*	je *vend__is__*	I sold
tu *vend__esti__*	tu *vend__is__*	you sold
lui\lei\Lei *vend__è__*	il\elle\on *vend__it__*	he\she\it sold
noi *vend__emmo__*	nous *vend__îmes__*	we sold
voi *vend__este__*	vous *vend__îtes__*	you sold
loro\Loro *vend__erono__*	ils\elles *vend__irent__*	they sold
3rd group		
Part__ire__	**Part__ir__**	*To leave*
io *part__ii__*	je *part__is__*	I left
tu *part__isti__*	tu *part__is__*	you left
lui\lei\Lei *part__ì__*	il\elle\on *part__it__*	he\she\it left
noi *part__immo__*	nous *part__îmes__*	we left
voi *part__iste__*	vous *part__îtes__*	you left
loro\Loro *part__irono__*	ils\elles *part__irent__*	they left

Irregular Verbs in the Preterite

Below is a table presenting irregular verbs in the preterite tense, which are common for all or several Romance languages:

Italian	French	
Essere (fui, fosti, fu, fummo, foste, furono)	**Être** (je fus, tu fus, il\elle\on fut, nous fûmes, vous fûtes, ils\elles furent)	*To be*

CHAPTER 6: VERBS

Italian	French	
Stare (stetti, stesti, stette, stemmo, steste, stettero)	**Être** (je fus, tu fus, il\elle\on fut, nous fûmes, vous fûtes, ils\elles furent)	*To be*
Avere (ebbi, avesti, ebbe, <u>avemmo</u>, <u>aveste</u>, ebbero)	**Avoir** (j'eus, tu eus, il\elle\on eut, nous eûmes, vous eûtes, ils\elles eurent)	*To have*
Mettere (misi, <u>mettesti</u> mise, <u>mettemmo</u>, metteste, misero)	**Mettre** (je mis, tu mis, il\elle\on mit, nous mîmes, vous mîtes, ils\elles mirent)	*To put*
Fare (feci, facesti, fece, facemmo, faceste, fecero)	**Faire** (je fis, tu fis, il\elle\on fit, nous fîmes, vous fîtes, ils\elles firent)	*To do*
Dire (dissi, dicesti, disse, dicemmo, diceste, dissero)	**Dire** (dis, dis, dit, dîmes, dîtes, dirent)	*To say*
Venire (venni, venne, vennero)	**Venir** (vins, vins, vint, vînmes, vîntes, vinrent)	*To come*
Sapere (seppi, seppe, seppero)	**Savoir** (sus, sus, sut, sûmes, sûtes, surent)	*To know*
Prendere (presi, prese, presero)	**Prendre** (pris, pris, prit, primes, prîtes, prirent)	*To take*

Italian	French	
Conoscere (conobbi, conobbe, conobbero)	**Connaître** (connus, connus, connut, connûmes, connûtes, connurent)	*To know* *To be acquainted*
Leggere (lessi, lesse, lessero)	**Lire** (lus, lus, lut, lûmes, lûtes, lurent)	*To read*
Scrivere (scrissi, scrisse, scrissero)	**Écrire** (écrivis, écrivis, écrivit, écrivîmes, écrivîtes, écrivirent)	*To write*
Tenere (tenni, tenne, tennero)	**Tenir** (tins, tins, tint, tînmes, tîntes, tînrent)	*To have,* *To hold*
Portare (regular)	**Apporter** (regular)	*To carry*

NOTE:

It should be noted that Italian irregular verbs of the preterite tense are only irregular in the 1st and 3rd person singular as well as the 3rd person plural. The other three forms are always regular.

Irregularities in Formation the Preterite

However, despite the majority of similar irregular verbs, Italian has its own number of irregular verbs with specific models of conjugation. In other words some verbs have specific spelling changes in order to preserve the pronunciation (sound) presented in the infinitive and others change their vowel within the stem. Therefore, it is important to consider the rules of the spelling or vowels change in a verb conjugation. Since the rules are very divergent and particular for each language, it makes it difficult to combine these changes in a verb conjugation of the Romance languages. So, it is necessary to consider them separately.

> **NOTE:**
>
> Unlike Italian, French has an insignificant number of irregular verbs with specific models of conjugation in the preterite. The most common of them were presented in the table of the irregular verbs (**See Irregular Verbs in the Preterite p.193**).

Italian

Verbs with a single -s-

There are a lot of verbs that operate the same as ***chiudere*** (*close*) and have a second, irregular root with a single **-s-** in the 1st, 3rd person singular and 3rd person plural forms of the preterite. To illustrate:

Did you know?

Turin (It. Torino) is a city and an important cultural and educational center in northern Italy. The city has Italy's best universities and academies, such as the University of Turin and the Turin Polytechnic.

Chiudere

io ***chiusi***

tu ***chiudesti***

lui, lei, Lei ***chiuse***

noi ***chiudemmo***

voi ***chiudeste***

loro, Loro ***chiusero***

Below are the verbs that are conjugated like *chiudere* in the preterite:

CHAPTER 6: VERBS

Italian	English
chiedere (chiesi, chiese, chiesero)	*to ask*
concludere (conclusi, concluse, conclusero)	*to conclude*
racchiudere (racchiusi, racchiudesti, racchiuse)	*to contain*
escludere (esclusi, escluse, esclusero)	*to exclude*
includere (inclusi, incluse, inclusero)	*to include*
decidere (decisi, decise, decisero)	*to decide*
coincidere (coincisi, coincise, coincisero)	*to coincide*
uccidere (uccisi, uccise, uccisero)	*to kill*
dividere (divisi, divise, divisero)	*to divide*
prendere (presi, prese, presero)	*to take*
accendere (accesi, accese, accesero)	*to light, to turn on*
attendere (attesi, attese, attesero)	*to wait*
apprendere (appresi, apprese, appresero)	*to learn*
difendere (difesi, difese, difesero)	*to defend*
offendere (offesi, offese, offesero)	*to offend*
scendere (scesi, scese, scesero)	*to descend*
sorprendere (sorpresi, sorprese, sorpresero)	*to surprise*
spendere (spesi, spese, spesero)	*to spend*
stendere (stesi, stese, stesero)	*to extend*
ridere (risi, rise, risero)	*to laugh*
sorridere (sorrisi, sorrise, sorrisero)	*to smile*
rimanere (rimasi, rimase, rimasero)	*to stay*
rispondere (risposi, rispose, risposero)	*to answer*

Italian	English
*mettere (misi, mise, misero)	to put

It should be remembered that:

- The vowel change in **mettere** should be noted. Also there are other verbs conjugated like **mettere**: **ammettere** - *to admit*; **commettere** - *to commit*; **permettere** - *to allow*; **promettere** - *to promise*; **rimettere** - *to return*; **smettere** - *to stop*; **trasmettere** - *to convey, to transmit*.

- The verb **porre** - *to put* follows the same rules as the above *-s-* verbs. To demonstrate:

Porre

io *posi*

tu ponesti

lui, lei, Lei *pose*

noi ponemmo

voi poneste

loro, Loro *posero*

There are also other verbs conjugated like **porre**: **comporre** - *to compose*; **disporre** - *to dispose, to arrange*; **opporre** - *to oppose, to object*; **proporre** - *to propose*.

- Also, the verbs **correre** - *to run*; **scegliere** - *to choose* and **volgere** - *to turn* also have a single *-s-* in the preterite. To illustrate:

Correre

io *corsi*

tu corresti

lui, lei, Lei *corse*

CHAPTER 6: VERBS

noi corremmo

voi correste

loro, Loro **corsero**

There are also other verbs conjugated like **correre**: **occorrere** - *to need, to be necessary*; **incorrere** - *to incur*; **rincorrere** - *to run after*; **scorrere** - *to slide*; **trascorrere** - *to spend, to pass by.*

Scegliere

io ***scelsi***

tu scegliesti

lui, lei, Lei ***scelse***

noi scegliemmo

voi sceglieste

loro, Loro ***scelsero***

There are also other verbs conjugated like **scegliere**: **accogliere** - *to welcome, to receive*; **cogliere** - *to pick, to catch*; **raccogliere** - *to collect*; **togliere** - *to remove.*

Volgere

io ***volsi***

tu volgesti

lui, lei, Lei ***volse***

noi volgemmo

voi volgeste

loro, Loro ***volsero***

Other verbs conjugated like **volgere** are: **dipingere** - *to paint*; **fingere** - *to pretend, to simulate*; **giungere** - *to reach, to arrive*; **piangere** - *to cry*; **scorgere** - *to sight, to notice, to make out*; **sorgere** - *to rise*; **spingere** - *to push*; **svolgere** - *to perform, to develop*.

It should be remembered that when a single **-s-** is preceded and followed by a vowel is pronounced like *z*. When a single **-s-** is preceded by a consonant, it is pronounces like *s*.

Verbs with a double -s- (-ss-)

Such verbs as **leggere** - *to read*, **scrivere** - *to write* and **vivere** - *to live*, as you might notice from the table of the irregular verbs, have a double *s* in the 1st person singular and the 3rd person singular and plural of the preterite. It is so because *s* is preceded by a vowel and must be doubled in order to preserve the *s* sound. Other verbs having a double *s* in the 1st person singular and the 3rd person singular and plural in the preterite are:

Italian	English
proddure (produssi, produsse, produssero)	*to produce*
trarre (trassi, trasse, trassero)	*to draw*
sottrarre (sottrassi, sottrasse, sottrassero)	*to subtract*
correggere (corressi, corresse, corressero)	*to correct*
eleggere (elessi, elesse, elessero)	*to elect*
proteggere (protessi, protesse, protessero)	*to protect*
reggere (ressi, resse, ressero)	*to hold*
descrivere (descrissi, descrisse, descrissero)	*to describe*
prescrivere (prescrissi, prescrisse, prescrissero)	*to prescribe*

CHAPTER 6: VERBS

Italian	English
trascrivere (trascrissi, trascrisse, trascrissero)	to transcribe
addurre (addussi, addusse, addussero)	to adduce
condurre (condussi, condusse, condussero)	to lead
indurre (indussi, indusse, indussero)	to induce
introdurre (introdussi, introdusse, introdussero)	to introduce
ridurre (ridussi, ridusse, ridussero)	to reduce
tradurre (tradussi, tradusse, tradussero)	to translate
contraddire (contraddissi, contraddisse, contraddissero)	to contradict
disdire (disdissi, disdisse, disdissero)	to cancel
indire (indissi, indisse, indissero)	to call
maledire (maledissi, maledisse, maledissero)	to curse
predire (predissi, predisse, predissero)	to predict
ridire (ridissi, ridisse, ridissero)	to object
attrarre (attrassi, attrasse, attrassero)	to attract
contrarre (contrassi, contrasse, contrassero)	to contract
detrarre (detrassi, detrasse, detrassero)	to deduct
distrarre (distrassi, distrasse, distrassero)	to distract

Italian	English
ritrarre (ritrassi, ritrasse, ritrassero)	to portray

Verbs with other double consonants

Such verbs as *cadere*, *tenere* and *volere* double the consonant of the root in the 1st person singular and 3rd person singular and plural in the preterite (*tenere* and *volere* are already presented in the list of the irregular verbs above (**See Irregular Verbs in the Preterite p.193**). Below is a list of verbs that double the consonant:

Italian	English
cadere (caddi, cadde, caddero)	to fall
decadere (decaddi, decadde, decaddero)	to decay
ricadere (ricaddi, ricadde, ricaddero)	to fall
appartenere (appartenni, appartenne, appartennero)	to belong
contenere (contenni, contenne, contennero)	to contain
mantenere (mantenni, mantenne, mantennero)	to maintain
sostenere (sostenni, sostenne, sostennero)	to support
bere (bevvi, bevve, bevvero)	to drink
divenire (divenni, divenne, divennero)	to prescribe
avvenire (avvenne)	to occur
convenire (convenni, convenne, convennero)	to agree

Italian	English
intervenire (intervenni, intervenne, intervennero)	*to intervene*
pervenire (pervenni, pervenne, pervennero)	*to reach*
rivenire (rivenni, rivenne, rivennero)	*to come back*
sovvenire (sovvenni, sovvenne, sovvennero)	*to remember*
svenire (svenni, svenne, svennero)	*to faint*
conoscere (conobbi, conobbe, conobbero)	*to know*
riconoscere (riconobbi, riconobbe, riconobbero)	*to recognize*

Verbs with -*qu*-

Verbs such as ***nascere*** and ***piacere*** get **-*qu*-** in the 1st person singular and the 3rd person singular and plural in the preterite. Below is a list of verbs that obtain **-*qu*-**:

Italian	English
nascere (nacqui, nacque, nacquero)	*to be born*
piacere (piacqui, piacque, piacquero)	*to please*
compiacere (compiacqui, compiacque, compiacquero)	*to satisfy*
dispiacere (dispiacqui, dispiacque, dispiacquero)	*to dislike*
giacere (giacqui, giacque, giacquero)	*to lie*

CHAPTER 6: VERBS

Use of the Preterite

The preterite in Italian and French is used to express:

- *actions that happened in the past without any relation to the present*:

Did you know?

Togo is a French-speaking country in West Africa located on the Gulf of Guinea. The capital, Lomé, hosts the world's largest voodoo market called the Fetish Market. It features monkey heads, skulls, crocodiles and skins of animals.

It. **aprirono** la finestra,

Fr. ils **ouvrirent** la fenêtre.

- *They **opened** the window.*

- *two or more completed continuous or consecutive actions in the past*:

It. **entrarono** nella sala e **aprirono** la finestra;

Fr. ils **entrèrent** dans la salle et **ouvrirent** la fenêtre.

- *They **entered** the room and **opened** the window.*

The following are the most common expressions that are usually used with the preterite:

Italian	French	English
ieri	**hier**	*yesterday*
ieri pomeriggio	**hier après-midi**	*yesterday afternoon*
ieri sera	**la nuit dernière**	*last night*
l'altro ieri	**la journée d'avant-hier**	*the day before yesterday*

Italian	French	English
l'altro giorno	l'autre jour	*the other day*
due giorni fa	il y a deux jours	*two days ago*
la settimana scorsa	la semaine dernière	*last week*
il mese scorso	le mois dernier	*last month*
l'anno scorso	l'année dernière	*last year*
stamattina	ce matin	*this morning*
di colpo	tout d'un coup	*suddenly*
per molto tempo	pendant longtemps	*for a long time*
l'estate scorsa	l'été dernier	*last summer*
poco fa	il y a peu	*a little while ago*
per poco tempo	pendant une courte période	*for a little while*

Special Use of the Preterite in French

It should be mentioned that **passé simple** (*the preterite*) is a literary tense used only in literary contexts in French. In conversational French **passé compose** (*the present perfect*) is used.

Difference between the Preterite and the Present Perfect in the Romance languages

In Romance languages the Preterite expresses a fully completed action in the past, whereas the Present Perfect expresses an action that started in the past and has been developing over a period of time and may or may not tend to continue into the future. Study the following:

CHAPTER 6: VERBS

> **Did you know?**
>
> The Vatican City is a UNESCO World Heritage Site; the only site to encompass a whole country.

It. **Incontrai** il mio amico in strada;

Fr. J'**<u>ai rencontré</u>** mon ami dans la rue.

- I **met** my friend in the street.

It. **Ho incontrato** il mio amico per strada;

Fr. J'**<u>ai rencontré</u>** mon ami dans la rue.

- I **have been meeting** my friend in the street (and I may still be continuing to meet him in the street).

Asking Questions

We have already looked at question words and now we will consider yes/no questions, which are questions that can be answered with "yes" or "no", and questions that get more detailed information.

Unlike in English, in Romance languages questions are formed differently. In English the verb **to do** is used to form questions: "**Do** you know him?", whereas in Romance languages this verb is never used. Generally speaking in Romance languages, asking a question which can be answered with "yes" or "no" is quite simple. In order to pose such a question, you should raise your intonation at the end of the question. For example:

It. Lo conosci?

Fr. Tu le connais?

- Do you know him?

Also, you can change a statement into a question by adding the word It. **no**? Fr. **non**? to the end of a statement in all the Romance languages. For instance:

> **Did you know?**
>
> Television was introduced in Belgium in 1953 with two channels, one in Dutch and one in French.

It. Vieni domani, **no**?

Fr. Tu viens demain, **non**?

- *You are coming tomorrow, **aren't you**?*

Peculiarities of Interrogation in the Romance languages

Italian

- In Italian you can make a question by placing the subject either at the end of the sentence or after the verb. Study the following:

    L'insegnante parla italiano. - Parla italiano l'insegnante? (Parla l'insegnante italiano?)

    - *The teacher speaks Italian. Does the teacher speak Italian?*

- Also, you can form a question by adding such expressions as **non è vero**?, **è vero**? or **vero**? to the end of a statement. For instance:

    Parli italiano, **non è vero**? - *You speak Italian, don't you? (lit. You speak Italian, **isn't it true**?)*

    Lavori in ufficio, **è vero**? - *You work in the office, **right**?*

    Hai un fratello, **vero**? - *You have a brother, **don't you**?*

French

- In French questions can also be formed by adding **n'est-ce pas**? to a statement. For example:

CHAPTER 6: VERBS

Did you know?

Venice (It. Venezia) gets between 20 million to 30 million tourists annually, which is around 60 thousand tourists per day. The population of the city, however, is only about 55 thousand people.

Tu parle français, **n'est-ce pas**? - *You speak French, **don't you**?*

Tu travailles dans le bureau, **n'est-ce pas**? - *You work in the office, **don't you**?*

Tu as un frère, **n'est-ce pas**? - *You have a brother, **don't you**?*

- Also, you can form a question by adding **est-ce que** or **est-ce qu'** (before vowels) at the beginning of the statement and putting a question mark at the end of a question.

Est-ce que tu parles français? - *Do you speak French?*

Est-ce qu'il travaille dans le bureau? - *Does he work in the office?*

- French questions can also be formed by means of inversion of the subject pronoun and verb in declarative sentences. It should be noted that the subject is connected to the verb with a hyphen. Study the following:

Parlez-vous français? - *Do you speak French?*

Travaillez-vous dans le bureau? - *Do you work in the office?*

It should be remembered that when inverting a 3rd person singular subject pronoun and a verb, a *t* should be added between the inverted verb and the subject when the verb ends in a vowel, for example:

Parle-t-il français? - *Does he speak French?*

Va-t-il à Paris? - *Does he go to France?*

With the 1st person singular subject *je* inversion is usually not used. In this case **est-ce que** should be used. For instance:

Est-ce que je joue bien? - *Do I play well?*

However, inversion with *je* is possible with certain frequently used verbs, which are **avoir** (*to have*), **être** (*to be*), **pouvoir** (*can*). The verb **pouvoir** becomes **puis** in the inversion with *je*.

Ai-je...? - *Do I have...?*; *Suis-je*...? - *Am I...?*; *Puis-je*...? - *Can I...?*

Did you know?

Réunion Island is a French overseas territory in the Indian Ocean, east of Madagascar. The island is known for its volcanos, coral reefs and tropical beaches. Its culture is a mix of various cultures influenced by people of African, Indian, European and Chinese origin.

Inversion is also possible in compound tenses in French. In this case, the subject pronoun and the auxiliary verb are inverted. Observe the following:

A-t-il travaillé au bureau? - *Does he work in the office?*

Es-tu venu? - *Have you come?*

Negation

Unlike in English, in Romance languages negation is also formed quite different. For instance, in English the verb **to do** is widely used to make a sentence negative: "*I don't know*", while in the Romance languages the verb to do is never used in negative sentences.

Furthermore, double negation, which is not acceptable in English, is frequently used in Romance languages, for example *I know nobody/I don't know anybody* (since it is not grammatically correct to say I don't know nobody):

It. Io **non** conosco **nessuno**,

Fr. Je **ne** connais **personne**.

- *I know nobody. / I don't know anybody.*

Formation of Negation in Simple Tenses

Italian negative sentences are formed by putting the word It. **non** before the verb.

In French the combination **ne...pas** is used where **ne** is placed before the verb and **pas** after it. It should be noted that **ne** becomes **n'** before words that begin with a *vowel* or *h*.

Below are the examples demonstrating the formation of negative sentences from affirmative in Romance languages:

Affirmative:	Negative:
It. Io lavoro;	It. Io **non** lavoro;
Fr. Je travaille	Fr. Je **ne** travaille **pas**
- I work.	- I don't work.
Affirmative:	**Negative:**
It. Lei scrive un libro;	It. Lei **non** scrive un libro;
Fr. Elle écrit un livre	Fr. Elle **n'**écrit **pas** un livre
- She writes a book.	- She doesn't write a book.

If an object pronoun (**See Object Pronoun p.90, p.99**) precedes the verb, the negative word should be placed before the object pronoun in Romance languages. In French **ne** is put before the object pronoun and **pas** is placed after the verb. For example:

Affirmative:	Negative:
It. La conosco;	It. **Non** la conosco;
Fr. Je la connais	Fr. Je **ne** la connais **pas**
- I know her.	- I don't know her.

If there is an infinitive which follows the verb in a sentence, the negative word is placed before the main verb. In French **ne** is put before the main verb and **pas** is placed after the main verb. For instance:

Affirmative:	Negative:
It. Voglio dormire;	It. Io **non** voglio dormire;
Fr. Je veux dormir	Fr. Je **ne** veux **pas** dormir
- *I want to sleep.*	- *I don't want to sleep.*

Omission of *Pas* in French

In French **pas** can be omitted in the negative sentences after such verbs as **pouvoir** (*can*), **savoir** (*to know*), **oser** (*dare*) and **cesser** (*to cease*) when they are accompanied by an infinitive, for example:

Je **ne** sais que dire - *I don't know what to say*;

Ils **ne** peuvent le faire - *They cannot do it*;

Tu **n'**oses y aller - *You don't dare go there*;

Il **ne** cesse de pleuvoir - *It doesn't stop raining.*

Negation of the Infinitive

In order to make an infinitive negative, you should put the negative words It. **non**, Fr. **ne pas** before the infinitive. Study the following:

Did you know?

The Vatican museums are over 9 miles (14,5 kilometers) long, and it is said that if you spent only 1 minute admiring each painting it would take you 4 years to complete the circuit.

It. Mi ha detto di **non** farlo;

Fr. Il m'a dit de **ne pas** le faire

- *He told me **not** to do it.*

It. Lei mi ha detto di **non** andarci;

Fr. Elle m'a dit de **ne pas** y aller.

- *She told me **not** to go there.*

Negation with Adjectives and the Adverb V*ery*

The negative words It. **non**, Fr. **pas** can also be used to negate adjectives or the adverb It. **molto**, Fr. **très** - *very*. For example:

> *Did you know?*
>
> The world's two first printed newspapers were both published in 1605. One was printed in Strasbourg, the other (the Nieuwe Tijdingen) was printed by Abraham Verhoeven in Antwerp.

It. un film **non interessante**;

Fr. un film **pas intéressant**.

- *An uninteresting film.*

It. una casa **non molto** grande;

Fr. une maison **pas très** grande.

- *A **not very** big house.*

Formation of Negation in Compound Tenses

Compound tenses in Italian negative sentences are formed by placing the negative word (It. **non**) before the auxiliary verb, while in French **ne** is put before and **pas** after the auxiliary verb.

In Romance languages auxiliary verbs are It. **avere**; Fr. **avoir** - *to have*. The auxiliary verb: It. **essere**; Fr. **être** - *to be* is also used in Italian and French with reflexive and intransitive verbs (**See Formation of the Present Perfect with the Verb *to be* in Italian and French p.257**)

For instance:

Affirmative:	**Negative:**
It. Ha finito;	It. **Non** ha finito;
Fr. Il a fini	Fr. Il **n'**a **pas** fini
- *He has finished.*	- *He hasn't finished.*

Other Negative Expressions

There are many other negative expressions, which are used in the Romance languages. Below is a table demonstrating the most common negative combinations and expressions, which consist of the negative word It. **non**, Fr. **ne** + **an adjective, pronoun** or **adverb**.

Italian	French	English
non...nessuno	ne...personne	*no one, nobody*
non...niente; non...nulla	ne...rien	*nothing*
non...né... né	ne...ni...ni	*neither...nor*
non...mai	ne...jamais	*never*
non...più	ne...plus	*no longer*
non...nessun (-o,-a,-i,-e)	ne...aucun (-e)	*not any, none*
non...affatto; non...punto; non...mica	ne...pas du tout; ne...point	*not at all, absolutely not*
non...neanche; non...nemmeno; non...neppure	ne...même pas	*not even*
non...che	ne...que	*only*

It should be remembered that the negative words It. **non**, Fr. **ne** always preceded the main verb in simple tenses or the auxiliary verb in compound tenses, while the placement of adjectives, pronouns or adverbs in the sentence can vary.

Therefore, it is important to consider all the expressions in order to demonstrate their positions in which they can be used in the sentence.

CHAPTER 6: VERBS

No one, Nobody
It. non...nessuno; Fr. ne...personne

1. If the pronouns *no one, nobody* (It. **nessuno**, Fr. **personne**) precede the verb, the negative wordsIt. **non** is omitted in Italian.

   NOTE:

   *In French **ne** is not omitted and the negative word **personne** is placed before it. Study the following:*

   It. **Nessuno** mi guarda;

   Fr. **Personne ne** me regarde.

   - *No one* looks at me.

   It. **Nessuno** è venuto;

   Fr. **Personne n**'est venu.

   - *No one* came.

2. If they are are used with the negative words It. **non**, Fr. **ne**, the pronouns *no one, nobody* (It. **nessuno**, Fr. **personne**) follow the main verb in simple tenses and the past participle in compound tenses in Italian and French. To illustrate:

   It. **Non** vedo **nessuno**;

   Fr. Je **ne** vois **personne**.

   - *I see no one*.

   It. **Non** ha visto **nessuno**;

   Fr. Il **n**'a vu **personne**.

   - *He has seen no one*.

CHAPTER 6: VERBS

It should be remembered that It. *nessuno*, Fr. *personne* are always placed after the verb when they function as the object. When they are the subject, they are put before the verb.

3. If an infinitive is used in the sentence, the negative words It. *non*, Fr. *ne* precede the main verb or the auxiliary verb and It. *nessuno*, Fr. *personne* follow the infinitive. For instance:

It. *Non* voglio vedere *nessuno*;

Fr. Je *ne* veux voir *personne*.

- *I want to see no one.*

Nothing
It. non...niente, non...nulla; Fr. ne...rien

Like *no one* and *nobody*, *nothing* has similar rules of placement in the sentence in the Romance languages.

1. If *nothing* (It. *niente* (*nulla*), Fr. *rien*) precedes the verb, the negative word It. *non* is dropped in Italian, whereas in French ne is not omitted and the pronoun rien is placed before it. Observe the following:

It. *Niente* mi piace;

Fr. *Rien ne* me plait.

- *I like nothing (Nothing pleases me).*

2. When they are used with the negative words It. *non*, Fr. *ne*, the pronouns nothing It. *niente* (*nulla*), Fr. *rien*) follow the main verb in simple tenses. In compound tenses they follow the past participle in Italian.

NOTE:

In French **rien** precedes the past participle in compound tenses.

It. ***Non*** vedo ***niente***;

Fr. Je ***ne*** vois ***rien***.

- *I see **nothing**.*

It. ***Non*** ho visto ***niente***;

Fr. Je ***n'***ai ***rien*** vu.

- *I have seen **nothing**.*

3. When there is an infinitive in the sentence, It. ***non***, Fr. ***ne*** precede the main verb or the auxiliary verb and Italian ***niente*** (***nulla***) follow the infinitive; in French ***rien*** is placed before the infinitive. For example:

It. ***Non*** voglio mangiare ***nulla***;

Fr. Je ***ne*** veux ***rien*** manger.

- *I want to eat **nothing**.*

Neither...nor
*It. **non...né...né**; Fr. **ne...ni...ni***

These negative words are usually placed after the main verb in simple tenses or after the past participle in compound tenses in the Romance languages. It should be mentioned that the negative words It. ***non***; Fr. ***ne*** always precede the main verb in simple tenses or the auxiliary verb in compound tenses. For instance:

It. ***Non*** parlano ***né*** spagnolo ***né*** portoghese;

Fr. Ils ***ne*** parlent ***ni*** espagnol, ***ni*** portugais.

- *They speak **neither** Spanish **nor** Portuguese.*

CHAPTER 6: VERBS

It. **Non** ho viaggiato **né** in Spagna **né** in Brasile;

Fr. Je **n'**ai voyagé **ni** en Espagne **ni** au Brésil.

- *I have travelled **neither** to Spain **nor** to Brazil.*

It worth noting that It. **né**; Fr. **ni** can be used in the sentence more than twice. Observe the following:

It. **Non** vuole **né** mangiare, **né** bere, **né** dormire;

Fr. Elle **ne** veut **ni** manger, **ni** boire, **ni** dormir.

- *She wants **neither** to eat, **nor** to drink, **nor** to sleep.*

Never
It. non...mai; Fr. ne...jamais

1. Unlike in French, in Italian the adverbs It. **mai** - *never* can be used before the main verb. In this case, the negative words It. **non** should be dropped.

   NOTE:
   *In French **jamais** must be used with **ne** where **ne** precedes the verb and **jamais** follows it.*

   It. It. **Mai** mi viene a trovare;

   Fr. Il **ne** me rend **jamais** visite.

   - *He **never** visits me.*

2. The adverbs It. **mai**; Fr. **jamais** - *never* are also used in combination with the negative words It. **non**; Fr. **ne**. In this case, *never* follows the main verb in simple tenses in all the Romance languages. In compound tenses it follows the past participle in Italian. However in Italian *never* can also be placed before the past participle.

NOTE:

In French **never** must precede the past participle in compound tenses.

It. **Non** mi viene **mai** a trovare;

Fr. Il **ne** me rend **jamais** visite.

- He **never** visits me.

It. **Non** ho **mai** viaggiato (or **Non** ho viaggiato **mai**);

Fr. Je **n'**ai **jamais** voyagé.

- I have **never** travelled.

NOTE:

In French **de** is used instead of the partitive article after **ne...jamais**. Example:

Fr. Je **ne** mange **jamais de** champignons

- I never eat mushrooms.

No longer, Anymore
It. non... più; Fr. ne...plus

The adverbs It. **più**; Fr. **plus** - *no longer, anymore* can only be used in combination with the negative words It. **non**; Fr. **ne**. Therefore, *no longer, anymore* follows the main verb in simple tenses in all the Romance languages. In compound tenses it follows the past participle in Italian. In Italian, however, *no longer, anymore* can also be placed before the past participle.

NOTE:

In French **no longer, anymore** Fr. **plus** must precede the past participle in compound tenses.

It. **Non** lavora **più** in ospedale;

Fr. Il **ne** travaille **<u>plus</u>** à l'hôpital.

- He doesn't work at the hospital **anymore**.

It. **Non** l'ho visto **più**;

Fr. Je **ne** l'ai **<u>plus</u>** vu.

- I haven't seen him **anymore**.

When there is an infinitive in the sentence, *no longer, anymore* is placed before the infinitive in Italian and French. For example:

It. **Non** voglio **più** mangiare;

Fr. Je **ne** veux **<u>plus</u>** manger.

- I don't want to eat **anymore**.

Not any, None
It. non...nessun; Fr. ne...aucun

It. **nessun**; Fr. **aucun** - *not any*, *none* are used as adjectives and must agree in gender and number with the noun. When used with the negative words It. **non**; Fr. **ne**, these adjectives always follow the main verb in simple tenses and the past participle in compound tenses in in all the Romance languages. For example:

It. **Non** vedo **nessun** uomo;

Fr. Je **ne** vois **aucun** homme.

- I don't see **any** man.

It. **Non** ho visto **nessuna** donna;

Fr. Je **n'**ai vu **aucune** femme.

*- I didn't see **any** woman.*

Not at all, Absolutely not
It. non...affatto, non...punto/mica; Fr. ne... pas du tout, ne...point

The negative expression *not at all* is quite different in Italian and French, so it needs to be considered separately in each Romance language.

Italian

Affatto, if used with ***non***, can be put either between the auxiliary verb and the past participle or after the past participle, while ***punto*** and ***mica*** always come before the past participle in compound tenses. Study the following:

It. Non è venuto ***affatto*** (***Non*** è ***punto/mica*** venuto).

*- He didn't come **at all**.*

French

Pas du tout, ***point***, if used with ***non***, should be placed after the main verb in simple tenses and after the auxiliary verb in compound tenses. For example:

Fr. Il ***n'***est pas ***du tout*** venu (Il ***n'***est ***point*** venu).

*- He didn't come **at all**.*

Not even
It. non...neanche, non...nemmeno, non... neppure; Fr. ne...même pas

It. **neanche**, **nemmeno**, **neppure** and Fr. **même pas** are usually placed after the main verb in simple tenses and after the auxiliary verb in compound tenses. However, in Italian they can be put either between the auxiliary verb and the past participle or after the past participle. For example:

It. It. **Non** mi ha **neanche** salutato (**Non** mi ha salutato **neanche/ nemmeno/ neppure**);

Fr. Elle **ne** m'a **même pas** salué.

- She **didn't even** greet me.

Only
It. non...che; Fr. ne...que

It. **che**; Fr. **que**, if used with **no/non/ne**, should be placed after the main verb in simple tenses and follow the past participle in compound tenses. For example:

Did you know?

Bologna, the capital of Emilia-Romagna region in Northern Italy, is popular for The Two Towers (Le due torri), that stand next to each other. The tower of Asinelli and the tower of Garisenda. The names derive from families who built them between 1109 and 1119. The construction was a competition between the two families to demonstrate which was the wealthier family.

It. **Non** ho **che** una sorella;

Fr. Je **n**'ai **qu'**une soeur.

- I have **only** one sister.

It. **Non** ha letto **che** un libro;

Fr. Elle **n'**a lu **qu'**un livre.

- She has read **only** one book.

The Imperfect Tense

Formation of the Imperfect

The imperfect tense (It. *l'imperfetto* Fr. *l'imparfait*) is formed by dropping the infinitive ending and adding the appropriate personal ending to the root of a verb.

> **NOTE:**
> In French the Imperfect tense is formed by dropping the ending **-ons** of the 1st person plural of the present tense and adding the appropriate endings.

Below is a table demonstrating the endings of the imperfect tense:

Italian	French
1st conj.: -ARE: -avo, -avi, -ava, -avamo, -avate, -avano;	
2nd conj.: -ERE: -evo, -evi, -eva, -evamo, -evate, -evano	**all the conj.:** -ais, -ais, -ait, -ions, -iez, -aient;
3 conj.: -IRE: -ivo, -ivi, -iva, -ivamo, -ivate, -ivano;	

Below is the table showing the example of conjugation of regular verbs in the imperfect tense:

Italian	French
1 conjugation	
It.: parl**are**	Fr.: parl**er**

CHAPTER 6: VERBS

Italian	French
io parl**avo** *tu* parl**avi** *lui\lei\Lei* parl**ava** *noi* parl**avamo** *voi* parl**avate** *loro\Loro* parl**avano**	*je* parl**ais** *tu* parl**ais** *il\elle\on* parl**ait** *nous* parl**ions** *vous* parl**iez** *ils\elles* parl**aient**
	2 conjugation
vend**ere**	vend**re**
vend**evo** vend**evi** vend**eva** vend**evamo** vend**evate** vend**evano**	vend**ais** vend**ais** vend**ait** vend**ions** vend**iez** vend**aient**
	3 conjugation
part**ire**	part**ir**
part**ivo** part**ivi** part**iva** part**ivamo** part**ivate** part**ivano**	part**ais** part**ais** part**ait** part**ions** part**iez** part**aient**

NOTE:

In French verbs ending in **-cer** and **-ger**, the spelling changes before **a** take place, which is in order to preserve the initial sound. For example:

Commencer (to begin): *je commençais - tu commençais - il/elle/on commençait - nous* *commencions - vous commenciez - ils/elles commençaient.*

Manger *(to eat): je mang**e**ais - tu mang**e**ais - il/elle/on mang**e**ait - nous mangions - vous mangiez - ils/elles mang**e**aient.*

Irregular Verbs in the Imperfect

The most common irregular verb of the imperfect tense in the Romance languages is the verb *to be*:

It. **Essere**: io **ero**; tu **eri**; lui\lei\Lei **era**; noi **eravamo**, voi **eravate**, loro\Loro **erano**.

Fr. **Être**: j'**étais**, tu **étais**, il\elle\on **était**, nous **étions**, vous **étiez**, ils\elles **étaient**.

- **To be**: *I **was**; you **were**; he, she, it **was**; we **were**; you **were**; they **were**.*

Use of the Imperfect

Generally speaking the imperfect tense in the Romance languages is used to talk about what someone was doing or used to do. Therefore, the imperfect tense in Italian and French is used to express:

‣ **Actions repeated habitually or regularly**

You use it when you talk about activities that you did repeatedly for a long period of undetermined time. The beginning and the end of the action is not specified. For example:

It. **Mangiavamo** in questo ristorante tutti i giorni;

Fr. Nous **mangions** dans ce restaurant tous les jours.

- *We **used to eat** at this restaurant every day.*

‣ **Two simultaneous actions**

Use it to talk about actions that were taking place at the same time in the past:

>It. Mentre lei ***dormiva***, lui ***leggeva*** il giornale;
>
>Fr. Pendant qu'elle ***dormait***, il ***lisait*** le journal.
>
>- *While she **was sleeping**, he **was reading** the newspaper.*

‣ Background actions that set stage for other actions

The background action is expressed in the imperfect, while the action that interrupts the background action is used in the preterite:

>It. ***Dormivi*** quando sono venuto;
>
>Fr. Tu ***dormais*** quand je suis arrivé.
>
>- *You **were sleeping** when I arrived.*

NOTE:
In Italian the background action can also be expressed by the imperfect progressive (**See The Continuous Tenses p.298**). Study the following:

>It. ***Stavi dormendo*** quando sono venuto.
>- *You **were sleeping** when I arrived.*

‣ Time and dates in the past

>It. ***Erano*** le due del pomeriggio;
>
>Fr. Il ***était*** deux heures de l'après-midi.
>
>- *It **was** two o'clock in the afternoon.*

CHAPTER 6: VERBS

It. ***Era*** lunedì;

Fr. C'***était*** lundi.

It ***was*** Monday.

- **Descriptions in the past**

The imperfect tense is used to describe a scene, circumstances or person in the past:

> *Did you know?*
>
> *Toulouse, the capital of France's southern Occitanie region, is known as La Ville Rose (The Pink City) owing to the pale coloured terra-cotta bricks used in most of its buildings.*

It. ***Faceva*** freddo quella note;

Fr. Il ***faisait*** froid cette nuit.

- *It **was** cold that night.*

It. Egli ***aveva*** quarant'anni;

Fr. Il ***avait*** quarante ans.

- *He **was** forty years old.*

It. ***Era*** alta e bella;

Fr. Elle ***était*** grande et belle.

- *She **was** tall and beautiful.*

- **Verbs denoting mental and emotional states, desires or conditions**

As most mental processes include duration, verbs of mental states or conditions are usually expressed in the imperfect when used in the past. The following is a list of the most common verbs describing mental states:

CHAPTER 6: VERBS

Italian	French	English
amare	**aimer**	*to love*
essere	**être**	*to be*
avere	**avoir**	*to have*
credere	**croire**	*to believe*
desiderare	**désirer**	*to desire*
sperare	**espérer**	*to hope*
pensare	**penser**	*to think*
potere	**pouvoir**	*to be able*
preferire	**préférer**	*to prefer*
sapere	**savoir**	*to know*
volere	**vouloir**	*to want*
riflettere	**refléter**	*to reflect*

Did you know?

The Vatican stamps its own coins. The €1 coin which has a portrait of the present Pope is in high demand with collectors.

It. **Volevo** andare in Francia;

Fr. Je **voulais** aller en France.

- *I wanted to go to France.*

It. Non **sapeva** la risposta;

Fr. Il ne **savait** pas la réponse.

- *He didn't know the answer.*

It. *da*; Fr. *depuis* + The Imperfect Tense

We have already studied the use of It. *da*; Fr. *depuis* (*for/since*) with the present indicative (**See Special Use of the Present Tense and Prepositions p.182**). In the Romance languages the prepositions It. *da*; Fr. *depuis* can also be used with the imperfect tense meaning *had been*. For instance:

It. ***Aspettavo da*** due ore;

Fr. J'***attendais depuis*** deux heures.

- *I **had been waiting** for two hours.*

The following are the most common adverbial expressions that are usually used with the imperfect tense:

Italian	French	English
sempre	toujours	*always*
a volte	parfois	*at times*
come sempre	comme toujours	*as always*
come d'uso, usual-mente	d'habitude, habituellement	*usually*
certe volte	quelquefois	*sometimes*
con frequenza, frequente-mente	fréquem-ment	*frequently*
spesso	souvent	*often*
continua-mente	continuellement	*continuously*
di quando in quando, di tanto in tanto	de temps en temps	*from time to time*
ininterrottamente	sans interrup-tion	*without interruption*
ripetuta-mente	à plusieurs reprises	*repeatedly*

Italian	French	English
senza sosta	sans cesse	*without stopping*
ogni giorno, tutti i giorni	chaque jour, tous les jours	*every day*
quotidianamente	quotidiennement	*daily*
la domenica	le dimanche	*on Sundays*
in quel momento	en ce moment	*at that moment*

Difference between the Preterite and the Imperfect in the Romance Languages

Generally speaking, the imperfect tense is used to express a continuing and habitual action in the past, whereas the preterite describes an action that began and finished in the past independently of its continuance. For instance:

The Preterite	The Imperfect
It. **Ho giocato** a tennis **ieri**;	It. **Giocavo** a tennis **di quando in quando**;
Fr. J'**ai joué** au tennis **hier**.	Fr. Je **jouais** au tennis **de temps en temps**.
- I **played** tennis **yesterday**.	- I **used to play** tennis *from time to time*.

Compound Tenses in The Past

Overview

The compound tenses in the Romance languages are formed in the same way by using the auxiliary verb (It. **avere** or **essere**, Fr. **avoir** or **être**) in the appropriate tense and the past participle.

CHAPTER 6: VERBS

The Pluperfect Tense

Formation of the Pluperfect

In Italian and French the pluperfect tense is formed by using the imperfect tense of the verb It. **avere** or **essere**, Fr. **avoir** or **être** with the past participle.

The formation of the pluperfect of the Romance languages is presented in the drawing below:

Pluperfect Formula

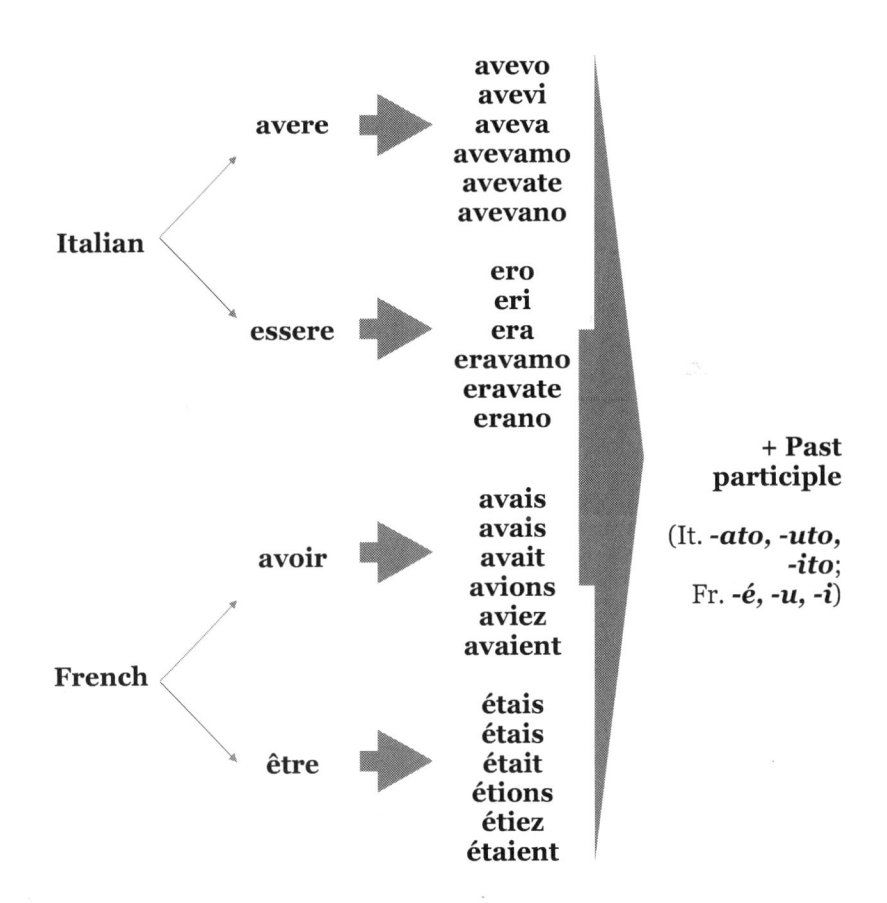

Italian
- avere → avevo, avevi, aveva, avevamo, avevate, avevano
- essere → ero, eri, era, eravamo, eravate, erano

French
- avoir → avais, avais, avait, avions, aviez, avaient
- être → étais, étais, était, étions, étiez, étaient

+ Past participle

(It. *-ato, -uto, -ito*;
Fr. *-é, -u, -i*)

CHAPTER 6: VERBS

> ***NOTE:***
>
> *Like in the Present Perfect, in the Pluperfect as well as other compound tenses the auxiliary verbs It. **essere**; Fr. **être** (to be) are also used with reflexive and intransitive verbs in Italian and French. Also, the past participle that is used with the auxiliary verb to be (It. **essere**, Fr. **être**) always agrees in gender and number with the subject. This means that the endings change in the feminine and plural forms the way they change in adjectives: in French **-e** is added to agree with the feminine and **-s-** is added for the plural, in Italian to agree with the feminine **-a** is used and **-i**, **-e** with the masculine and feminine plurals respectively.*

Below is the table showing the example of conjugation of verbs in the pluperfect tense:

Italian	French
Avere	*Avoir*
io **avevo parlato**	j`avais parlé
tu **avevi parlato**	tu **avais parlé**
lui/lei/Lei **aveva parlato**	il/elle **avait parlé**
noi **avevamo parlato**	nous **avions parlé**
voi **avevate parlato**	vous **aviez parlé**
loro/Loro **avevano parlato**	ils/elles **avaient parlé**
Essere	*Être*
io **ero partito**(-a)	j'étais **parti**(-e)
tu **eri partito**(-a)	tu **étais parti**(-e)
lui/lei/Lei **era partito**(-a)	il/elle **était parti**(-e)
noi **eravamo partiti**(-e)	nous **étions parti**(-e)s
voi **eravate partiti**(-e)	vous **étiez parti**(-e)s
loro/Loro **erano partiti**(-e)	ils/elles **étaient parti**(-e)s

CHAPTER 6: VERBS

> *Did you know?*
>
> Verona, an Italian city of 270 thousand inhabitants, is the city where 3 of William Shakespeare's plays are set: Romeo and Juliet, The Two Gentlemen of Verona and The Taming of the Shrew. Verona is considered one of the most beautiful cities in the world due to its architecture.

For example:

It. **Avevamo parlato** e poi è andata via;

Fr. Nous **avions parlé** et puis elle est partie.

- We **had spoken** and then she left.

It. **Era** già **partita** quando sono arrivato;

Fr. Elle **était** déjà **partie** quand je suis arrivé.

- She **had** already **left** when I arrived.

Use of the Pluperfect Tense

The pluperfect tense is used the same in the Romance languages as in English to express:

- **Past action completed prior to another action in the past**. Study the following:

It. Non sapevo se mi **aveva visto**;

Fr. Je ne savais pas si elle m'**avait vu**.

- I didn't know if she **had seen** me.

Peculiarities of Use of the Pluperfect in the Romance Languages

In Italian and French this tense is used in spoken language.

The Past Perfect (Anterior) Tense

Formation of The Past Perfect (Anterior)

In the Romance languages the past perfect (anterior) tense is formed by using the preterite of the verb It. ***avere*** or ***essere***, Fr. ***avoir*** or ***être*** with the past participle.

> **NOTE:**
> It should be remembered that in Italian and French the past perfect (anterior) tense is used mostly in literary contexts.

Below is the drawing demonstrating the formation of the past perfect (anterior) in Italian and French:

Past Perfect (Anterior) Formula

Italian

avere → ebbi, avesti, ebbe, avemmo, aveste, ebbero

essere → fui, fosti, fu, fummo, foste, furono

French

avoir → eus, eus, eut, eûmes, eûtes, eurent

être → fus, fus, fut, fûmes, fûtes, furent

+ Past participle

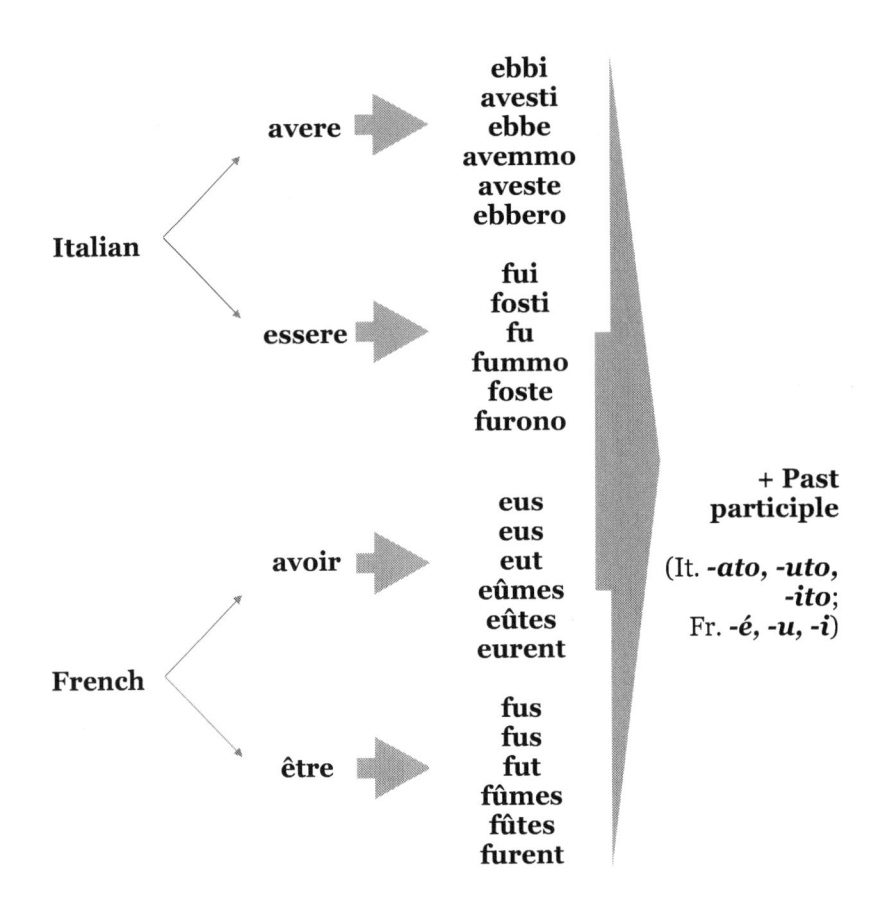

(It. *-ato, -uto, -ito*; Fr. *-é, -u, -i*)

CHAPTER 6: VERBS

Below is the table showing the example of conjugation of verbs in the past perfect (anterior) tense:

Italian	French
Avere	*Avoir*
io **ebbi parlato**	j'**eus parlé**
tu **avesti parlato**	tu **eus parlé**
lui/lei/Lei **ebbe parlato**	il/elle **eut parlé**
noi **avemmo parlato**	nous **eûmes parlé**
voi **aveste parlato**	vous **eûtes parlé**
loro/Loro **ebbero parlato**	ils/elles **eurent parlé**
Essere	*Être*
io **fui partito(-a)**	je **fus parti(-e)**
tu **fosti partito(-a)**	tu **fus parti(-e)**
lui/lei/Lei **fu partito(-a)**	il/elle **fut parti(-e)**
noi **fummo partiti(-e)**	nous **fûmes parti(-e)s**
voi **foste partiti(-e)**	vous **fûtes parti(-e)s**
loro/Loro **furono partiti(-e)**	ils/elles **furent parti (-e)s**

Did you know?

The Central African Republic is a landlocked nation situated in Central Africa. The CAR's 2 official languages are French and Sango. The country has 5 national parks and 33 protected areas. They are home to around 3,500 species of plants, 660 birds, 130 mammals, 185 reptiles and 25 amphibians.

For example:

It. Dopo che **ebbe finito** il lavoro, è partito;

Fr. Après qu'il **eut terminé** le travail, il est parti.

- When he **had finished** the work, he left.

It. Quando *fu partita*, sono arrivato;

Fr. Quand elle *fut partie*, je suis arrivé.

- *When she* **had left**, *I arrived.*

Use of the Past Perfect (Anterior) Tense

Like the pluperfect tense, the past perfect (anterior) is also used to express a past action that *had* occurred before another action in the past. This tense is generally used in subordinate clauses after temporal conjunctions, which indicate a past action instantly preceding another. In such sentences the main verb is in the preterite.

The following are the most common temporal conjunctions that are usually used in the past perfect (anterior) tense:

Italian	French	English
dopo che (dopoché)	**après que**	*after*
quando	**quand (lorsque)**	*when*
come, appena	**dès que (aussitôt que), à peine**	*as soon as, scarcely (hardly)*

It. **Appena fui tornato** a casa, mi ha chiamato;

Fr. **Dès que** je **fus rentré** à la maison, elle m'a appelé.

- *As soon as I* **had returned** *home, she called me.*

NOTE:

In French the subject and verb are inverted after ***à peine***.

Fr. **À peine fus-je rentré** à la maison, qu'elle m'a appelé.

- *I had hardly returned home when she called me.*

However, in modern spoken language the past perfect (anterior) is usually replaced by the preterite in the Romance languages:

It. **Appena sono tornato** a casa, mi ha chiamato;

Fr. **Dès que** je **suis rentré** à la maison, elle m'a appelé.

- *As soon as I returned home*, she called me.

The Future Tense

Regular Formation of the Future

The future tense of most verbs is formed by adding the appropriate endings to the infinitive in all the conjunctions.

Below is the table demonstrating the endings of the future tense in Italian and French:

	Italian	French
1st, 2nd and 3rd person singular	-ò, -ai, -à,	-ai, -as, -a,
1st, 2nd and 3rd person plural	-emo, -ete, -anno;	-ons, -ez, -ont;

> **NOTE:**
>
> The final **-e** of the 2nd conjunction (**-re** verbs) in French, as well as the final **-e** of all the conjunctions in Italian is dropped before adding the future endings (e.g. It. parti**re** (to leave) io partirò - I will leave; Fr. **attendre** (to wait) j'attendrai - I will wait).
>
> Also, Italian future tense of the 1st conjunction (**-are** verbs) is formed by changing the infinitive ending **-are** into **-er** (we changed the initial **-a-** to **-e-** and dropped the final **-e-**) before adding the appropriate future endings

(e.g. It. aspettare (to wait) io aspetterò - I will wait).

The following is the table showing the example of conjugation of regular verbs in the future tense:

Italian	French
parlare	**parler**
io parlerò tu parlerai lui\lei\Lei parlerà noi parleremo voi parlerete loro\Loro parleranno	je parlerai tu parleras il\elle\on parlera nous parlerons vous parlerez ils\elles parleront

NOTE:

In French the 2nd and 3rd person singular forms sound alike (e.g. tu parler**as**; il\elle parler**a**); the 1st person singular and the 2nd person plural sound alike (e.g. je parler**ai**; vous parler**ez**), and then the 1st and 3rd person plurals also sound alike (e.g. nous parler**ons**; ils\elles parler**ont**). However, these forms are all spelled differently.

Irregular Verbs in The Future

The following is a table presenting irregular verbs in the future tense, which are common for all or several Romance languages:

Italian	French
essere (sarò, sarai, sarà, saremo, sarete, saranno)	**être** (serai, seras, sera, serons, serez, seront)
stare (starò, starai, starà, staremo, starete, staranno)	—

CHAPTER 6: VERBS

Italian	French
avere (avrò, avrai, avrà, avremo, avrete, avranno)	**avoir** (aurai, auras, aura, aurons, aurez, auront)
tenere (terrò, terrai, terrà, terremo, terrete, terrano)	**tenir** (tiendrai, tiendras, tiendra, tiendrons, tiendrez, tiendront)
fare (farò, farai, farà, faremo, farete, faranno)	**faire** (ferai, feras, fera, ferons, ferez, feront)
venire (verrò, verrai, verrà, verremo, verrete, verrano)	**venir** (viendrai, viendras, viendra, viendrons, viendrez, viendront)
sapere (saprò, saprai, saprà, sapremo, saprete, sapranno)	**savoir** (saurai, sauras, saura, saurons, saurez, sauront)
vedere (vedrò, vedrai, vedrà, vedremo, vedrete, vedranno)	**voir** (verrai, verras, verra, verrons, verrez, verront)
morire (morrò, morrai, morrà, morremo, morrete, morranno)	**mourir** (mourrai, mourras, mourra, mourrons, mourrez, mourront)
dare (darò, darai, darà, daremo, darete, daranno)	**donner** (regular)
dire (regular)	**dire** (regular)
volere (vorrò, vorrai, vorrà, vorremo, vorrete, vorranno)	**vouloir** (voudrai, voudras, voudra, voudrons, voudrez, voudront)
dovere (dovrò, dovrai, dovrà, dovremo, dovrete, dovranno)	**devoir** (devrai, devras, devra, devrons, devrez, devront)
potere (potrò, potrai, potrà, potremo, potrete, potranno)	**pouvoir** (pourrai, pourras, pourra, pourrons, pourrez, pourront)

Italian	French
andare (andrò, andrai, andrà, andremo, andrete, andranno)	**aller** (irai, iras, ira, irons, irez, iront)

As it is seen from the table, Italian and French have almost the same set of regular and irregular verbs.

Irregularities in Formation of the Future in French

Did you know?

Italians are allowed to donate 8% of their yearly taxes to the Vatican (this is instead of paying it to the Italian Government).

However, despite the majority of similar irregular verbs with Italian, French has its own number of irregular verbs with specific models of conjugation. Some verbs, in order to form the future tense, use the 3rd person singular of the present tense rather than the infinitive.

Below are the most common verbs that use the 3rd person singular form while forming the future tense in French:

Infinitive	the 3rd form singular	Future
acheter (*to buy*)	**achète**	*j'achèterai*
appeler (*to call*)	**appelle**	*j'appellerai*
employer (*to employ*)	**emploie**	*j'emploierai*
ennuyer (*to be bored*)	**ennuie**	*j'ennuierai*
essayer (*to try*)	**essaie**	*j'essaierai*
essuyer (*to dry*)	**essuie**	*j'essuierai*
jeter (*to throw*)	**jette**	*je jetterai*
lever (*to lift*)	**lève**	*je lèverai*
mener (*to lead*)	**mène**	*je mènerai*

nettoyer (*to clean*)	**nettoie**	*je nettoierai*
payer (*to pay*)	**paie**	*je paierai*
peser (*to weigh*)	**pèse**	*je pèserai*

Use of The Future Tense

Like in English, the future tense in Italian and French is used:

➤ **to express an action that will occur in the future:**

It. Lo **visiterò** domani;

Fr. Je le **visiterai** demain.

*- I **will visit** him tomorrow.*

Also, the present tense can be used to express an action or intention that will occur in the future:

Did you know?

The first Belgian car was built in 1894, it was called the Vincke. The brand Vincke stopped existing in 1904.

It. **vado** a Parigi domani;

Fr. je **vais** à Paris demain.

*- I **am going** to Paris tomorrow.*

➤ **to express probability and assumption:**

In conversational Italian and French the future can be used to express probability. In questions it is used to express surprise. As it is used in conversation, it is necessary to convey the meaning with intonation and use it in context. In Italian and French the verbs *to be* and *to have* (It. **essere**, **avere**; Fr. **être**, **avoir**) are generally used in order to express probability in the future.

It. Dove **sarà** tuo fratello? - **Sarà** a casa;

Fr. Où **sera** ton frère? - Il **sera** à la maison.

- Where **will** your brother **be**? - He **will be** at home.

The Informal Future

In the Romance languages the informal future is used primarily in colloquial language in order to express future actions. In French it is formed by the verb *to go* of the present tense which is placed right before the infinitive. This expression is the equivalent of the English *to be going to*.

The formula of the informal future of French is the following:

> Fr. **aller** + **Infinitive**

In Italian this expression is formed by using the verb **stare** (*to be*) and the preposition **per**, which are put before an infinitive:

> It. **stare per** + **Infinitive**

It. **Sta per leggere** un libro,

Fr. Il **va lire** un livre

- He **is going to** read a book.

Special Use of the Future

In Romance languages the future tense can also be used after certain conjunctions when the verb of the main clause is in the future tense, as well as in the dependent clause. It should be noted that, unlike in the Romance languages, in English the verb of the main clause is used in the present tense.

The following are the most common conjunctions used with the future tense:

Italian	French	English
quando	quand, lorsque, au moment où	when
come, appena	dès que, aussitôt que	as soon as
mentre (ché), intanto che	pendant que, tandis que	while

It. ***Quando sta per arrivare***, sto per vederla (***Quando arriverà***, la vedrò);

Fr. ***Quand elle va arriver***, je vais la voir (***Quand elle arrivera***, je la verrai).

- **When she arrives**, I will see her.

Did you know?

The Italian language has a co-official status in Slovenia. About 4000 Slovenian people speak Italian as their mother tongue. Around 15% Slovenians speak Italian as a second language.

It. Stiamo per parlare ***appena sto per venire*** (Parleremo ***appena verrò***).

Fr. On va parler ***dès que je vais arriver*** (Nous parlerons ***dès que j'arriverai***).

- We will talk **as soon as I come**.

The Future Perfect Tense

Formation of the Future Perfect

Like other compound tenses, The future perfect in the Romance languages is formed similarly by using the auxiliary verb (It. ***avere*** or ***essere***, Fr. ***avoir*** or ***être***) in the future tense and the past participle.

CHAPTER 6: VERBS

The future perfect is generally used to express an action that *will have been* completed at a certain moment in the future.

The drawing below shows the ways of forming the future perfect in Italian and French:

Future Perfect Formula

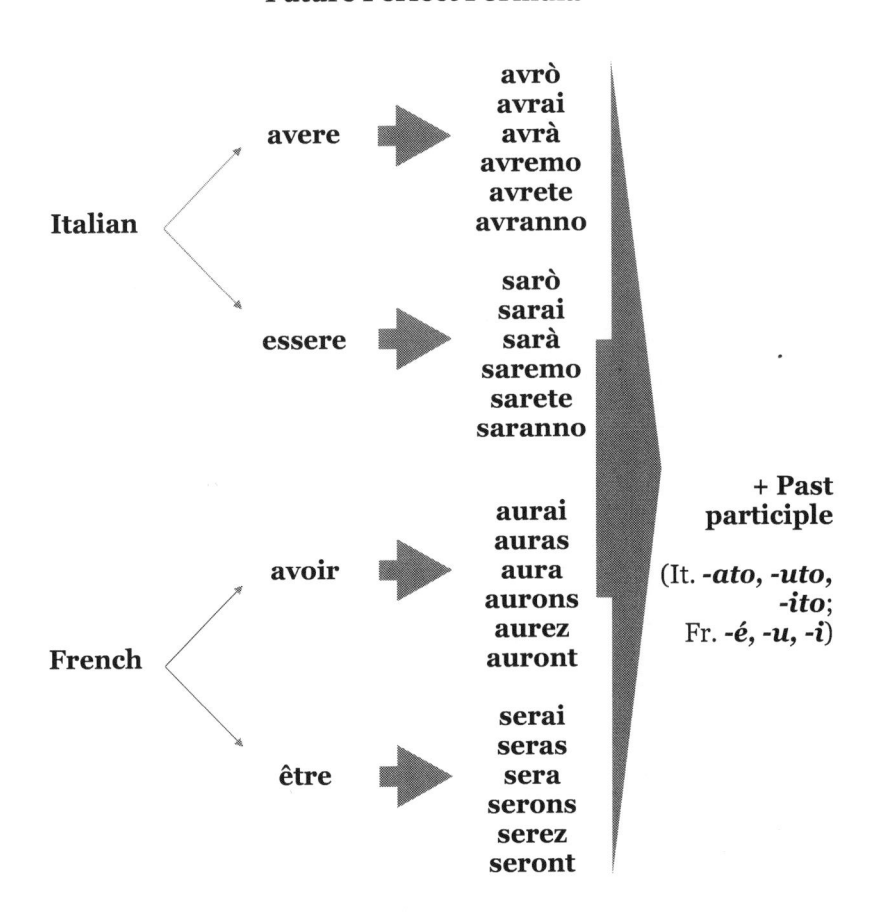

Italian
- avere → avrò, avrai, avrà, avremo, avrete, avranno
- essere → sarò, sarai, sarà, saremo, sarete, saranno

French
- avoir → aurai, auras, aura, aurons, aurez, auront
- être → serai, seras, sera, serons, serez, seront

+ Past participle

(It. *-ato, -uto, -ito*; Fr. *-é, -u, -i*)

Below is the table that demonstrates the example of conjugation of verbs in the future perfect tense:

Italian	French
Avere	*Avoir*
io **avrò parlato**	j`**aurai parlé**

Italian	French
tu **avrai parlato**	tu **auras parlé**
lui/lei/Lei **avrà parlato**	il/elle **aura parlé**
noi **avremo parlato**	nous **aurons parlé**
voi **avrete parlato**	vous **aurez parlé**
loro/Loro **avranno parlato**	ils/elles **auront parlé**
Essere	*Être*
io **sarò partito** (-a)	je **serai parti** (-e)
tu **sarai partito** (-a)	tu **seras parti** (-e)
lui/lei/Lei **sarà partito**(-a)	il/elle **sera parti**(-e)
noi **saremo partiti**(-e)	nous **serons parti**(-e)s
voi **sarete partiti**(-e)	vous **serez parti**(-e)s
loro/Loro **saranno partiti**(-e)	ils/elles **seront parti**(-e)s

Observe the example:

It. Quando lei arriverà, *sarò partito*;

Fr. Quand elle arrivera, je *serai parti*.

- *I will have already left* when she arrives.

Use of the Future Perfect Tense

In Italian and French the future perfect tense is used:

* To express a future action that will have been completed before another action in the future:

It. Domani alle nove, *saranno arrivati* a Buenos Aires;

Fr. Demain à neuf heures, ils **seront arrivés** à Buenos Aires.

- *Tomorrow at nine o'clock, they **will have arrived** in Buenos Aires.*

It. **Avremo terminato** il lavoro per gennaio;

Fr. Nous **aurons fini** le travail pour janvier.

- *We **will have finished** the work by January.*

- Like the future tense, the future perfect is also used to express probability in the Romance languages. However, it is used in this way with all verbs (**See Use of the Future Tense p.240**).

Did you know?

Monaco is a French-speaking micro-state in Western Europe. It is surrounded by France on 3 sides while the other side borders the Mediterranean Sea. The most famous Casino de Monte-Carlo was opened in Monaco 155 years ago, in 1863.

It. lei **avrà lasciato** Madrid;

Fr. Elle **sera partie de** Madrid.

- *She **must have left** Madrid.*

Special Use of the Future Perfect

Like the future tense, the future perfect tense can also be used after certain conjunctions with the future or future perfect in the main clause in Romance languages.

The following are the most common conjunctions that are usually used in the future perfect tense in Italian and French:

Italian	French	English
dopo che (dopoché)	après que	*after*
quando	quand	*when*

Italian	French	English
come, appena	dès que, aussitôt que	as soon as, scarcely

Study the following:

It. ***Dopo che avrà comprato*** un biglietto aereo, volerà in Italia;

(***Dopo che comprerà*** un biglietto aereo, volerà in Italia).

Fr. ***Après qu'il aura acheté*** un billet d'avion, il volera en Italie;

(***Après qu'il achètera*** un billet d'avion, il volera en Italie).

- ***After he has bought*** *a plane ticket, he'll fly to Italy.*

The Conditional Tense

Overview

Like in English, in the Romance languages the conditional tense is generally used to express what *would* happen in the future, which means that it refers to possible and hypothetical situations.

Formation of the Present Conditional

The present conditional is formed by adding the appropriate endings to the future stem of the verb in the Romance languages. It should also be noted that the endings are similar to those of the imperfect tense in French. However, Italian has different endings, which requires more attention while memorizing them.

Below is the table displaying the endings of the present conditional tense in Italian and French:

CHAPTER 6: VERBS

	Italian	French
1st, 2nd and 3rd person singular	-ei, -esti, -ebbe,	-ais, -ais, -ait,
1st, 2nd and 3rd person plural	-emmo, -este, -ebbero;	-ions, -iez, -aient;

The following is the table showing the example of conjugation of regular verbs in the present conditional tense:

Italian	French
parlare	**parler**
io parler**ei** tu parler**esti** lui\lei\Lei parler**ebbe** noi parler**emmo** voi parler**este** loro\Loro parler**ebbero**	je parler**ais** tu parler**ais** il\elle parler**ait** nous parler**ions** vous parler**iez** ils\elles parler**aient**

NOTE:

In Italian verbs that end in *-ciare* and *-giare* drop the i get *-ce* and *-ge* respectively in the present conditional root. Also, verbs ending in *-care* and *-gare* add an h in order to preserve the sound of the **c** and **g**, and therefore get *-che* and *-ghe*.

Irregular Verbs in the Conditional

The very verbs that are irregular in the future are also irregular in the conditional in Italian and French, which definitely makes it easier to learn and memorize them.

The following is a table presenting some irregular verbs in the conditional tense, which are common for all or several Romance languages:

CHAPTER 6: VERBS

Italian	French
essere (sarei, saresti, sarebbe, saremmo, sareste, sarebbero)	**être** (serais, serais, serait, serions, seriez, seraient)
stare (starei, staresti, starebbe, staremmo, stareste, starebbero)	—
avere (avrei, avresti, avrebbe, avremmo, avreste, avrebbero)	**avoir** (aurais, aurais, aurait, aurions, auriez, auraient)
tenere (terrei, terresti, terrebbe, terremmo, terreste, terrebbero)	**tenir** (tiendrais, tiendrais, tiendrait, tiendrions, tiendriez, tiendraient)
fare (farei, faresti, farebbe, faremmo, fareste, farebbero)	**faire** (ferais, ferais, ferait, ferions, feriez, feraient)
venire (verrei, verresti, verrebbe, verremmo, verreste, verrebbero)	**venir** (viendrais, viendrais, viendrait, viendrions, viendriez, viendraient)
sapere (saprei, sapresti, saprebbe, sapremmo, sapreste, saprebbero)	**savoir** (saurais, saurais, saurait, saurions, sauriez, sauraient)
vedere (vedrei, vedresti, vedrebbe, vedremmo, vedreste, vedrebbero)	**voir** (verrais, verrais, verrait, verrions, verriez, verraient)
morire (morrei, morresti, morrebbe, morremmo, morreste, morrebbero)	**mourir** (mourrais, mourrais, mourrait, mourrions, mourriez, mourraient)
dare (darei, daresti, darebbe, daremmo, dareste, darebbero)	**donner** (regular)
dire (regular)	**dire** (regular)

Italian	French
volere (vorrei, vorresti, vorrebbe, vorremmo, vorreste, vorrebbero)	**vouloir** (voudrais, voudrais, voudrait, voudrions, voudriez, voudraient)
dovere (dovrei, dovresti, dovrebbe, dovremmo, dovreste, dovrebbero)	**devoir** (devrais, devrais, devrait, devrions, devriez, devraient)
potere (potrei, potresti, potrebbe, potremmo, potreste, potrebbero)	**pouvoir** (pourrais, pourrais, pourrait, pourrions, pourriez, pourraient)
andare (andrei, andresti, andrebbe, andremmo, andreste, andrebbero)	**aller** (irais, irais, irait, irions, iriez, iraient)

Irregularities in Formation the Conditional in French

French has a number of verbs that have irregular stems in the conditional. Some of them are the same as in the future tense.

Infinitive	Conditional
acheter (to buy)	**j'achèterais**
appeler (to call)	**j'appellerais**
employer (to employ)	**j'emploierais**
envoyer (to send)	**j'enverrais**
falloir (to need)	**il faudrait**
recevoir (to receive)	**je recevrais**
valoir (to value)	**je vaudrais**
apercevoir (to notice)	**j'apercevrais**
décevoir (to disappoint)	**je décevrais**

| courir (to run) | je courrais |

Use of the Conditional Tense

In the Romance languages the conditional is used:

- **To express and describe an action that would happen if it were not for some other circumstances.** It is expressed by *would* in English (**See Conditional Clauses p.254**):

> **Did you know?**
>
> The Italian language is an officially recognized minority language in Croatia. It is spoken by around 7% of the population in Istria County. Native Italian speakers are mainly concentrated along the western coast of the Istrian peninsula.

It. Se avessi tempo, **andrei** a Lisbona;

Fr. Si j'avais le temps, j'**irais** à Lisbonne.

- *If I had time, I **would** go to Lisbon.*

- **To express a polite request, desire or advice:**

It. **Vorrei** andare a Lisbona;

Fr. J'**aimerais** aller à Lisbonne.

- *I **would like** to go to Lisbon.*

It. **Potrei** avere un bicchiere d'acqua?;

Fr. **Pourrais**-je avoir un verre d'eau?

- ***Could** I have a glass of water?*

- **To express a future action in indirect speech** when the main verb is in the past tense. In this case, the present conditional can be equivalent to a simple future in the past in English:

> **Did you know?**
>
> The Republic of the Congo (or simply Congo) is a country in Central Africa with great rainforest reserves. The Nouabalé-Ndoki National Park is known as the world's "Last Eden". This region of swampy forest is home to western lowland gorillas, chimpanzees, bongo and forest elephants. In 2012, Unesco declared the Park a World Heritage Site.

It. lei ha detto che **verrebbe**;

Fr. Elle m'a dit qu'elle **viendrait**.

- She told me that she **would come**.

It should be remembered that if the verb in the main sentence is in the present tense, the future tense is used.

Observe the following:

It. lei dice che **verrà**;

Fr. Elle dit qu'elle **viendra**.

- She says that she **will come**.

The Conditional Perfect Tense

Overview

Like in English, in Italian and French the conditional tense expresses an action in the past that *would have* happened but did not because of another event.

Formation of the Conditional Perfect

The conditional perfect is formed by using the present conditional of the auxiliary verb (It. **avere** or **essere**; Fr. **avoir** or **être**) and the past participle in the Romance languages.

CHAPTER 6: VERBS

The drawing below demonstrates the ways of forming the conditional perfect in Italian and French:

Conditional Perfect Formula

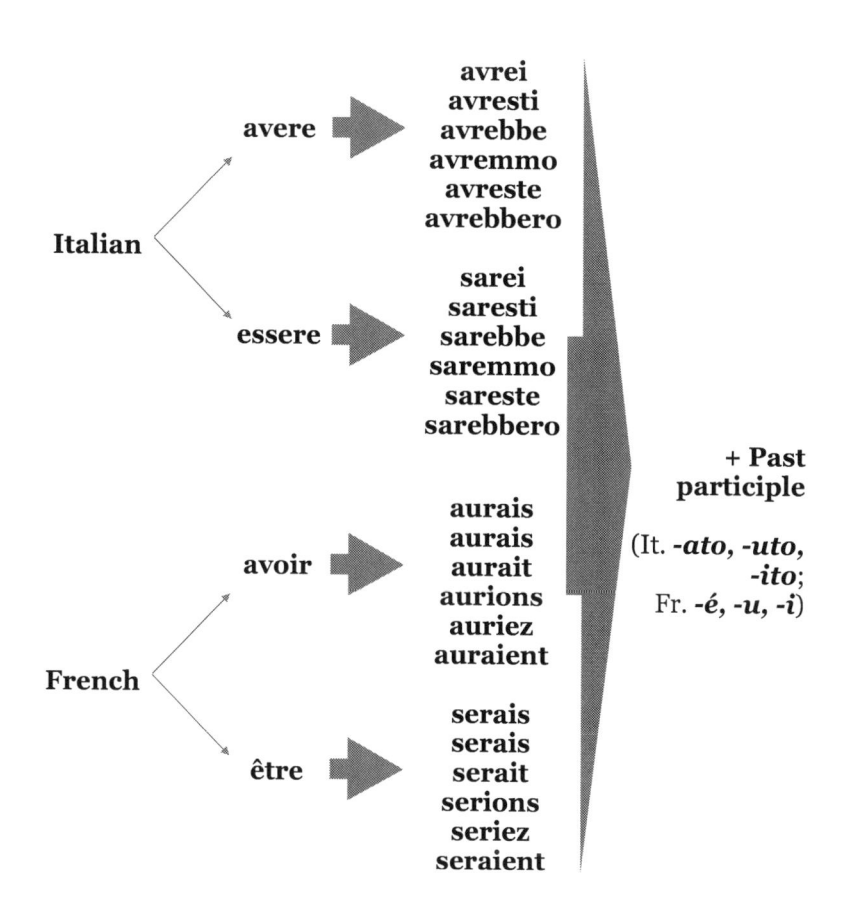

Italian:
- avere → avrei, avresti, avrebbe, avremmo, avreste, avrebbero
- essere → sarei, saresti, sarebbe, saremmo, sareste, sarebbero

French:
- avoir → aurais, aurais, aurait, aurions, auriez, auraient
- être → serais, serais, serait, serions, seriez, seraient

+ Past participle (It. *-ato, -uto, -ito*; Fr. *-é, -u, -i*)

Below is the table demonstrating examples of verb conjugation in the conditional perfect tense:

Italian	French
Avere	*Avoir*
io **avrei parlato**	j'**aurais parlé**

Italian	French
tu **avresti parlato**	tu **aurais parlé**
lui/lei/Lei **avrebbe parlato**	il/elle **aurait parlé**
noi **avremmo parlato**	nous **aurions parlé**
voi **avreste parlato**	vous **auriez parlé**
loro/Loro **avrebbero parlato**	ils/elles **auraient parlé**
Essere	*Être*
io **sarei partito(-a)**	je **serais parti(-e)**
tu **saresti partito(-a)**	tu **serais parti(-e)**
lui/lei/Lei **sarebbe partito(-a)**	il/elle **serait parti(-e)**
noi **saremmo partiti(-e)**	nous **serions parti(-e)s**
voi **sareste partiti(-e)**	vous **seriez parti(-e)s**
loro/Loro **sarebbero partiti(-e)**	ils/elles **seraient parti(-e)s**

Use of the Conditional Perfect Tense

In Italian and French the conditional perfect tense is used:

- **To express what would have happened if something else had not prevented it (See Conditional Clauses p.254):**

    It. Se avessimo avuto tempo, ***saremmo andati*** a Lisbona;

    Fr. Si nous avions eu le temps, nous ***serions allés*** à Lisbonne.

    - *If we had had time, we **would have gone** to Lisbon.*

    It. ***Avrei comprato*** questo libro, se avessi avuto i soldi;

Fr. J'*aurais acheté* ce livre, si j'avais de l'argent.

- *I **would have bought** this book if I had had the money.*

Conditional Clauses

A conditional clause refers to an event (ofter hypothetical), which may or may not happen in reality. Conditional sentences have two parts: the conditional or *if* clause, and the main clause, for instance: "*If you have time, we will go to the cinema*". In this sentence the conditional clause or *if* clause "*If you have time*" refers to a hypothetical event, the main clause "*we will go to the cinema*" shows what will happen if the condition of the *if* clause is met.

Normally, conditional clauses are introduced by *if* (It. *se*; Fr. *si*) in the Romance languages.

Conditional clauses have a particular sequence of tenses that needs to be followed. However, the sequence of tenses slightly differs in Italian and French, which requires more attention while learning. There are three types of *if* clauses in Italian and French.

1. Possible Condition

Below is the formation of the first type of *if* clause in Italian and French, which is **Possible Condition**:

If Clause	Main Clause
It. *se*; Fr. *si* + *Present Indicative*	*Present Indicative* or *Future* or *Imperative*

The first type of the conditional clause is used to demonstrate that the condition is likely to be implemented and therefore the consequence is regarded as possible. Observe the following:

It. *Se hai* fame, *compro* qualcosa da mangiare;

Fr. *Si tu as* faim, *j'achète* quelque chose à manger.

- *If you're* hungry, *I'll buy* something to eat.

CHAPTER 6: VERBS

Did you know?

The Vatican City came into existence in 1929 after the Lateran Treaty signed between Italy and the Holy See.

It. *Se lui ha* abbastanza tempo, *andrà* in America del Sud;

Fr. *S'il a* assez de temps, *il ira* en Amérique du Sud.

- *If he has* enough time, *he will go* to South America.

It. *Se sai* dov'è lui, *dimmelo*;

Fr. *Si tu sais* où il est, *dis-le moi*.

- *If you know* where he is, *tell me*!

2. Impossible condition

The following is the formation of the second type of *if* clause in Italian and French, which is called **impossible condition**:

NOTE:

In Italian **the Imperfect Subjunctive** is used in the *if* clause, whereas in French **the Imperfect Indicative** is used in this case.

The second type of conditional clause is contrary to the reality of the present and so the consequence is considered to be impossible. For example:

It. *Se io avessi* abbastanza tempo, *andrei* in Sud America;

Fr. *Si j'avais* assez de temps, *j'irais* en Amérique du Sud.

- *If I had* enough time, *I would go* to South America.

3. Impossible condition in the past

The following is the formation of the third type of *if* clause in Italian and French, which is called **impossible condition in the past**:

If Clause	Main Clause
It. *se*; Fr. *si* + **Pluperfect Tense**	**Past Conditional**

> **NOTE:**
> In Italian **the Pluperfect Subjunctive** is used in the **if** clause, whereas in French **the Pluperfect Indicative** is used in this case.

The third type of conditional clause is predominantly used for the situations that are contrary to the reality of the past. Therefore, it describes an unrealized past possibility. For instance:

It. *Se io avessi avuto* abbastanza tempo, *sarei andato* in Sud America;

Fr. *Si j'avais eu* assez de temps, *je serais allé* en Amérique du Sud.

- *If I had had* enough time, *I would have gone* to South America

The Subjunctive Mood

Overview

The subjunctive is one of the most difficult features of language for those who speak English, since the subjunctive is rarely used in English, whereas it is widely used in Italian and French.

At first let's look at the difference between the indicative and subjunctive moods in the Romance languages. *The indicative mood* is used to express a truth, fact, probability or action which is not dependent on an opinion or condition, while *the subjunctive mood* conveys desires, doubts, emotions or actions which are possible, uncertain, doubtful or unreal. Such ideas are dependent on an opinion or condition.

Basic Rules for Indicative and Subjunctive

CHAPTER 6: VERBS

The Indicative mood is

- generally used to talk about events, states or actions that are considered to be facts or true;
- quite common in speech to make real, accurate and factual statements or for describing evident qualities while referring to a situation or person.

The Subjunctive mood is

- generally used to talk about desires, doubts, emotions, the abstract and other unreal situations;
- commonly used in speech for making recommendations and expressing how particular things make you feel;
- widely used to express opinions concerning another action.

Study the following:

Indicative mood	Subjunctive mood
Example 1	Example 1
It. So che lei **arriva**;	It. Dubito che **arrivi**;
Fr. Je sais qu'elle **arrive**.	Fr. Je doute qu'elle **arrive**.
- *I know that she is coming.*	- *I doubt that she is coming.*
Example 2	Example 2
It. John **va** al cinema;	It. Egli vuole che John **vada** al cinema;
Fr. John **va** au cinéma.	Fr. Il veut que John **aille** au cinéma.
- *John goes to the cinema.*	- *He wants John to go to the cinema.*

In the second example, it can be seen that even though he wants John to go to the cinema, it is uncertain whether John will fulfill his desire, and so the action is conveyed in the subjunctive. In this case, in English an infinitive is used (he wants John **to go** to the cinema).

NOTE:

It should be mentioned that the subjunctive mood has many of the same verb tenses as the indicative mood, but not all. Moreover, the number of tenses in the subjunctive mood differs among Romance languages. Subjunctive in Italian and French has four tenses, which are present subjunctive, present perfect subjunctive, past subjunctive and past perfect subjunctive.

The Present Subjunctive

Formation of the Present Subjunctive

In Italian regular verbs form the present subjunctive by dropping the final *-o* of the 1st person singular of the present indicative and adding the appropriate personal ending to the root of a verb.

NOTE:

However, in French the **-ent** ending from the 3rd person plural of the indicative is dropped before adding the endings in order to form the present subjunctive.

Below is a table demonstrating the endings of the present subjunctive in the Romance languages:

Italian	French
1st conj.: -ARE: -i, -i, -i, -iamo, -iate, -ino;	**1st, 2nd and 3rd conj.: -ER, -RE and -IR:** -e, -es, -e, -ions, -iez, -ent;
2nd and 3rd conj.: -ERE and -IRE: -a, -a, -a, -iamo, -iate, -ano;	

Below is the table displaying the examples of conjugation of regular verbs in the present subjunctive in Italian and French:

Italian	French
1 conjugation	
parl**are**	parl**er**

CHAPTER 6: VERBS

Italian	French
che io parl**i**	que je parl**e**
che tu parl**i**	que tu parl**es**
che lui\lei\Lei parl**i**	qu'il\elle parl**e**
che noi parl**iamo**	que nous parl**ions**
che voi parl**iate**	que vous parl**iez**
che loro\Loro parl**ino**	qu'ils\elles parl**ent**
2 conjugation	
vend**ere**	vend**re**
che vend**a**	que je vend**e**
che vend**a**	que tu vend**es**
che vend**a**	qu'il\elle vend**e**
che vend**iamo**	que nous vend**ions**
che vend**iate**	que vous vend**iez**
che vend**ano**	qu'ils\elles vend**ent**
3 conjugation	
part**ire**	part**ir**
che part**a**	que je part**e**
che part**a**	que tu part**es**
che part**a**	qu'il\elle part**e**
che part**iamo**	que nous part**ions**
che part**iate**	que vous part**iez**
che part**ano**	qu'ils\elles part**ent**

Irregular Verbs in the Present Subjunctive

Below is a table presenting irregular verbs in the present subjunctive, which are common for all or several Romance languages:

CHAPTER 6: VERBS

Italian	French
essere (sia, sia, sia, siamo, siate, siano)	**être** (sois, sois, soit, soyons, soyez, soient)
stare (stia, stia, stia, stiano)	—
avere (abbia, abbia, abbia, abbiamo, abbiate, abbiano)	**avoir** (aie, aies, ait, ayons, ayez, aient)
tenere (tenga, tenga, tenga, tengano)	**tenir** (tienne, tiennes, tienne, tiennent)
fare (faccia, faccia, faccia, facciamo, facciate, facciano)	**faire** (fasse, fasses, fasse, fassions, fassiez, fassent)
venire (venga, venga, venga, vengano)	**venir** (vienne, viennes, vienne, viennent)
sapere (sappia, sappia, sappia, sappiamo, sappiate, sappiano)	**savoir** (sache, saches, sache, sachions, sachiez, sachent)
vedere (vegga (veda), vegga (veda), vegga (veda), veggano (vedano))	**voir** (voie, voies, voie, voyions, voyiez, voient)
morire (muoia, muoia, muoia, muoiano)	**mourir** (meure, meures, meure, meurent)
dare (dia, dia, dia, diano)	**donner** (regular)
dire (dica, dica, dica, diciamo, diciate, dicano)	**dire** (dise, dises, dise, disions, disiez, disent)
volere (voglia, voglia, voglia, vogliamo, vogliate, vogliano)	**vouloir** (veuille, veuilles, veuille, veuillent)

Italian	French
dovere (debba (deva), debba (deva), debba (deva), dobbiamo, dobbiate, debbano (devano)	**devoir** (doive, doives, doive, doivent)
potere (possa, possa, possa, possiamo, possiate, possano)	**pouvoir** (puisse, puisses, puisse, puissions, puissiez, puissent)
andare (vada, vada, vada, vadano)	**aller** (aille, ailles, aille, aillent)

Use of the Present Subjunctive

As it has been explained before, the present subjunctive is used in clauses following verbs which designate desires, doubts, emotions, feelings, requests, uncertainty, necessity, etc. in Italian and French. The subjunctive verb is usually introduced by It. *che*, Fr. *que*.

The present subjunctive is commonly used after the following verbs and expressions in the Romance languages:

1. **Verbs expressing wishing, desire or preference:**

Italian	French	English
volere che	**vouloir que**	*to want*
desiderare che	**desirer que**	*to wish, to desire*
preferire che	**préférer que**	*to prefer*
augurare che	**souhaiter que**	*to wish*
sperare che	<u>**espérer que**</u> (*indicative*)	*to hope*

CHAPTER 6: VERBS

Italian	French	English
suggerire che	**suggérer que** (proposer)	to suggest
—	—	if only

NOTE:
French **espérer** is followed by the indicative.

Study the following examples:

Did you know?

The first stock exchange building was built in Bruges (Belgium).

It. **Voglio che** lei **venga**.

Fr. Je **veux qu'**elle **vienne**.

- I want her to come.

It. **Spero che tu possa** venire domani.

Fr. J'**espère que tu peux** venir demain.

- I hope you can come tomorrow.

Hope or *If Only* in Italian and French

It. **Spero** (or **Se solo/magari/soltanto**); Fr. **J'espère** (or **Si seulement**) - I hope or if only. Observe the following:

It. **Se soltanto** sapesse!

Fr. **Si seulement** il savait!

- If only he knew!

2. Verbs of denial:

Italian	French	English
negare che	nier que	to deny

It. **Negano che** ci **conoscano**.

Fr. Ils **nient qu'**ils nous **connaissent**.

- They deny that they know us.

3. Verbs of doubt:

Italian	French	English
dubitare che	douter que	to doubt

Did you know?

Padua (It. Padova) is a city in Northern Italy. The University of Padua, one of the oldest universities in Italy, was founded in 1222. It established the first anatomy hall in Europe in 1594. Galileo Galilei was a lecturer at the university (1592-1610).

It. **Dubito che** lei lo **sappia**.

Fr. Je **doute qu'**elle le **sache**.

- I doubt that she knows.

4. Verbs which express emotions and feelings:

Italian	French	English
essere contento che	être content que	to be glad that
essere felice che	être heureux que	to be happy that
essere arrabbiato che	être fâché que	to be angry that

CHAPTER 6: VERBS

Italian	French	English
essere triste che	être triste que	to be sad that
essere dispiaciuto che	être désolé que	to be sorry that
essere orgoglioso che	être fier que	to be proud that
essere sorpreso che	être surpris que	to be surprised that
essere furioso che	être furieux que	to be furious that
avere paura che	avoir peur que	to be afraid that
___	avoir crainte que	to be afraid that
temere che	craindre que	to fear that
lamentare che	regretter que	to be sorry that
arrabbiarsi che	se fâcher que	to get angry
gioire che	se réjouir que	to rejoice, to be delighted

It. **Sono felice che tu sia** qui.

Fr. **Je suis heureux que tu sois** ici.

- I am happy that you are here.

It. **Sono sorpreso che ti piaccia** questa canzone.

Fr. **Je suis surpris que tu aimes** cette chanson.

- I am surprised that you like this song.

It. **Siamo tristi che tu lasci** il lavoro.

Fr. **Nous sommes tristes que tu quittes** le travail.

- We are sad that you are leaving the work.

5. Verbs expressing commands or requirements:

Italian	French	English
comandare che	commander que	to command
esigere che	exiger que	to demand
ordinare che	ordonner que	to order
richiedere che	requérir que	to require

It. Lei *esige che* Lei *venga* a tempo domani.

Fr. Elle *exige que* vous *veniez* à temps demain.

- *She demands that you be on time tomorrow.*

6. Verbs demonstrating permission or refusal of permission:

Italian	French	English
permettere che	permettre que	to permit
consentire che	consentir que	to consent
proibire che	interdire que	to forbid
impedire che	empêcher que	to prevent

It. Lei *permette che* lui ci *vada*.

Fr. Elle *permet qu*'il y *aille*.

- *She permits him to go there.*

It. Ti *proibisco che* tu *faccia* questo.

Fr. J'*interdis que* tu *fasses* cela.

- *I forbid you to do that.*

7. **Impersonal expressions that convey opinion or emotions:**

Italian	French	English
è tempo che	il est temps que	*it is time that/for*
è meglio che	il vaut (vaudrait) mieux que	*it is better that/for*
è preferibile che	il est préférable que	*it is better that/for*
è necessario che	il est nécessaire que	*it is necessary that*
bisogna che	il faut (faudrait) que	*it is necessary that*
è importante che	il est important que	*it is important that*
importa che	il importe que	*it is important that*
è essenziale che	il est essentiel que	*it is essential that*
è giusto che	il est juste que	*it is right that*
è sufficiente che	il suffit que	*it is enough that*
è indispensabile che	il est indispensable que	*it is indispensable that*
è conveniente che	il est convenable que	*it is proper that*
conviene che	il convient que	*it is fitting that*
è possibile che	il est possible que	*it is possible that/for*
si può che	il se peut que	*it is possible that/for*
è impossibile che	il est impossible que	*it is impossible that/for*
è utile che	il est utile que	*it is useful that/for*

Italian	French	English
è inutile che	il est inutile que	*it is useless that/for*
è dubbio che (si dubita che)	il est douteux que	*it is doubtful that*
è poco probabile che	il est peu probable que	*it is unlikely that*
non è certo che	il n'est pas certain que	*it is uncertain that*
è fortunato che	il est heureux que	*it is fortunate that*
è bene che	il est bon que	*it is good that*
è un peccato che	c'est (il est) dommage que	*it is a pity that*
sembra che	il semble que	*it seems that*
è vergognoso che	il est honteux que	*it is shameful that*
è triste che	il est triste que	*it is sad that*
è sorprendente che (sorprende che)	il est surprenant que (il surprend que)	*it is surprising that*
è stupefacente che	il est étonnant que	*it is astonishing that*
è urgente che	il est urgent que	*it is urgent that*

It. ***È necessario che*** tu **studi**;

Fr. ***Il est nécessaire que*** tu ***étudies***.

- *It is necessary that you to study.*

It. ***È possibile che*** mi **chiami** oggi;

Fr. ***Il est possible qu'***elle m'***appelle*** aujourd'hui.

- *It is possible that she will call me today.*

It. ***È un peccato che*** lui ***sia*** malato.

Fr. ***Il est dommage qu'***il ***soit*** malade.

- *It is a pity that he is ill.*

It. ***È triste che partano*** così presto.

Fr. ***Il est triste qu'***ils ***partent*** si tôt.

- *It is sad that they are leaving so early.*

Use of the Present Indicative instead of Subjunctive

The present indicative is normally used with the verbs and expressions that involve certainty in Italian and French.

The following is a list of the most common verbs and expressions that are used in the present indicative:

Italian	French	English
pensare che	**penser que**	*to think*
credere che	**croire que**	*to believe*
è certo che	**il est certain que**	*it is certain that*
è sicuro che	**il est sûr que**	*it is sure that*
è probabile che	**il est probable que**	*it is probable that*
è evidente che	**il est évident que**	*it is evident that*
è esatto che	**il est exact que**	*it is correct that*
è chiaro che	**il est clair que**	*it is clear that*
è vero che	**il est vrai que**	*it is true that*

CHAPTER 6: VERBS

> **Did you know?**
>
> Corsica (Fr.Corse) is a French mountainous island in the Mediterranean Sea. Corsica was sold to France in 1768. A year later, in 1769, Napoleon Bonaparte was born in the Corsican capital of Ajaccio. Today, his home "Maison Bonaparte" is used as a museum.

It. **Penso che vengono**;

Fr. Je **pense qu'**ils **viennent**.

- I think they are coming.

It. **È vero che** lui **sa** nuotare;

Fr. **Il est vrai qu'**il **sait** nager.

- It is true that he can swim.

However, Italian and French forms of the above expressions are used in the subjunctive for the negative and interrogative, since uncertainty is expressed:

It. **Non credo che vengano**;

Fr. Je **ne crois pas qu'**ils **viennent**.

- I don't believe they are coming.

It. **Non è certo che** lui **sappia** nuotare;

Fr. **Il n'est pas certain qu'**il **sache** nager.

- It is not certain that he can swim.

Subjunctive with Subordinate Conjunctions

The following is a list of conjunctions that require the subjunctive in the Romance languages:

1. Conjunctions of time:

CHAPTER 6: VERBS

Italian	French	English
prima che	avant que	*before*
dopo che	**après que** (*indicative*)	*after*
non appena che	**aussitôt que** (*indicative*)	*as soon as*
mentre che	**pendant que** (*indicative*)	*while*
quando	**quand** (*indicative*)	*when*
finché (fino a quando)	en attendant que (jusqu'à ce que)	*until*

> **NOTE:**
> In French **après que, aussitôt que, pendant que** and **quand** always take the indicative.

It. Parleremo **prima che** lei **esca**;

Fr. Nous parlerons **avant qu'**elle **sorte**.

- *We will talk before she leaves.*

2. **Conjunctions of cause or negation:**

Italian	French	English
non che; (nonché)	non que	*not that*
senza che	sans que	*without*

It. Lui è partito **senza que** io le **parlassi**;

Fr. Il est parti **sans que** je lui **parle**.

- *He left without me speaking to him.*

NOTE:

In Italian the Imperfect Subjunctive It. ***parlassi*** (the Present Subjunctive ***parli***) should be used in the above example.

3. **Conjunctions of purpose:**

Italian	French	English
affinché	afin que	*in order that, so that*
perché	pour que	*in order that, so that*
in maniera che, in forma che, in modo che	de manière que, de façon que, de sorte que	*so that*
per paura che	de crainte que, de peur que	*for fear that*

It. Lo diciamo **perché** tu lo **sappia**;

Fr. Nous le disons **pour que** tu le **saches**;

- We say it so that you know it.

NOTE:

However, in certain cases, It. **in maniera che, in forma che, in modo che**; Fr. **de manière que, de façon que, de sorte que** are followed by the indicative, especially when the result is an implemented and supposedly irrevocable fact or action.

In this case, these expressions can be translated in English as **so**. For example:

It. Sono venuto presto **in modo che** nessuno mi **ha visto**;

*Fr. Je suis venu tôt **de façon que** personne ne m'a vu.*
- I came early (in a way) so (that) nobody saw me.

4. Conjunctions of concession:

Italian	French	English
benché, quantunque, sebbene	bien que, quoique, encore que	although, though
malgrado che	malgré que	despite that

It. **Benché** io **sia** molto impegnato, ti telefonerò.

Fr. **Bien que** je **sois** très occupé, je vais te téléphoner.

- Although I am very busy, I will call you.

5. Conjunctions of condition:

Italian	French	English
a condizione che	à condition que	on the condition that
in caso che	en cas que	in the case that
purché	pourvu que	provided that
supposto che, posto che	supposé que	supposing that
a meno che (non)	à moins que	unless
sia che...sia che	soit que...soit que	whether...or

It. Sto per fare una passeggiata **a condizione che faccia** bel tempo;

Fr. Je vais faire un tour *à condition qu'*il *fasse* beau.

- I will go for a walk on the condition that the weather is good.

> **NOTE:**
> In French the negative particle **ne** is normally used after **à moins que, avant que, de peur que, de crainte que, de manière que, de sorte que** when the verb in the dependent clause is affirmative. **Ne...pas** is used if the verb is negative. For instance:

Fr. J'irai au marché *à moins qu'il ne* fasse mauvais.

- I will go to the market unless the weather is bad.

Fr. Je viens plus tôt *de crainte qu'il ne* m'attende *pas*.

- I come early for fear that he will not wait for me.

The following conjunction does not take the subjunctive in Italian and French:

Italian	French	English
perché	**parce que**	because

Indirect Commands in Romance languages

The present subjunctive may be used in indirect commands, which are quite common for stating a wish or hope that something will occur. They are normally used to refer to a third person.

The following is the formula to form indirect commands in Italian and French:

Fr. *Que*, It. *Che* + *Present Subjunctive*

Study the following:

It. ***Che*** lei ***lavori***!

Fr. ***Qu'***elle ***travaille***!

- *Let her work!*

Subjunctive after Affirmation in Romance Languages

The subjunctive is used with the following expression of affirmation in Italian and French:

Italian	French	English
che io sappia	**que je sache**	*as far as I know*

Observe the following:

It. Nessuno lo sa, ***che io sappia***;

Fr. Personne ne le sait, ***que je sache***.

- *No one knows **as far as I know**.*

Subjunctive in Relative Clauses

The subjunctive is usually used in relative clauses when the antecedent is indefinite, meaning a noun or pronoun that represents somebody or something that is not yet found or identified. The indicative is used when the antecedent is definite. Compare the following:

It. ***Conosciamo*** un uomo che ***può*** viaggiare con noi;

Fr. Nous ***connaissons*** un homme qui ***peut*** voyager avec nous.

- *We know a man who can travel with us.*

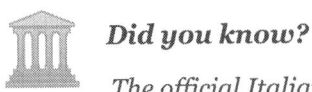

> **Did you know?**
>
> The official Italian name of the Vatican City is *Stato della Citta del Vaticano*.

It. **Cerchiamo** un uomo che **possa** viaggiare con noi;

Fr. Nous **cherchons** un homme qui **puisse** voyager avec nous.

- We are looking for a man who can travel with us.

Subjunctive with the Superlative and It. *solo, unico*; Fr. *seul, unique*

The present subjunctive is also used in a relative clause after a superlative expression and after It. *solo, unico*; Fr. *seul, unique* that are preceded by the appropriate definite article when these expressions express judgment or exaggeration. For instance:

It. È *il miglior film che* io *conosca*;

Fr. C'est *le meilleur film que* je *connaisse*.

- It is the best film that I know.

It. Egli è *l'unico studente che studi* bene;

Fr. Il est *le seul étudiant qui étudie* bien.

- He is the only student who studies well.

Subjunctive with Indefinite Words

The subjunctive is also used after the following indefinite words in Italian and French:

Italian	French	English
comunque...che	**si... que**	*however*

Italian	French	English
in qualche modo che	de quelque manière que	however
qualunque cosa...	quoi que ce soit...	whatever
qualunque...che	quelque (s)...que, quel que soit...que	whatever/whichever (with a noun)
chiunque..., chicche-ssia...	qui que ce soit...	whoever
ovunque.., dovunque...	où que...	wherever

Did you know?

The name "Belgium" dates back to the Romans. They called their province in the north of Gaul Gallia Belgica after its previous inhabitants, the Celtic and German Belgae.

It. **Qualunque** libro **che** tu **legga**, devi finirlo;

Fr. **Quel que soit** le livre **que** tu **lises**, tu dois le finir.

- Whichever book you read, you must finish it.

It. **Chiunque** lo **dica**, non crederci;

Fr. **Qui que ce soit qui** te le **dise**, ne le crois pas.

- Whoever says it, do not believe him.

The Present Perfect Subjunctive

Formation of the Present Perfect Subjunctive

The present perfect subjunctive in the Romance languages is formed by using the present subjunctive of the auxiliary verb (It. **avere** or **essere**, Fr. **avoir** or **être**) and the past participle.

The drawing below demonstrates the ways of forming the present perfect subjunctive in Italian and French:

CHAPTER 6: VERBS

Present Perfect Subjunctive Formula

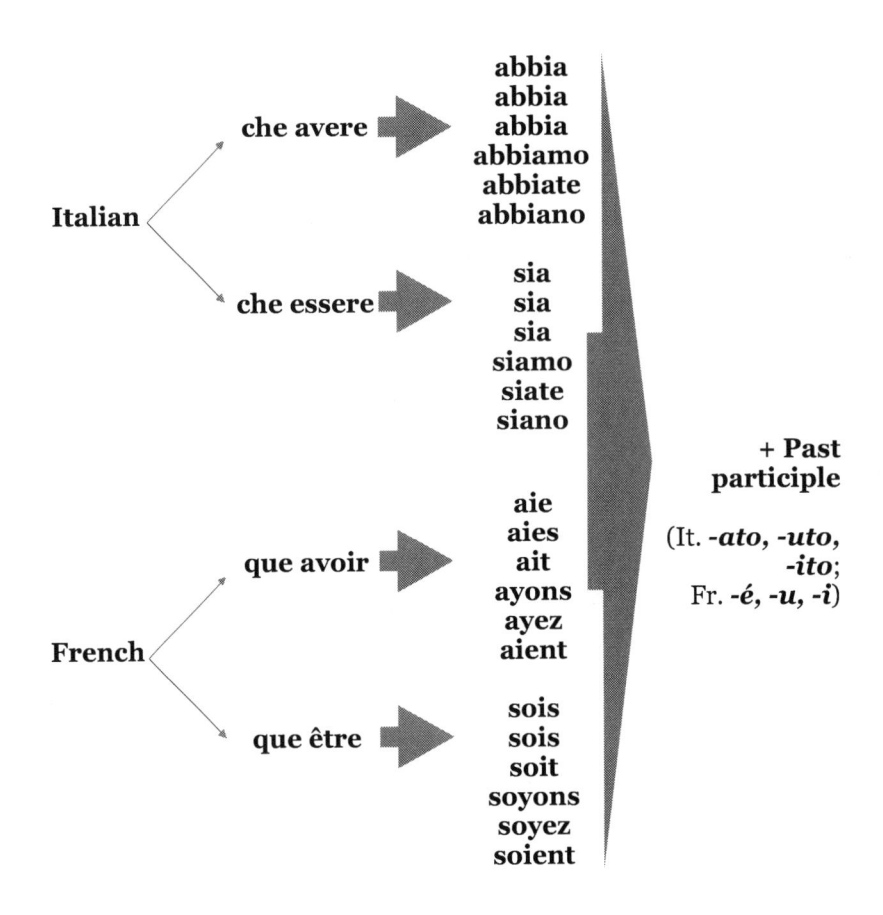

Italian:
- che avere → abbia, abbia, abbia, abbiamo, abbiate, abbiano
- che essere → sia, sia, sia, siamo, siate, siano

French:
- que avoir → aie, aies, ait, ayons, ayez, aient
- que être → sois, sois, soit, soyons, soyez, soient

+ Past participle

(It. *-ato, -uto, -ito*; Fr. *-é, -u, -i*)

Below is the table that illustrates the example of verb conjugation in the present perfect subjunctive in Italian and French:

Italian	French
Avere	*Avoir*
che io **abbia parlato**	que j`**aie parlé**
che tu **abbia parlato**	que tu **aies parlé**
che lui/lei/Lei **abbia parlato**	que il/elle **ait parlé**

277

CHAPTER 6: VERBS

Italian	French
che noi **abbiamo parlato**	que nous **ayons parlé**
che voi **abbiate parlato**	que vous **ayez parlé**
che loro/Loro **abbiano parlato**	que ils/elles **aient parlé**
Essere	*Être*
che io **sia partito(-a)**	que je **sois parti(-e)**
che tu **sia partito(-a)**	que tu **sois parti(-e)**
che lui/lei/Lei **sia partito(-a)**	que il/elle **soit parti(-e)**
che noi **siamo partiti(-e)**	que nous **soyons parti(-e)s**
che voi **siate partiti(-e)**	que vous **soyez parti(-e)s**
che loro/Loro **siano partiti(-e)**	que ils/elles **soient parti(-e)s**

Use of the Present Perfect Subjunctive

In Italian and French the present perfect subjunctive is used:

- when a present indicative or future verb in a main clause governs a verb that requires the subjunctive which refers to a past action in a dependent clause, for example:

Did you know?

Until 1934 Italian was the official language of Malta. Even though Italian has since been replaced by English as the official language, today, 68% of the Maltese population speaks Italian, and 10% of the population use it in everyday conversations.

It. ***Sono felice che tu sia venuto***;

Fr. ***Je suis heureux que tu sois venu***.

- *I am happy that you came.*

It. ***Sono triste che lei mi abbia lasciato***;

Fr. ***Je suis triste qu'elle m'ait laissé***.

- *I am sad that she left me.*

The Imperfect Subjunctive

Formation of the Imperfect Subjunctive

In Italian and French the imperfect subjunctive is formed by dropping the Fr. *-s* and It. *-sti* of the 2nd person singular of the preterite tense (Fr. *le passé simple*; It. *il passato remoto*) and adding the appropriate endings. In French the diacritic mark must be put above the stressed vowel in the 3rd person singular, which is also before the attached ending of the imperfect subjunctive (e.g. que travaill**ât** - *that he works*). However, Italian does not have any diacritical marks in the imperfect subjunctive.

The following is a table demonstrating the endings of the imperfect subjunctive in Italian and French:

Italian	French
-ssi, -ssi, -sse,-ssimo,-ste, -ssero;	-sse, -sses, -t, -ssions, -ssiez, -ssent;

Below is the table illustrating the example of conjugation of regular verbs of all conjugations in the imperfect subjunctive:

Italian	French
1 conjugation	
It.: parl**are**	Fr.: parl**er**
che io parla**ssi**	que je parla**sse**
che tu parla**ssi**	que tu parla**sses**
che lui\lei parla**sse**	que il\elle parl**ât**
che noi parla**ssimo**	que nous parla**ssions**
che voi parla**ste**	que vous parla**ssiez**
che loro parla**ssero**	que ils\elles parla**ssent**
2 conjugation	
vend**ere**	vend**re**

Italian	French
che vende**ssi**	que vendi**sse**
che vende**ssi**	que vendi**sses**
che vende**sse**	que vend**ît**
che vende**ssimo**	que vendi**ssions**
che vende**ste**	que vendi**ssiez**
che vende**ssero**	que vendi**ssent**
	3 conjugation
part**ire**	part**ir**
che parti**ssi**	que parti**sse**
che parti**ssi**	que parti**sses**
che parti**sse**	que part**ît**
che parti**ssimo**	que parti**ssions**
che parti**ste**	que parti**ssiez**
che parti**ssero**	que parti**ssent**

Irregular Verbs in the Imperfect Subjunctive

All verbs that are considered to be irregular in the preterite are also irregular in the imperfect subjunctive in the Romance languages. (**See The Preterite p.191**)

Use of the Imperfect Subjunctive

In the Romance languages the imperfect subjunctive is used:

- in subordinate or dependent clauses when the verb in the main clause is in the preterite, imperfect indicative, present perfect or conditional. That is to say the imperfect subjunctive expresses emotions, doubts and etc. that occurred in the past. Study the following:

CHAPTER 6: VERBS

Did you know?

French is one of the prestige languages in Morocco. It is often used in international commerce, media, government and diplomacy. French is taught at all schools. 34% of Moroccans speak French fluently.

It. ***Volevo che*** lui ***andasse*** in ospedale;

Fr. Je ***voulais qu'il allât*** à l'hôpital.

- I wanted him to go to the hospital.

NOTE:

In French the imperfect subjunctive is used only in written language. In spoken language, the present subjunctive normally replaces the imperfect subjunctive, for example:

Fr. Je ***voulais qu'il aille*** à l'hôpital.

The Pluperfect (Past Perfect) Subjunctive

Overview

The pluperfect subjunctive expresses a completed action that *had* happened before another action in the past in all the cases that the subjunctive would be used in the Romance languages.

It is worth saying that the pluperfect is usually used with conditional perfect independent clauses to show hypothetical situations.

Formation of The Pluperfect Subjunctive

In Italian and French the pluperfect subjunctive is formed by using the imperfect subjunctive of the verb It. ***avere*** or ***essere***, Fr. ***avoir*** or ***être*** with the past participle.

The formula of the pluperfect subjunctive of the Romance languages is presented in the drawing below:

Pluperfect Subjunctive Formula

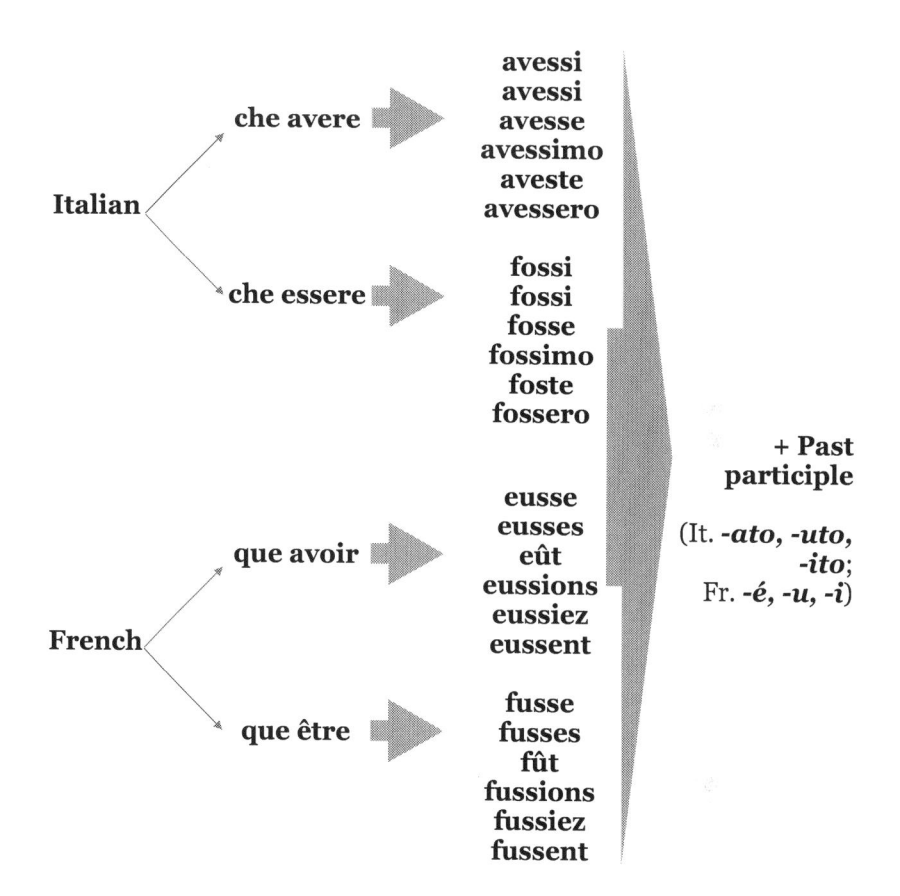

Italian
- che avere → avessi, avessi, avesse, avessimo, aveste, avessero
- che essere → fossi, fossi, fosse, fossimo, foste, fossero

French
- que avoir → eusse, eusses, eût, eussions, eussiez, eussent
- que être → fusse, fusses, fût, fussions, fussiez, fussent

+ Past participle
(It. *-ato, -uto, -ito*; Fr. *-é, -u, -i*)

NOTE:

*It should be remembered that in the pluperfect subjunctive as well as other compound tenses, the auxiliary verbs It. **essere**; Fr. **être** (to be) are also used with reflexive and intransitive verbs in Italian and French. Also, the past participle which is used with the auxiliary verb to be (It. **essere**, Fr. **être**) always agrees in gender and number with the subject. This means that the endings change in the feminine and plural forms the way they change in adjectives: in French -e is added to agree with the feminine and -s- is added for the plural, in*

*Italian to agree with the feminine -**a** is used and -**i**, -**e**- with the masculine and feminine plurals respectively.*

Below is the table demonstrating the example of conjugation of verbs in the pluperfect subjunctive:

Italian	French
Avere	*Avoir*
che io **avessi parlato**	que j'**eusse parlé**
che tu **avessi parlato**	que tu **eusses parlé**
che lui/lei/Lei **avesse parlato**	que il/elle **eût parlé**
che noi **avessimo parlato**	que nous **eussions parlé**
che voi **aveste parlato**	que vous **eussiez parlé**
che loro/Loro **avessero parlato**	que ils/elles **eussent parlé**
Essere	*Être*
che io **fossi partito(-a)**	que je **fusse parti(-e)**
che tu **fossi partito(-a)**	que tu **fusses parti(-e)**
che lui/lei/Lei **fosse partito(-a)**	que il/elle **fût parti(-e)**
che noi **fossimo partiti(-e)**	que nous **fussions parti(-e)s**
che voi **foste partiti(-e)**	que vous **fussiez parti(-e)s**
che loro/Loro **fossero partiti(-e)**	que ils/elles **fussent parti(-e)s**

Use of the Pluperfect Subjunctive

In the Romance languages the pluperfect subjunctive is used:

- in completed actions that had happened before another action in the past where the pluperfect is used in clauses that require the subjunctive and the main verb is put in a past tense. Observe the following:

CHAPTER 6: VERBS

Did you know?

The Vatican City has a two-mile border with Italy. The city is 1/8th the size of Ney Work's Central Park.

It. Lei **dubitava che** lui **avesse detto** questo;

Fr. Elle **doutait qu**'il **eût dit** cela.

- She doubted that he had said that.

It. **Sembrava che** lei *fosse andata* in Brasile;

Fr. Il **semblait qu**'elle *fût allée* au Brésil.

- It seemed that she had gone to Brazil.

NOTE:

In French the pluperfect subjunctive is also used in written language. In conversation, the past subjunctive usually replaces the pluperfect subjunctive, for example:

Fr. Elle **a regretté qu**'elle **ait dit** cela.
- She was sorry that she had said that.

The Sequence of Tenses with the Subjunctive

As there are fewer subjunctive tenses than indicatives in the Romance languages, it might be helpful to demonstrate the most common sequence of these subjunctive tenses with their indicative equivalents. However, it should be mentioned that it as a common pattern in the sequence of tenses rather than a fixed rule since everything depends on contexts while conveying the correct meaning of a phrase.

The following is a table that illustrates the common sequence of indicative tenses with their subjunctive counterparts in Italian and French:

Verbs in main clause	Subjunctive in subordinate clause
present, future, perfect indicative	*present, perfect*
preterite, imperfect, pluperfect indicative, conditional	*imperfect, pluperfect*
command	*present*

NOTE:

Instead of the preterite, the Italian and French conversational past tense (it. <u>passato prossimo</u>; fr. <u>passé composé</u>) - **present perfect** is followed by **the imperfect and pluperfect subjunctive**.

It. **Sono orgoglioso che** lei **abbia guadagnato**;

Fr. **Je suis fier qu'**elle **ait gagné**.

- *I am proud that she won.*

It. **Sarà utile che faccia** gli esercizi la mattina;

Fr. **Il sera utile qu'il fasse** les exercices le matin.

- *It will be useful for him to do exercices in the morning.*

It. **L'ho proibito che** mi **molestassi**;

Fr. Je lui **ai interdit qu'**il me **dérangeasse**

(Je lui **ai interdit qu'**il me **dérange**)

- *I prohibited him to disturb me.*

Did you know?

French Guiana is an overseas department of France, situated on the north Atlantic coast of South America. It Boarders Brazil and Suriname. French Guiana is home to the Guiana Space Centre (Fr. Le Centre Spatial Guyanais), which is a European spaceport.

CHAPTER 6: VERBS

The Imperative Mood

The imperative mood is usually used to express commands. The exclamation marks must be used in the imperative. The Romance languages have several categories of commands that include both affirmative and negative commands. They are: **informal commands, formal commands, let's commands** and **indirect commands**.

1. Informal Commands

Affirmative informal commands, are used to tell your friend, family member or child to do something. The singular form of the affirmative informal command, or It. **tu**, Fr. **tu** command is identical with the 3rd person of the present indicative in Italian, whereas in French the 2nd person singular is used for all conjugations except for *-er* verbs where *s* is usually dropped from the 2nd person singular in order to form the imperative. The plural form of the affirmative informal command (It. **voi**, Fr. **vous**) is also formed differently in the Romance languages.

> **NOTE:**
>
> To form Italian and French plural form of the affirmative informal command, or It. **voi**, Fr. **vous** command we should use the 2nd person plural form of the present indicative.

Observe the example of the singular and plural forms of the affirmative informal commands in the Romance languages:

	Italian	French
Singular form of the informal command	**Parla!** **Scrivi!**	**Parle!** **Écris!**
Plural form of the informal command	**Parlate!** **Scrivete!**	**Parlez!** **Écrivez!**

2. Formal Commands

Formal commands, or It. **Lei** (**Loro**), Fr. **vous** commands are usually used while addressing people you do not know very well, people older than you or people you show respect, such as teachers, bosses and etc.

In Italian *-i* is added to the *-are* verbs and *-a* to the *-ere* and *-ire* verbs for singular form of the formal commands. Italian plural form of the formal commands is obtained by adding *-ino* to the *-are* verbs and *-ano* to the *-ere* and *-ire* verbs.

> *NOTE:*
> *It should be noted that French has a similar form for the plural informal commands and formal commands.*

Study the example of the singular and plural forms of the affirmative formal commands in Italian and French:

	Italian	French
Singular form of the formal command	**Parli!** **Scriva!**	**Parlez!** **Écrivez!**
Plural form of the formal command	**Parlino!** **Scrivano!**	**Parlez!** **Écrivez!**

3. Let's Commands

The let's commands, or It. **noi**, Fr. **nous** commands are normally used when someone suggests an action to be fulfilled by a group of people.

	Italian	French
Let's commands	**Parliamo!** **Scriviamo!**	**Parlons!** **Écrivons!**

CHAPTER 6: VERBS

NOTE:

In Italian and French such commands are formed by simply using the 2nd person plural of the present indicative.

*In French the imperative forms of the verb **aller** are **va, allons** and **allez**. It should be remembered that **va** becomes **vas** and the familiar form of the imperative of the -er verbs adds **s** before such pronouns as **y** and **en**, for example: Va**s-y**! - Go there!; Parle**s-en**! - Speak about it!*

Irregular Imperative

There are several verbs that have completely irregular imperative forms in Italian and French:

Italian	French
Essere (tu) **Sii**! (voi) **Siate**! (Lei) **Sia**! (Loro) **Siano**!	**Être** (tu) **Sois**! (nous) **Soyons**! (vous) **Soyez**!
Stare (tu) **Sta'**! (voi) **State**! (Lei) **Stia**! (Loro) **Stiano**!	—
Tenere (regular)	**Tenir** (regular)
Fare (tu) **Fa'**! (Lei) **Fai**! (Loro) **Facciano**!	**Faire** (regular)
Venire (regular)	**Venir** (regular)
Sapere (tu) **Sappi**! (voi) **Sappiate**! (Lei) **Sappia**! (Loro) **Sappiano**!	**Savoir** (tu) **Sache**! (vous) **Sachez**!
Vedere (regular)	**Voir** (regular)

Italian	French
Dare (tu) **Da'**!	**Donner** (regular)
Dire (tu) **Di'**!	**Dire** (regular)
Andare (tu) **Vai**!	**Aller** (regular)

The Negative Imperative

Negative commands are formed differently in Italian and French. Thus, they should be regarded separately.

Italian

The negative singular forms of informal commands, or **tu** commands are formed by placing a negative word **non** before the infinitive in Italian. For example:

It. **Non aprire** il libro.

- Do not open the book.

The negative plural forms of informal commands, or **voi** command forms are formed by putting the negative word **non** in front of the affirmative **voi** form.

It. **Non partite** domani.

- Do not leave tomorrow.

The *let's not commands* are expressed by placing the negative word non before the command in Italian, for example:

It. ***Non parliamo***.

- Let's not talk.

French

In French the negative commands are formed by placing ***ne*** or ***n'*** in front of the verb and ***pas*** after it, regardless whether the negative commands are informal or formal. In French object pronouns also precede the verb in negative commands. Observe the following:

Fr. ***N'ouvre pas*** le livre.

- Do not open the book.

Fr. ***Ne partez pas*** demain.

- Do not leave tomorrow.

Fr. ***Ne le dis pas***.

- Do not say it.

Softened Commands in the Romance Languages

In Italian and French there are special formulas that can be used to soften the commands to sound more polite.

Below are the most common patterns to use in polite speech:

Italian	French	English
mi faccia il favore di + inf.	**faites-moi la faveur de + inf.**	*do me a favor*
per favore; per piacere	**s'il te plaît; s'il vous plaît**	*please*

CHAPTER 6: VERBS

> **Did you know?**
>
> Trieste is a city in northeast Italy, which occupies a narrow strip of land between the Adriatic Sea and Slovenia. Italian, Germanic and Slavic cultural influences are visible in its layout. The most iconic landmark of the city is Unity of Italy Square (It. Piazza Unità d'Italia). It is the main square in Trieste located between the 19th-century avenues and the old medieval city.

It. **Mi faccia il favore di aprire** la finestra;

Fr. **Faites-moi la faveur d'ouvrir** la fenêtre.

- Do me a favor - open the window.

It. Chiudi la porta, **per favore**;

Fr. Ferme la porte, **s'il te plaît**.

- Close the door, please.

Alternatively softened commands can be expressed as questions in the Romance languages. For example:

It. **Mi dai un po' d'acqua?**

Fr. **Vous me donnez un peu d'eau?**

- Would you give me some water?

The Present Participle (Gerund)

Overview

The present participles (gerunds) are used to indicate several continuous actions in Italian and French. Generally speaking the present participle (gerund) expresses the concept of *"while doing"*, *"in doing"* or *"by doing"* in the Romance languages.

The present participle (gerund) in Italian ends in It. **-ando**, **-endo** and Fr. **-ant** in French, which is the equivalent to the English form of *-ing*.

It should be noted that nouns and adjectives that end in *-ing* in English cannot be expressed by a gerund in the Romance languages.

Formation of the Present Participle (Gerund)

In Italian, the present participle (gerund) is formed by dropping the infinitive ending and adding *-ando* to the stem of *-are* verbs and *-endo* to the verb root of *-ere* and *-ire* verbs.

Whereas, in French, the present participle is formed by dropping the ending -ons from the 1st person plural of the present tense and adding the present participle (gerund) ending *-ant* in all the conjugations.

Below is a table presenting how the present participle (gerund) is formed:

	1st conj.	*2nd conj.*	*3rd conj.*
Italian	-are; -ando (parl**are** – parl**ando**)	-ere; -endo (vend**ere** – vend**endo**)	-ire; -endo (part**ire** – part**endo**)
French	-er; -ant (parl**er** – parl**ant**)	-re; -ant (vend**re** – vend**ant**)	-ir; -ant (part**ir** – part**ant**)

Irregularities in Formation of the Present Participle (Gerund) in Italian

Unlike French, Italian have a considerable number of irregularities in formation of the present participle (gerund), which should be remembered by learners.

Italian

In Italian, most verbs form the present participle (gerund) with the root of the 1st person singular (*io*) of the present indicative form without the personal ending.

Infinitive	Root (the 1st person)	Present Participle (Gerund)

CHAPTER 6: VERBS

bere	bev	bevendo
dire	dic	dicendo
fare	fac	facendo
tradurre	traduc	traducendo

Use of Present Participle (Gerund)

Present participle (gerund) is generally used:

- **To indicate several ongoing actions:**

Present participles (Gerunds) can be used to express several continuous actions that occur at the same time in the Romance languages.

NOTE:

In French, in this case, the present participle (gerund) is used after the preposition **en**.

Did you know?

Vanuatu is a Pacific island nation situated in the South Pacific Ocean. The official languages are Bislama, French and English. The city is home to the Vanuatu National Museum situated in the capital, Port Vila. It specializes in exhibits of the nation's Melanesian culture.

It. Lei ha letto il libro, **mangiando**;

Fr. Elle a lu le livre, **en mangeant**.

- **While eating**, she read the book.

It. Mi guardò **sorridendo**;

Fr. Il me regarda **en souriant**.

- *He looked at me **smiling**.*

However, the French preposition **en** plus the present participle is not used after the verbs **commencer** and **finir**. The preposition **par** with the infinitive is normally used with these verbs (e.g. Elle *a fini par travailler* - *She finally started to work*; Il *a commencé par faire la cuisine* - *He began by cooking*.).

- **In place of a relative clause**

    Present participles (Gerunds) are also used to modify or qualify a noun, in place of a relative clause in Spanish, Portuguese, Italian and French.

> *NOTE:*
>
> *In French, this usage is common in official language. In spoken language the relative clause is more likely to be used.*

It. L'uomo **attraversando** (che sta attraversando) la strada è mio padre;

Fr. Un homme **traversant** (qui est en train de traverser) la rue est mon père.

- The *man* **crossing** *the street is my father.*

> *NOTE:*
>
> *This use of the present participle (gerund) is only possible in the case of action verbs. A relative clause must be used with other verbs in the Romance languages. Study the following:*

It. un libro **che descrive** la storia della sua vita;

Fr. un livre **qui décrit** l'histoire de sa vie.

- a book **that describes** the story of his life.

- **To express the continuous tenses. (See The Continuous Tenses p.298).**

CHAPTER 6: VERBS

No Use of Present Participle (Gerund)

There are some situations in which English uses words with -ing ending that cannot be expressed by a gerund in Italian and French.

- **As a verbal noun**

The infinitive is used, rather than the gerund in order to form a verbal noun. Study the following:

It. Mi piace **nuotare**;

Fr. J'aime **nager**.

- *I like **swimming**.*

- **As an adjective**

In English, the present participle (the *-ing* form) is used to express an adjective-like function (e.g. *a smiling girl*). In the Romance languages, the present participle (gerund) cannot be used to convey it. Instead, there is a number of ways to reflect this. Observe the following:

1. By adding the appropriate ending in order to make an adjective from some verbs. Thus, adjectives are formed by dropping the infinitive ending and adding the appropriate personal ending to the stem of a verb.

   Below is a table showing the endings that transform some verbs into adjectives in the Romance languages:

	Italian	French
1st conj.	-ante	
2nd conj.	-ente	-ant(e)
3rd conj.		

NOTE:
In this case, the present participle is used in French (**See The Present Participle p.291**).

Also, if the French present participle is used as an adjective, it agrees with the noun it modifies.

*It. madre **sorridente**;*
*Fr. mère **souriante**.*
*- **smiling** mother.*

2. By using the following prepositional phrase:

> It. ***di***, Fr. ***de (d')*** + *a noun* or ***infinitive***.

It. una lezione ***di equitazione***;

Fr. une leçon ***d'équitation***.

*- a **riding** lesson.*

- **After prepositions**

With prepositions, the infinitive must be used rather than the present participle (gerund) in the Romance languages. (**See Use of The Infinitive p.301**).

How to Avoid Using the Present Participle (Gerund)

In order to avoid using the gerund one should use the following words to start the sentence in the Romance languages:

Italian	French	English
quando	**quand**	*when*
mentre	**tandis que**	*while*
poiché, siccome	**puisque, comme**	*since*
sebbene, benché	**même si, bien que**	*although, even though*
nonostante	**nonobstant**	*notwithstanding*

Italian	French	English
malgrado	malgré	in spite of

> **NOTE:**
> The majority of these words are followed by the subjunctive in the Romance languages. (**See The Subjunctive Mood p.256**).

It. **Commettendo** errori, io imparo. - **Quando faccio** degli errori, imparo;

Fr. **En faisant** des erreurs, j'apprends - **Quand** je **fais** des erreurs, j'apprends.

- By **making** mistakes, I learn; (**When I make** mistakes, I learn).

Did you know?

St. Peter's Basilica of the Vatican City is the largest Catholic Church in the world.

It. Parlavano, **cucinando**. - **Mentre cucinavano**, parlavano;

Fr. Ils parlaient, **en cuisinant**. - **Tandis qu'**ils **cuisinaient**, ils parlaient.

- **While** cooking, they talked.

The Compound Present Participle (Gerund) in Italian

The compound present participle (gerund) is particular only to Italian and doesn't exist in French.

Formation of the Compound Present Participle (Gerund) in Italian

The Italian compound present participle (gerund) is formed with the present participle of the verbs It. ***avere*** or ***essere*** plus the past participle of the action verb.

Below is the formula of the compound present participle in Italian:

Italian
avendo or **essendo** + Past Participle
(***avendo mangiato*** - *having eaten*)   (***essendo stato*** - *having been*)

Use of the Compound Present Participle in Italian

Did you know?

Rwanda is a landlocked state in Central and East Arica and one of the smallest countries in Africa. This country has a lot of lakes, the largest being Lake Kivu. It is one of the deepest lakes in the world with a depth of 480 meters.

Like in English, in Italian the compound present participle is used to indicate contemporaneity of several actions where one action precedes another. Something also worth noting is that the compound present participle never follows a preposition. For example:

It. ***Avendo terminato*** la lettera, lei l'ha portata all'ufficio postale.

- ***Having finished*** *the letter, she brought it to the post office.*

The Continuous Tenses

Formation of Continuous Tenses

The progressive tenses show that the action of the verb is in the process of taking place in the Romance languages. In Italian, the continuous tenses are formed with the present participle (gerund) of the verb with an appropriate form of the verb It. ***stare***.

CHAPTER 6: VERBS

Whereas in French, there is only one combination used in order to express progressive tense, which is: the present tense of the verb *être* + *en train de* + *Infinitive*.

> **NOTE:**
> However, the French present simple along with the adverb **maintenant** *(now)* is frequently used in order to express the continuous action.

It. *Sta lavorando*;

Fr. Il *est en train de travailler* (Il *travaille maintenant*).

- *He is working.*

The Italian language has a different number of progressive tenses, except for French, which has only one progressive form (the present progressive). Nevertheless, in Italian the continuous forms are most commonly used with the present indicative and the imperfect indicative, while the preterite, the present perfect, the past perfect, the pluperfect, the future, the present subjunctive, the imperfect subjunctive, and the conditional are rarely used.

Thus, regard the continuous constructions that demonstrate the present and imperfect indicative of the 1st person singular of the verb It. *lavorare*; Fr. *travailler* - *to work*.

	Italian	**French**
Present Continuous	**sto lavorando** (I am working)	**je suis en train de travailler** (I am working)
Imperfect Continuous	**stavo lavorando** (I was working at the moment)	____

Use of Continuous Tenses

Like in English, in the Romance languages continuous tenses are normally used with action verbs in order to express that an action *is taking place*.

The Present Continuous

In Italian and French the present continuous is primarily used:

- **for an action that is taking place at the present moment**. For example:

It. Che cosa **stai facendo**? - ***Sto mangiando***;

Fr. Qu'est-ce que tu ***fais maintenant***? - Je **suis en train de manger**.

- *What **are** you **doing**? - I **am eating**.*

The Imperfect Continuous

In Italian this tense is used similarly as the present continuous, but referring to a past time.

NOTE:

In French, the present perfect or imperfect indicative is used in this case. Observe the following:

It. Quando sono arrivato **stava leggendo**;

Fr. Quand je suis arrivé elle **lisait**.

- *When I arrived she **was reading**.*

CHAPTER 6: VERBS

The Infinitive

Overview

The Infinitive is the basic form of the verb in any language. In English, the infinitive is preceded by the preposition *to* (e.g. *to go, to speak, to do* etc.), while in the Romance languages, infinitives are separated into three conjugations according to their endings. Italian infinitives are ended in *-ARE, -ERE,* and *-IRE* and French infinitive forms have the endings *-ER, -RE,* and *-IR*.

The infinitive forms show what an action is, but show nothing about who is doing the action or at what time the action is performed. In the Romance languages, in order to conjugate a verb, one needs to remove the infinitive ending and add the appropriate tense's ending to the stem of the verb.

Below is a table helping to find the stem from the infinitive of the regular verbs in Italian and French:

	1st conj. (-AR, -ARE, -ER)		2nd conj. (-ER, -ERE, -RE)		3rd conj. (-IR, -IRE)	
	Infinitive	Stem	Infinitive	Stem	Infinitive	Stem
Italian	parl**are**	parl-	vend**ere**	vend-	part**ire**	part-
French	parl**er**	parl-	vend**re**	vend-	part**ir**	part-

Use of The Infinitive

The infinitive is generally used:

- **As a noun**

In Italian and French, when a verb functions as a noun, the infinitive must be used, whereas in English the gerund (verb with *-ing* ending) is used in this case. In the Romance languages, the gerund is only used to express an action in progress. The infinitive can be used as the subject of a sentence or the object of another verb or preposition in Italian and French. Study the following:

CHAPTER 6: VERBS

> **Did you know?**
>
> The Swiss Guard is the official guard of the Vatican and the Pope. This unit was originally established in about 1505 by Pope Julius II. There are 110 soldiers and 6 officers in the unit. They all wear very colorful and unique uniforms that some say were designed by Michelangelo.

It. **Viaggiare** è allegro ed educativo;

Fr. **Voyager** est allègre et éducatif.

- **Travelling** is enjoyable and educational.

It. Le **piace nuotare**;

Fr. Elle **aime nager**.

- She **likes swimming**.

- **After conjugated verbs without a preposition**

If one verb follows another, the second verb takes the infinitive when the subject of the first verb is the same as that of the second in the Romance languages. It is common for the modal verbs (e.g. *can, should, must*), which are usually followed by an infinitive with no in-between preposition and also for verbs expressing feelings, necessity, and accomplishment in Italian and French. Observe the following:

It. **Posso parlare** con lui;

Fr. Je **peux parler** avec lui.

- I **can talk** to him.

Below is the list of the most common verbs which are followed by an infinitive without preposition in the Romance languages:

Italian	French	English
dovere	devoir	must, should
potere	pouvoir	to be able to, can
sapere	savoir	to know how to
volere	vouloir	to want to

Italian	French	English
preferire	préférer	to prefer to
amare	aimer	to love to
desiderare	désirer	to desire to
raggiungere	atteindre	to manage to
piangere	regretter	to regret
*<u>pensare di</u>	penser	to plan to, to intend to
*<u>sperare di</u>	espérer	to hope to, to expect to
affermare	affirmer	to affirm
apparire	apparaître	to seem

NOTE:

In Italian the verbs **pensare** and **sperare** are followed by the preposition **di**, which should be remembered.

- **After conjugated verbs with a preposition:**

In the Romance languages certain verbs are followed by prepositions and there is no common principal in terms of which prepositions follow which verbs, and therefore, this has to be memorized on a case-by-case basis. Nevertheless, there are a few generalizations that may help learners:

1. **Verbs followed by the preposition *a* (*Italian*) and *à* (*French*) + an infinitive.**

Verbs meaning *beginning* and verbs that express preparation or readiness to perform an action or verbs of movement towards someplace or goal are usually followed by *a* (*à*) plus an infinitive in the Romance languages.

Below is the list of the most frequent verbs followed by *a* (*à*) + *infinitive* in Italian and French:

CHAPTER 6: VERBS

Italian	French	English
aiutare a	aider à	to help to
apprendere a, imparare a	apprendre à	to learn how to
insegnare a	enseigner à	to teach how to
cominciare a, iniziare a	commencer à	to begin to, to start to
mettersi a	se mettre à	to start to, to set about
invitare a	inviter à	to invite to
prepararsi a	se préparer à	to prepare to
dedicarsi a	se consacrer à, se vouer à	to dedicate oneself to
decidersi a	se décider à	to decide to, to make up one's mind
tornare a	retourner à	to do something again
abituarsi a	s'habituer à	to become accustomed to
obbligare a	obliger à	to oblige
esitare a	hésiter à	to hesitate

It. Ha **cominciato (iniziato) a sorridere**;

Fr. Elle **a commencé à sourire**.

- She **started to smile**.

It. **Imparo a parlare** una lingua straniera;

Fr. J'**apprends à parler** une langue étrangère.

- I **learn how to speak** a foreign language.

2. **Verbs followed by the preposition *de* (French) and *di* (Italian) + *an infinitive*.**

In the Romance languages, the preposition Fr. *de* and It. *di* is used after verbs that indicate movement away from, like refraining from, which corresponds to English *"from"* + *the gerund*, and also used after verbs meaning *"to stop"* and *"to finish"*.

Below is the list of the most frequent verbs followed by *de* (*di*) + *infinitive* in Italian and French:

Italian	French	English
—	**venir de**	*to have just done smth.*
ricordarsi di	<u>**se rappeler (de)**</u>	*to remember*
rallegrarsi di	**se réjouir de**	*to be happy to*
pentirsi di	**se repentir de, regretter de**	*to regret, to repent of*
stancarsi di	**se lasser de, se fatiguer de**	*to tire of, to grow tired of*
smettere di, cessare di	**arrêter de, cesser de**	*to stop doing smth.*
dipendere da	**dépendre de**	*to depend on*
vantarsi di	**se vanter de**	*to boast of*
dimentic-are di	**oublier de**	*to forget*
lamentarsi di	**se plaindre de**	*to complain of*
finire di	**finir de**	*to finish (doing smth.*
tentare di, cercare di	**tenter de, essayer de**	*to try to*
astenersi da	**se retenir de**	*to refrain from*
dissuadere da	**dissuader de**	*to dissuade from*

Italian	French	English
contempl-are di	**envisager de**	*to contemplate doing smth.*

> **NOTE:**
> In Italian, the meaning *"having just done something"* is conveyed by the word **appena** and the verb *finire* in the present perfect indicative (e.g. **Ho appena finito** *la mia lettera.* - *I have just finished my letter.*)
> In French, the verb *se rappeler* is used with the preposition **de** when: 1) it is followed by a noun (ex. *Je me rappelle de lui*); 2) one wants to remind someone of something so he/she does not forget it. In this case the preposition **de** is usually followed by an infinitive.

It. **Ha cercato (tentato) di convincerlo**;

Fr. Elle **a essayé (tenté) de le convaincre**.

- She tried to convince him.

It. **Ricordati di telefonarmi** più tardi oggi!

Fr. **Rappelle-toi de** me **téléphoner** plus tard aujourd'hui!

- Remember to call me later today!

It. **Sono appena arrivato** a casa;

Fr. Je **viens d'arriver** à la maison.

- I have just arrived home.

3. **Verbs followed by the preposition *per* (*Italian*) and *par* (*French*) + *an infinitive*.**

In Italian and French, these prepositions are found with verbs indicating *to begin* or *end by* or *opt to*.

CHAPTER 6: VERBS

Observe the list of the most frequent verbs followed by It. *per*; Fr. *par* + *infinitive* in the Romance languages:

Italian	French	English
finire per	**finir par**	to end (by doing something)
optare per	***opter pour**	to opt to

NOTE:
In French, the verb **opter** (to opt for) is used with the preposition **pour**.

It. Lui finisce sempre **per dire** questo;

Fr. Il finit toujours **par dire** cela.

- *He always **ends by saying** this.*

It. Alla fine, **ha optato per imparare** francese;

Fr. En fin de compte, elle **a opté pour apprendre** français.

- *In the end she **opted to learn** French.*

4. **Verbs followed by the preposition *de* (*French*) and *di* (*Italian*) + an infinitive.**

In Italian and French the following verbs are used with the prepositions *de* and *di* plus an infinitive. Observe the following:

Italian	French	English
minacciare di	**menacer de**	to threaten with (to)
contare di	**compter de**	to rely on, to remember
sognare di	**rêver de**	to think about, to contemplate doing smth.

It. Lui **sogna di vivere** in Brasile;

Fr. Il **rêve de vivre** au Brésil.

- He **dreams of living** in Brazil.

5. **Verbs followed by the preposition *de* (*French*) and *di* (*Italian*) + *an infinitive*.**

Below are the verbs and verbal combinations that express necessity and are used with the preposition **de** and **di** in French and Italian.

Italian	French	English
avere bisogno di	**avoir besoin de**	*to have to*
***bisogna**	***il faut**	*must (used impersonally)*

NOTE:

In Italian and French the modal verb <u>must</u> which is used impersonally does not require any preposition at all.

It. **Ho bisogno di partire** ora;

Fr. **J'ai besoin de partir** maintenant.

- **I have to leave** now.

Other verbs that are used with prepositions in the Romance languages must be learned individually since they are followed by different prepositions, which makes it difficult to combine them.

- **After independent prepositions:**

In the Romance languages some prepositions are used independently, which means that they are not associated with a preceding verb.

Below are the most common independent prepositions after which the infinitive is used in Italian and French:

Italian	French	English
prima di	avant de	*before*
per, allo scopo di	pour, afin de	*in order to*
senza	sans	*without*

It. Egli è uscito **senza guardar**mi;

Fr. Il est sorti **sans** me **regarder**.

- *He went out without looking at me.*

It. Ho detto che **per ricordar**gli;

Fr. Je l'ai dit **pour** lui **rappeler**.

- *I said it to remind him.*

- **After set phrases containing a preposition:**

    There are also a few set phrases consisting of the verbs *to have* or *to be*, a noun or an adjective and a preposition after which an infinitive is used in the Romance languages. This pattern corresponds to English "*to have/to be + adjective or noun + preposition +infinitive or gerund*". The following is a formula of such set phrases in the Romance languages.

Italian	French
avere (essere/stare) + adjective/noun + preposition + infinitive	**avoir (être)** + adjective/noun + preposition + infinitive

This occurs with a few common set phrases in Italian and French:

CHAPTER 6: VERBS

Italian	French	English
avere il tempo di	avoir le temps de	to have time
avere voglia di	avoir envie de	to have an inclination (to feel like)
avere vergogna di	avoir honte de	to be ashamed
avere paura di	avoir peur de	to be afraid of
avere fretta di	avoir hâte de	to be in a hurry
avere la possibilità di	avoir la possibilité de	to have an opportunity to
avere la fortuna di / essere fortunati	avoir de la chance / être chanceux	to be lucky
esser degno di	être digne de	to be worthy of
essere / stare contento di	être content de	to be glad to
essere / stare felice di	être heureux de	to be happy to

It. *Ho la fortuna di vivere qui*;

Fr. *J'ai de la chance de vivre ici.*

- *I am lucky to live here.*

It. *Ho voglia di andare in spiaggia*;

Fr. *J'ai envie d'aller à la plage.*

- *I feel like going to the beach.*

- **After expression with to be plus an adjective:**

CHAPTER 6: VERBS

In Italian, if used impersonally, expressions with It. ***essere + an adjective*** are usually followed by an infinitive, with no preceding preposition, while in French the preposition ***de*** is placed before an infinitive in this case. Also, the pronoun ***Il*** must be put before ***être*** (*to be*) when conjugated in French (e.g. ***il est***), which is equivalent to English "*It is*". Observe the formula:

Italian	French
It. ***essere + an adjective + infinitive***	***Il + être + adjective + de + infinitive***

It. *È facile cantare*;

Fr. *Il est facile de chanter*.

- *It is easy to sing.*

It. *È difficile tradurre* questo testo;

Fr. *Il est difficile de traduire* ce texte.

- *It is difficult to translate this text.*

NOTE:

Nevertheless, when this type of combination describes something particular or personal, ***da*** is used in Italian before the infinitive. French always retains ***de*** before the infinitive in this sort of expressions. It is worth saying that it happens basically with such adjectives as <u>easy</u> and <u>difficult</u>. Study the following:

It. Questa canzone? *È facile da* cantare;

Fr. Cette chanson? Elle est *facile de* chanter.

- *This song? It is easy to sing.*

It. Questo testo è ***difficile da*** tradurre;

Fr. Ce texte est ***difficile de*** traduire.

311

CHAPTER 6: VERBS

- This text is difficult to translate.

- **As an indirect command:**

    In Italian and French the infinitive is used to give instruction in the affirmative in different situations. For example:

    It. ***Spingere!***

    Fr. ***Pousser!***

    - Push!

NOTE:

In Italian, if the indirect command is in the negative, the past participle ***vietato*** (prohibited) normally precedes the infinitive:

It. ***Vietato Correre!***

Fr. ***Ne pas Courir!***

- Do not run!

Make in Causative Constructions in The Romance Languages

In the Romance languages the verb It. *fare*, Fr. *faire* - *make* is used to express the causative, which indicates the idea of having someone do something or having something made or done, and which corresponds to English causative construction "*make someone do something or have something done or made*".

NOTE:

In Italian and French the verb It. ***fare***, Fr. ***faire*** is followed by an infinitive and the object is normally put at the end of the phrase.

Study the following:

CHAPTER 6: VERBS

It. *Faccio cenare i bambini*;

Fr. *Je fais dîner les enfants.*

- *I make the children eat dinner.*

It should be mentioned that when the object is a noun, it follows the infinitive in Italian and French. However, when the object is a pronoun, it must precede the verb It. *fare*, Fr. *faire* in all the Romance languages, whereas in English it is placed after the verb *make*. For example:

It. *Faccio cenare i bambini - Li faccio cenare*;

Fr. *Je fais dîner les enfants - Je les fais dîner.*

- *I make (have) the children eat dinner - I make (have) them eat dinner.*

Did you know?

Belgium is the sixth largest importer of coffee with 4.3 million bags per year.

It must be remembered that in the affirmative imperative, the direct object noun must follow the infinitive, but nevertheless the direct object pronoun always precedes the infinitive in Italian and French.

It. *Fa' lavare il cane - Fallo lavare*;

Fr. *Fais laver le chien - Fais-le laver.*

- *Have the dog washed - Have it washed.*

When there are two objects in a causative sentence, one becomes the indirect object and the other will be the direct object. The indirect object is the person or thing being made to do something. The indirect object is introduced by the preposition *a* (in Italian) or *à* (in French) alone or in its articulated form.

Remember that all pronoun objects precede It. *fare*, Fr. *faire* except in the affirmative imperative in the Romance languages.

One object:

CHAPTER 6: VERBS

It. La madre fa leggere **la** figlia;

Fr. La mère fait lire **la** fille.

- *The mother has (makes) the daughter read.*

Two objects:

It. La madre fa leggere il testo **alla** figlia;

Fr. La mère fait lire le texte **à** la fille.

- *The mother has (makes) the daughter read the text.*

If either one or more of the objects is a pronoun, the object pronouns must precede the verb It. *fare*, Fr. *faire* in Italian and French. If necessary, revise object pronouns. Study the following:

Italian	French	English
La madre fa leggere il testo alla sua figlia.	La mère fait lire le texte à sa fille.	The mother has her daughter read the text.
La madre lo fa leggere alla sua figlia.	La mère le fait lire à sa fille.	The mother has her daughter read it.
La madre le fa leggere il testo.	La mère lui fait lire le texte.	The mother has her read the text.
La madre glielo fa leggere.	La mère le lui fait lire.	The mother has her read it.

Note that in Italian, the indirect pronoun is **loro** follows the infinitive, for example:

It. La madre ha fatto leggere i testi agli bambini.

La madre li ha fatti leggere ai bambini.

La madre ha fatto leggere **loro** i testi.

La madre li ha fatti leggere a **loro**.

- *The mother had the children read the texts.*

The mother had the children read them.

The mother had them read the texts.

The mother had them read them.

In Italian and French, in order to avoid possible ambiguity with the indirect object, the person doing the action can be introduced by **da** (in *Italian*) instead of **a**, and **par** (in *French*) instead of **à**. For instance, the sentence:

It. ***Lei fa pulire una macchina a John***;

Fr. ***Elle fait nettoyer une voiture à John***

can mean 1) *She has John clean a car* or 2) *She has a car cleaned to John*. If the first meaning is intended, It. **da** and Fr. **par** can replace It. **a** and Fr. **à**. Observe the following:

It. ***Lei fa pulire una macchina da John***;

Fr. ***Elle fait nettoyer une voiture par John***.

- *She has John clean a car.*

A reflexive pronoun can also be used with the verb It. ***fare***, Fr. ***faire*** in causative constructions in the Romance languages.

Let and Verbs of Perception + the Infinitive in the Romance Languages

In the Romance languages, after the verb It. ***lasciare*** and Fr. ***laisser*** - *let* and after the verbs of perception the infinitive is used. A few common verbs of perception are:

CHAPTER 6: VERBS

Italian	French	English
udire (sentire)	entendre	to hear
vedere	voir	to see
ascoltare	écouter	to listen
guardare	regarder	to look at
sentire	sentir	to feel

Unlike in English, in Italian and French, the infinitive precedes the noun. The pronoun is placed before the main verb. Generally, these verbs function similarly to the verb It. *fare*, Fr. *faire* in causative constructions. Study the following:

It. Lascio Paula terminare la lezione -> Le lascio terminare la lezione -> Gliela lascio terminare.

Fr. Je laisse Paula terminer la leçon -> Je lui laisse terminer la leçon -> Je la lui laisse terminer or Je lui laisse la terminer.

- I let Paula finish the lesson -> I let her finish the work -> I let her finish it.

Did you know?

Lucca is a city in Tuscany, Central Italy near the Tyrrhenian Sea. The city is famous for its well-preserved Renaissance walls encircling the historic city center.

It. Vedo leggere Ana -> La vedo leggere.

Fr. Je vois lire Ana -> Je la vois lire.

- I see Ana reading -> I see her reading.

It. Ha sentito cantare sua moglie -> L'ha sentita cantare.

Fr. Il a entendu chanter sa femme -> Il l'a entendue chanter.

- He heard his wife singing -> He heard her singing.

NOTE:

In Italian and French the past participle agrees with the preceding direct object when the object fulfills the action indicated by the infinitive.

That is to say, in the expression It. <u>la moglie che lui ha sentita cantare</u> and Fr. <u>la femme qu'il a entendue chanter</u>, the wife did the singing and, thus, the past participle agrees.

*But nevertheless, if the expression were It. **Ha sentito cantare la canzone** => **L'ha sentita cantare**; Fr. **Il a entendu chanter la chanson** => **il l'a entendu chanter** - He heard the song sung => He heard it sung, the past participle would not agree as it. canzone, Fr. chanson is the object of It. cantare and fr. chanter.*

The Compound Infinitive

In the Romance languages, the compound infinitive is formed with the auxiliaries It. **essere/avere** and Fr. **être/avoir** plus the past participle of the acting verb, which is the equivalent of *having + the past participle* in English. Remember that the past participle which is used with the auxiliary verb to be (It. **essere**, Fr. **être**) always agrees in gender and number with the subject in Italian and French.

Below is the table showing an example of the compound infinitive in the Romance languages:

Italian	French
avere parlato *essere venuto(a)(i)(e)*	*avoir parlé* *être venu(e)(s)(es)*

NOTE:

In Italian it is quite common to drop the final *-e* of the auxiliary verb (It. **avere, essere**) in the compound infinitive, for example: **aver parlato, esser venuto**.

Use of the Compound Infinitive

The compound infinitive is usually used after the prepositions:

Italian	French	English
dopo	**après**	*after*
senza	**sans**	*without*

Did you know?

Chad is a landlocked nation in Central Africa. It is the 5th biggest country in Africa in terms of area. The country's official languages are Arabic and French. The main religions of Chad are Islam (over 50%) and Christianity (around 5%). Its capital N'Djamena is the largest city.

It. **Dopo aver terminato** il lavoro, è andato al bar;

Fr. **Après avoir terminé** le travail, il est allé au bar.

- **After having finished** his work, he went to the bar.

It. Lei è tornata dal Brasile **senza essere stata** a Rio de Janeiro;

Fr. Elle est revenue du Brésil **sans avoir été** à Rio de Janeiro.

- She returned from Brazil **without having been** to Rio de Janeiro.

Reflexive Verbs

Overview

In the Romance languages, reflexive verbs are always used with an object pronoun which refers to the same person or things as the verb's subject. In other words, the action of reflexive verbs is executed and received by the subject. In English, the object pronoun of reflexive verbs has such suffixes as -*self* or -*selves* (e.g. *I wash myself, they wash themselves*).

Formation of Reflexive Verbs

In Italian and French, reflexive verbs are formed by using the appropriate reflexive pronouns (**See Reflexive Pronouns p.91**), which

CHAPTER 6: VERBS

can change according to the subject of the verb. In the infinitive form, the reflexive pronouns is put after the verb in Italian, while in French it is placed before the verb (e.g. It. *lavarsi*; Fr. *se laver*).

> **NOTE:**
> In Italian the *-e* of the infinitive ending is dropped before attaching a reflexive pronoun to it.

When conjugated, reflexive pronouns are placed before the verb in Italian and French.

It must be remembered that in contrast with English, reflexive pronouns cannot be omitted in Italian and French.

Observe the following forms of the present tense of It. *lavarsi*, Fr. *se laver* - *to wash*:

Italian	French	English
io **mi lavo**	je, j'**me lave**	*I wash myself*
tu **ti lavi**	tu **te laves**	*you wash yourself*
lui/lei/Lei **si lava**	il,elle,on **se lave**	*he/she/it wash himself/ herself/itself*
noi **ci laviamo**	nous **nous lavons**	*we wash ourselves*
voi **vi lavate**	vous **vous lavez**	*you wash yourselves*
loro/Loro **si lavano**	ils/elles **se lavent**	*they wash themselves*

> **NOTE:**
> In French *me* becomes *m'*, *te* becomes *t'* and *se* becomes *s'* before a vowel or a mute h (e.g. je *m'amuse*; tu *t'habille*; il *s'arrête*.).

319

Reflexive Verbs with a Reflexive Meaning

Below is a list of the most common reflexive verbs of the Romance languages:

Italian	French	English
alzarsi	se lever	*to get up*
arrabbiarsi	se fâcher	*to get angry*
chiamarsi	s'appeler	*to be called*
coricarsi	se coucher	*to go to bed*
coprirsi	se couvrir	*to cover oneself*
divertirsi	se divertir/s'amuser	*to have fun*
ferirsi	se blesser	*to wound oneself*
fidarsi di	se fier à	*to trust*
innamorarsi di	tomber amoureux de	*to fall in love with*
lamentarsi di	se plaindre	*to complain about*
lavarsi	se laver	*to wash oneself*
mettersi	se mettre	*to put on (clothing)*
pentirsi di	se repentir de	*to repent of*
prepararsi per	se préparer pour	*to get ready*
pulirsi	se nettoyer	*to clean oneself*
radersi	se raser	*to shave*
ricordarsi di	se rappeler (de)/se souvenir de	*to remember*
sedersi	s'asseoir	*to sit down*
sentirsi	se sentir/se porter	*to feel*
spogliarsi	se déshabiller	*to undress*

CHAPTER 6: VERBS

Italian	French	English
sposarsi con	se marier avec	to get married
svegliarsi	se réveiller	to wake up
vestirsi	s'habiller	to get dressed
voltarsi	se tourner	to turn
sbrogliarsi/cavarsi (togliersi) d'impiccio	se débrouiller/ se tirer (d'affaire)	to manage, to handle a situation
chiedersi	se demander	to wonder
affrettarsi	se dépêcher/se presser	to hurry
interessarsi a	s'intéresser à	to be interested in
farsi beffe di	se moquer de	to make fun of
occuparsi di	s'occuper de	to be busy with, to take care of
accadere	se passer	to happen
pettinarsi	se peigner	to comb one's hair
riposarsi	se reposer	to rest
trovarsi	se trouver	to be located
annoiarsi	s'ennuyer	to get bored
passeggiare	se promener	to take a walk
addormentarsi	s'endormir	to fall asleep
bagnarsi	se baigner	to bathe
pulirsi	se brosser	to brush oneself
distrarsi	se distraire	to distract oneself
docciarsi	se doucher	to shower
andarsene	s'en aller	to leave
truccarsi	se maquiller	to put on makeup

CHAPTER 6: VERBS

Italian	French	English
azzittirsi	se taire	*to be quiet*

The verbs in *italics* are not reflexive.

It. ***Mi corico*** più presto oggi;

Fr. ***Je me couche*** plus tôt aujourd'hui.

- I go to bed earlier today.

Did you know?

The flag of Vatican City has two bands of yellow, which are vertical and white, in the center of which are the crossed keys of Saint Peter and papal miter.

It. Questa donna ***si lamenta*** tutto il tempo;

Fr. Cette femme ***se plaint*** tout le temps.

- This woman complains all the time.

Italian and French Compound Tenses with Reflexive Verbs

It must be memorized that all reflexive verbs are used with the appropriate conjugated verb ***essere*** (in *Italian*) and ***être*** (in *French*) - *to be* when forming compound tenses. Also, the past participle of reflexive verbs agrees in gender and number with the subject in Italian and French.

It. ***Si è alzata*** alle 6 di ieri;

Fr. ***Elle s'est levée*** à 6 heures hier.

- She got up at 6 a.m. yesterday.

It. I miei genitori ***si sono sposati*** vent'anni fa;

Fr. Mes parents ***se sont mariés*** il y a vingt ans.

CHAPTER 6: VERBS

- My parents got married twenty years ago.

Reflexive Verbs with Parts of the Body

In the Romance languages, if a part of the body is used with reflexive verbs, one should utilize the definite article rather than the possessive adjective. Study the following:

Did you know?

Europe's first skyscraper was built in Antwerp in 1928. It's called "De Boerentoren" ("Farmer's Tower") and is still the second tallest structure in the city, after the Cathedral of Our Lady.

It. Mary si lava **la** faccia;

Fr. Mary se lave **le** visage.

- Mary washes her face.

It. Mary si lava **le** mani;

Fr. Mary se lave **les** mains.

- Mary washes her hands.

Reciprocal Reflexive Verbs

Reciprocal reflexive verbs refer to persons that are acting upon one another. This corresponds to English *"each other"* or *"one another"*. Below is a partial list of the most frequent reflexive verbs with a reciprocal meaning in Italian and French:

Italian	French	English
abbracciarsi	s'embrasser	*to embrace each other (one another)*
aiutarsi	s'aider	*to help each other (one another)*
amarsi	s'aimer	*to love each other (one another)*
ammirarsi	s'admirer	*to admire each other (one another)*

CHAPTER 6: VERBS

Italian	French	English
baciarsi	s'embrasser	to kiss each other (one another)
conoscersi	se connaître	to know each other (one another)
incontrarsi	se rencontrer	to meet each other
innamorarsi	tomber amoureux	to fall in love (with each other)
piacersi	se plaire	to like each other (one another)
riconoscersi	se reconnaître	to recognize each other (one another)
rispettarsi	se respecter	to respect each other (one another)
rivedersi	se revoir	to see each other again (one another)
salutarsi	se saluer	to greet each other (one another)
scriversi	s'écrire	to write to each other (one another)
sposarsi	se marier	to get married
vedersi	se voir	to see each other (one another)
visitarsi	se visiter	to visit each other (one another)
volersi bene	s'aimer bien	to like/love each other (one another)
consolarsi	se consoler	to comfort each other (one another)

It. Non *si vedono* molto frequentemente;

Fr. Ils ne *se voient* pas très fréquemment.

- *They do not **see each other** very often.*

> **Did you know?**
>
> *Bari is a port and university city on the Adriatic Sea, in southern Italy. It is known for its narrow streets, the 11th century Basilica of Saint Nicholas and the Cathedral of San Sabino. The Murat quartier has 19th-century architecture, a promenade on the sea, and major shopping areas.*

It. Gli insegnanti *si salutano* all'università ogni mattina;

Fr. Les enseignants *se saluent* à l'université tous les matins..

- *Teachers **greet each other** in the university every morning.*

Since the reflexive and the reciprocal forms are similar in the Romance languages, confusion may occur in some cases. For instance the phrase:

It. Loro *si amano*;

Fr. Ils *s'aiment*.

could mean "*They love themselves*" or "*They love each other*". In order to avoid ambiguity, the following phrases may be supplemented to reflexive verbs:

Italian	French	English
l'un l'altro	**l'un l'autre**	each other/ one another
reciproca-mente (a vicenda)	**réciproque-ment**	mutually

It. ***Ci amiamo l'un l'altro***;

Fr. ***Nous nous aimons l'un l'autre***.

- We love each other.

It. Gli avversari **si rispettano reciprocamente**;

Fr. Les opposants **se respectent mutuellement**.

- Opponents respect each other.

Reflexive Verbs Versus Non-Reflexive Verbs

In the Romance languages, verbs can function both reflexively and non-reflexively. Remember if the action is performed and received by the same subject, the verb is reflexive. However, when the action is executed on another person or object, the verb is not reflexive. Study the following sentences:

Reflexive	*Non-reflexive*
It. Tom **si lava**; Fr. Tom **se lave**. *- Tom washes himself.*	It. Tom **lava il cane**; Fr. Tom **lave le chien**. *- Tom washes the dog.*
It. Sarah **si corica**; Fr. Sarah **se couche**. *- Sarah goes to bed.*	It. Sarah **corica i bambini**; Fr. Sarah **couche les enfants**. *- Sarah puts the children to bed.*

It is noticeable that the non-reflexive verbs are transitive, i.e. they take a direct object. Observe the difference in meaning between the following reflexive and non-reflexive verbs in Italian and French:

	Reflexive	*Non-reflexive*
Italian	**aiutarsi**	**aiutare**
French	**s'aider**	**aider**
English	to help each other	to help (someone)
Italian	**alzarsi**	**alzare**

French	**se lever**	**lever**
English	*to get up*	*to raise, to lift*
Italian	**chiamarsi**	**chiamare**
French	**s'appeler**	**appeler**
English	*to be called*	*to call (someone)*
Italian	**prepararsi**	**preparare**
French	**se préparer**	**préparer**
English	*to get ready*	*to prepare (someone or something)*
Italian	**ricordarsi di**	**ricordare**
French	**se rappeler (de)**	**rappeler**
English	*to remember*	*to remind (someone or something)*
Italian	**vestirsi**	**vestire**
French	**s'habiller**	**habiller**
English	*to get dressed*	*to dress (someone), to wear (something)*

Reflexive Verbs in the Infinitive in the Romance languages

In Italian, the reflexive pronoun either follows the reflexive verb, attaching to it, or precedes the first conjugated verb in the sentence. In French, the reflexive pronoun invariably precedes the reflexive verb in the infinitive. Remember that the pronoun always agrees with the subject in all the Romance languages.

Did you know?

Burkina Faso is a francophone, landlocked country in West Africa. The two words "Burkina" and "Faso" come from different languages spoken in the country. "Burkina" comes from Mossi and means "honest". "Faso" comes from the Dyula language and means "fatherland".

It. *Ti* devi *affrettare* or *Devi affrettarti*

Fr. Tu as besoin de *te dépêcher*.

- *You need to hurry up.*

It. Sto per *vestirmi* or *Mi* sto per *vestire*;

Fr. Je vais *m'habiller*.

- *I am going to get dressed.*

Reflexive *se* (French) and *si* (Italian) as an Indefinite Subject

The reflexive pronoun *se* in French and *si* in Italian can be used as an impersonal or indefinite subject, which is equivalent to English *people, they, one* or *we*. In the Romance languages the verb is invariably 3rd person singular (**See also Alternatives to Passive Voice in the Romance Languages p.337**).

NOTE:

In French, the impersonal pronoun **on** *must be used in this case.*

It. *Si può* fumare qui?

Fr. *Peut-on* fumer ici?

- *Can we smoke here?*

CHAPTER 6: VERBS

Frequent Reflexive Verb of *Becoming*

The following verb meaning "*to become*" must be memorized since it is very common and can be useful for the learners to apply. This verb implies intentional effort made by the subject.

Italian	French	English
farsi	se faire	to become

It. Lui *si è fatto* conoscere;

Fr. Il *s'est fait* connaître.

- He **became** successful.

Affirmative Imperative of Reflexive verbs in the Romance Languages

In the affirmative imperative, in Italian, the reflexive pronoun is attached to the end of the verb to form one word, while in French, the reflexive pronoun is joined to the verb by a hyphen.

NOTE:

*In Italian, the reflexive pronoun is separated from the verb in **loro** form. In French, te changes to **toi** in the affirmative imperative.*

Did you know?

ATM users in Vatican City are still given the option to use Latin to perform transactions. The Vatican Bank is the only one in the world to do so.

It. **Siedi_ti_** qui!

Fr. **Assieds-_toi_** ici!

- Sit down here!

It. **Alzate_vi_**!

Fr. **Levez-_vous_**!

- Get up! (polite form)

329

CHAPTER 6: VERBS

Negative Imperative of Reflexive Verbs in the Romance Languages

In the negative imperative, the reflexive pronoun always precedes the verb in French.

> **NOTE:**
> In Italian, the reflexive pronoun can be either joined to the verb or be separated and put before the verb. it is also notable that with formal **Lei**, the pronoun is always placed before the verb.

It. Non **lamentarti**! or Non **ti lamentare**!

Fr. **Ne te plains pas**!

- *Do not complain!*

> **NOTE:**
> In French, the reflexive pronoun **te** does not alter in the negative imperative.

The Passive Voice

Overview

Generally, passive constructions are formed when the objects of active constructions become the subjects of the passive verbs. The following is the example of a passive construction in English:

Active voice	Passive voice
My friend wrote the book.	**The book was written by my friend.**

The passive voice in the Romance languages is not very different from English but it is used less frequently in Spanish, Portuguese, Italian and French than in English. Moreover, passive constructions are often replaced by alternatives in the Romance languages.

Formation of the Passive Voice

The passive voice is formed by using the conjugated forms of the verbs It. *essere* and Fr. *être* - *to be* plus the past participle of the verb. However, unlike in English, in the Romance languages the past participle agrees in gender and in number with the subject of the passive phrase. The person or the agent performing the action is normally introduced by the preposition *da* (in *Italian*) and *par* (in *French*), which corresponds to English *by*.

NOTE:

In Italian the preposition It. *da* contract with the definite articles (**See Articles p.61**):

Italian
il, lo, la, l' + da = dal, dallo, dalla, dall'

Below is the table that shows the formation of the passive voice in the Romance languages:

Italian	*essere*	+ Past Participle +	*da*	**Italian**
French	*être*		*par*	**French**

Active voice	Passive voice
It. **Mio padre ha comprato la casa.** Fr. **Mon père a acheté la maison.** - *My father bought the house.*	It. **La casa è stata comprata da mio padre.** Fr. **La maison a été achetée par mon père.** - *The house was bought by my father.*

CHAPTER 6: VERBS

Like in English, in the Romance languages the passive voice can be used in all tenses, which means that all tenses in the active voice can be replaced by an equivalent with the verb in the passive voice.

Below is the illustration of all forms of the passive voice in Italian and French. The 1st person singular of the regular verb It. **amare**; Fr. **aimer** - *to love* was taken as an example.

	Italian	French
	Indicative mood	
	Present tenses	
Present tense	io sono amato(a)	je suis aimé(e)
Present Perfect	io sono stato amato(a)	j'ai été aimé(e)
	Past tenses	
Preterite	io fui amato(a)	je fus aimé(e)
Imperfect	io ero amato(a)	j'étais aimé(e)
Past Perfect	io fui stato amato(a)	j'eus été aimé(e)
Pluperfect	io ero stato amato(a)	j'avais été aimé(e)
	Future tenses	
Future	io sarò amato(a)	je serai aimé(e)
Future Perfect	io sarò stato amato(a)	—
	Conditionals	
Conditional	io sarei amato(a)	je serais aimé(e)
Conditional Perfect	io sarei stato amato(a)	j'aurais été aimé(e)
	Subjunctive mood	
	Present tenses	

CHAPTER 6: VERBS

	Italian	French
Present tense	che io sia amato(a)	que je sois aimé(e)
Present Perfect	che io sia stato amato(a)	que j'aie été aimé(e)
	Past tenses	
Past (Imperfect) tense	che io fossi amato(a)	que je fusse aimé(e)
Past Perfect	che io fossi stato amato(a)	que j'eusse été aimé(e)
	Future tenses	
Future tense	——	——
Future Perfect	——	——
	Imperative mood	
	sii amato(a) (tu) sia amato(a) (Lei) siamo amati(e) (noi) siate amati(e) (voi) siano amati(e) (Loro)	sois aimé(e) (tu) soyez aimé(e)s(es) (vous) soyons aimé(e)s (nous) soyez aimé(e)s(es) (vous) soyez aimé(e)s(es) (vous)
	Infinitive	
	essere amato(a)	être aimé(e)
	Compound infinitive	
	essere stato amato(a)	avoir été aimé(e)
	Present Participle (Gerund)	
	(gerund) essendo amato(a) (part.pres) essere amato(a)	étant aimé(e)
	Compound Present Participle	
	——	——

	Italian		French
	Past Participle (Gerund)		
	essendo stato amato (a)i	stato amato (a)i	aimé(e)s; ayant été aimé(e)s

Here are examples of all the forms of the passive voice used in sentences in the Romance languages. Even though some of the examples below may seem odd to a native speaker, they are given just in order to illustrate the usage of the passive voice:

Present simple:

It. La lettera *è inviata* da sua moglie.

Fr. *La lettre est envoyée* par sa femme.

- *The letter is sent by his wife.*

Present Perfect:

It. Ultimamente, la lettera *è stata inviata* da sua moglie.

Fr. Récemment, la lettre *a été envoyée* par sa femme.

- *Lately, the letter has been sent by his wife.*

Preterite:

> *Did you know?*
>
> The largest Freemason temple on the European continent is the Great Temple in Brussels (at 79, Rue de Laeken).

It. La lettera *fu inviata* da sua moglie.

Fr. La lettre *fut envoyée* par sa femme.

- *The letter was sent by his wife.*

CHAPTER 6: VERBS

Imperfect:

It. Anticamente, le lettere ***erano inviate*** da sua moglie.
Fr. Anciennement, les lettres ***étaient envoyées*** par sa femme.
- *In the past, the letters **used to be sent** by his wife.*

Past Perfect:

It. Molte lettere ***furono state inviate*** da sua moglie.
Fr. Beaucoup de lettres ***eurent été envoyées*** par sa femme.
- *Many letters **had been sent** by his wife.*

Pluperfect:

It. La lettera ***era stata inviata*** da sua moglie.
Fr. La lettre ***avait été envoyée*** par sa femme.
- *The letter **had been sent** by his wife.*

Future:

It. La lettera ***sarà inviata*** da sua moglie.
Fr. La lettre ***sera envoyée*** par sa femme.
- *The letter **will be sent** by his wife.*

Future Perfect:

It. Domani alle nove, la lettera ***sarà stata inviata*** da sua moglie.

Fr. Demain à neuf heures, la lettre **aura été envoyée** par sa femme.
- *Tomorrow at nine o'clock, the letter **will have been sent** by his wife.*

Conditional:

It. La lettera **sarebbe inviata** da sua moglie.
Fr. La lettre **serait envoyée** par sa femme.
- *The letter **would be sent** by his wife.*

Conditional Perfect:

It. La lettera **sarebbe stata inviata** da sua moglie.
Fr. La lettre **aurait été envoyée** par sa femme.
- *The letter **would have been sent** by his wife.*

Present Subjunctive:

It. **È urgente che** la lettera **sia inviata** da sua moglie.
Fr. **Il est urgent que** la lettre **soit envoyée** par sa femme.
- ***It is urgent that** the letter **be sent** by his wife.*

Present Perfect Subjunctive:

It. **Sono felice che** la lettera **sia stata inviata** da sua moglie.
Fr. **Je suis heureux que** la lettre **ait été envoyée** par sa femme.
- ***I am happy that** the letter **has been sent** by his wife.*

CHAPTER 6: VERBS

> **Did you know?**
>
> *Ferrara, a city in northern Italy, is known for its palaces erected by the powerful Renaissance clan, the Este family. The Este Castle (It. Castello Estense), located in the center of the town, is one of the iconic landmarks of Ferrara.*

Past (Imperfect) Subjunctive:

It. ***Era urgente che*** la lettera ***fosse inviata*** da sua moglie.

Fr. ***Il était urgent que*** la lettre ***fût envoyée*** par sa femme.

- ***It was urgent for*** the letter ***to be sent*** by his wife.

Past Perfect Subjunctive:

It. ***Io speravo che*** la lettera ***fosse stata inviata*** da sua moglie.

Fr. ***J'espérais que*** la lettre ***eût été envoyée*** par sa femme.

- ***I hoped that*** the letter ***had been sent*** by his wife.

French Passive Voice with *de*

In French ***de*** is normally used with verbs that indicate condition or emotion, for example:

Fr. La mère est aimé ***de*** ses enfants.

- *The mother is loved **by** her children.*

Fr. La rue est couverte ***de*** neige.

- *The street is covered **with** snow.*

Alternatives to Passive Voice in the Romance Languages

It is noticeable that the passive voice is not frequently used in the Romance language and it can be sometimes overused by English speakers. Usually there is a number of equivalent constructions which are more commonly utilized instead in everyday speech in Italian and French:

- **To convert a passive construction into an active voice.**

    If the agent is expressed, the passive voice in Italian and French should be avoided, especially in informal speech, by converting a passive construction into an active one. Observe the following:

	Passive		*Active*
Italian	Questa canzone è stata scritta da un cantante popolare.	>	Un cantante popolare ha scritto questa canzone.
French	Cette chanson a été écrite par un chanteur populaire.	>	Un chanteur populaire a écrit cette chanson.
English	- *This song was written by a popular singer.*	>	- *A popular singer wrote this song.*

- **Using an indefinite 3rd person plural active verb** (*in Italian*) **or indefinite pronoun *on*** (*in French*).

    When the agent is not given, it may be possible to replace the passive voice by using an indefinite 3rd person plural in Italian or *on* in French meaning "*they*", "*people*" and an active verb.

NOTE: *in French, when **on** is used, the verb is conjugated in the 3rd person singular.*

It. ***Mi hanno sorpreso***;

Fr. ***On m'a surpris.***

- *I was surprised.*

CHAPTER 6: VERBS

- **Using the reflexive.**

Constructions with the reflexive pronoun *se* (*in French*) and *si* (*in Italian*) with the 3rd person singular or plural form of the verb are rather common in the Romance languages. However, there are a few points to be remembered.

A. These constructions are predominantly used when the subject (the agent) by whom the action is fulfilled is not a person or unimportant. In this case the verb agrees with the subject in number:

It. ***Lo spagnolo si parla*** in questo paese;

Fr. ***L'espagnol se parle*** dans ce pays.

- *Spanish is spoken in this country.*

Did you know?

Senegal is a country in West Africa. The name "Senegal" comes from the Wolof language "Sunuu Gaal", that means "Our Pirogue". It resulted from a misunderstanding between Portuguese sailors and Wolof fishermen in the 15th century.

It. ***I libri si vendono*** in questo negozio;

Fr. ***Les livres se vendent*** dans ce magasin.

- *The book are sold in this shop.*

B. When an indirect object is involved, French utilizes ***on***. Study the following:

Fr. ***On*** a donné les billets d'avion à Ana.

- *Ana was given the flight tickets.*

CHAPTER 7: NUMBERS, TIME AND DATE

Numbers

Overview

In the Romance languages, numerals can be in four forms, i.e. **cardinals** (e.g. *one, two, three, four,* etc.), **ordinals** (e.g. *first, second, third, fourth,* etc.), **fractions** (e.g. *half, one third,* etc.) and **collectives** (e.g. *a couple, a dozen*).

Cardinal Numbers

The Italian and French cardinal numbers are as follows:

	Italian	French
0	zero	zéro
1	uno/una	un/une
2	due	deux
3	tre	trois
4	quattro	quatre
5	cinque	cinq
6	sei	six
7	sette	sept
8	otto	huit
9	nove	neuf
10	dieci	dix

CHAPTER 7: NUMBERS, TIME AND DATE

	Italian	French
11	undici	onze
12	dodici	douze
13	tredici	treize
14	quattordici	quatorze
15	quindici	quinze
16	sedici	seize
17	diciassette	dix-sept
18	diciotto	dix-huit
19	diciannove	dix-neuf
20	venti	vingt
21	ventuno	vingt et un
22	ventidue	vingt-deux
23	ventitré	vingt-trois
24	ventiquattro	vingt-quatre
25	venticinque	vingt-cinq
26	ventisei	vingt-six
27	ventisette	vingt-sept
28	ventotto	vingt-huit
29	ventinove	vingt-neuf
30	trenta	trente
31	trentuno	trente et un
32	trentadue	trente-deux

CHAPTER 7: NUMBERS, TIME AND DATE

	Italian	French
33	trentatré	trente-trois
40	quaranta	quarante
50	cinquanta	cinquante
60	sessanta	soixante
70	settanta	soixante-dix
80	ottanta	quatre-vingts
90	novanta	quatre-vingt-dix
100	cento	cent
101	cento uno (centouno, centuno)	cent un
102	cento due (centodue)	cent deux
103	cento tre (centotré)	cent trois
200	duecento	deux cents
201	duecento uno (duecento-uno, duecent-uno)	deux cent un
202	duecento due (duecentodue)	deux cent deux
300	trecento	trois cents
400	quattro-cento	quatre cents
500	cinque-cento	cinq cents
600	seicento	six cents
700	settecento	sept cents
800	ottocento	huit cents

CHAPTER 7: NUMBERS, TIME AND DATE

	Italian	French
900	novecento	neuf cents
1000	mille	mille
1001	mille uno	mille un
1100	mille cento	mille cent
1101	mille cento uno	mille cent un
1200	mille duecento	mille deux cents
2 000	due mila (duemila)	deux mille
10 000	dieci mila (diecimila)	dix mille
20 000	venti mila (ventimila)	vingt mille
100 000	cento mila (centomila)	cent mille
200 000	duecento mila (duecentomila)	deux cent mille
1 000 000	un milione	un million
2 000 000	due milioni	deux millions
10 000 000	dieci milioni	dix millions
100 000 000	cento milioni	cent millions
1 000 000 000	un miliardo	un milliard
2 000 000 000	due miliardi	deux milliards
1 000 000 000 000	un trilione	un billion
2 000 000 000 000	due trilioni	deux billions

CHAPTER 7: NUMBERS, TIME AND DATE

In the Romance languages, It. **uno**; Fr. **un** agree in gender with a noun. Observe the following:

| It. **un** libro;
Fr. **un** livre.
- *one book.* | It. **una** casa;
Fr. **une** maison.
- *one house.* |

NOTE:

*Italian **uno** is predominantly used while counting. It becomes **un** before a masculine noun and **una** in front of a feminine noun.*

However, the feminine form of It. **una**; Fr. **una** is not widely used before It. **mille**; Fr. **mille**. It also should be mentioned that It. **un** and Fr. **un** are not usually used before It. **cento** and **mille** and Fr. **cent** and **mille** in Italian and French.

Did you know?

San Marino, one of the smallest republics in the world, is located in the Emilia-Romagna region of Italy, south of the city of Rimini on the northern part of the Adriatic coast.

Study the following:

It. **cento / mille** libri;

Fr. **cent / mille** livres.

- *a hundred / a thousand books.*

In the Romance languages It. **un milione** (*due milioni*), **un miliardo** (*due milliardi*), **un trilione** (*due trilioni*); Fr. **un million, un milliard, un billion** take the preposition **de** (in French) and **di** (in Italian) before a noun. Below is a table demonstrating this rule:

Italian	un milione, un miliardo, un trilione	+ **di** (Italian)	+ **noun**
French	un million, un milliard, un billion	+ **de** (French)	

It. ***un milione di*** euro

Fr. ***un million d'***euros

- *a million euros*

Italian and French use dots to separate thousands while English uses a comma, and a comma is used to mark the decimal in the Romance languages whereas English utilizes a point. Observe the following:

Italian and French	English
1.250.300 2,50	1,250,300 2.50

Peculiarities of Spelling Rules of Cardinal Numbers in the Romance Languages

Despite a certain number of common rules, each Romance language has its own set of peculiar spelling rules of cardinal numbers, which ought to be regarded individually.

Italian

It is notable that Italian numbers 11-99 are combined into one word. Also, the final vowel of ***venti, trenta, quaranta, cinquanta, sessanta, settanta, ottanta*** and ***novanta*** is dropped while the numbers *uno* and *otto* are added. When ***tre*** is added to ***venti, trenta, quaranta, cinquanta***, etc. the final *-e* of ***tre*** is accented (e.g. ***ventitré, trentatré, quarantatré, cinquantatré***, etc.). Remember that the final vowel of ***ventuno, trentuno, quarantuno, cinquantuno, sessantuno, settantuno, ottantuno*** and ***novantuno*** is dropped before nouns (e.g. ***ventun libri***, etc.).

Italian ***cento*** is invariable. The numbers that designate tens and units - *one, two*, etc. are usually added but not attached. However, some people attach them. The compounds of ***cento*** are attached (e.g. ***duecento, trecento, quattrocento***, etc.).

French

It must be noted that in numbers 21, 31, 41, 51, 61, 71 the *et* is used and there is no hyphen. Observe the following:

21	vingt et un	51	cinquante et un
31	trente et un	61	soixante et un
41	quarante et un	71	soixante et onze

French *et* is not used in 81, 91, 101 and a hyphen is used in 81 and 91. Study the following:

| 81 | quatre-vingt-un | 101 | cent un |
| 91 | quatre-vingt-onze | | |

If **vingt** and **cent** are multiplied, they become plural (e.g. *quatre vingts, deux cents*). However, if **vingt** and **cent** are followed by another number, they remain singular (e.g. *vingt-huit, cent cinq*).

In French **mille** never becomes plural (e.g. *quatre mille, trois mille soixante*).

Phrases of Approximation Used with Cardinal Numbers

Following are phrases of approximation which are used with cardinal numbers in the Romance languages:

Italian	French	English
approssimativamente	approximativement	*approximately*
all'incirca	autour de	*about, around*
più o meno	plus ou moins	*more or less*
circa	à peu près de	*near, close to*
su	environ	*about, around*

CHAPTER 7: NUMBERS, TIME AND DATE

Italian	French	English
qualcosa di	**chose de**	*about*
qualcosa così	**quelque chose comme ça**	*thereabouts*
come	**comme**	*some*

It. È situato a **approssimativamente** 15 (quindici) chilometri dalla spiaggia;

Fr. Il est situé à **approximativement** 15 (quinze) kilomètres de la plage.

- *It is situated at **approximately** 15 kilometres from the beach.*

It. Duecento chilometri o **qualcosa così**;

Fr. Deux cents kilomètres ou **quelque chose comme ça**.

- *Two hundred kilometres or **thereabouts**.*

Did you know?

Belgium has more comic book makers per square kilometer than any other country in the world (even Japan).

It. **Più o meno** venti euro;

Fr. **Plus ou moins** vingt euros.

- ***More or less** twenty euros.*

It. Ha **all'incirca** cinquant'anni;

Fr. Il a **autour de** cinquante ans.

- *He is **about** fifty years old.*

Use of Cardinal Numbers

In Italian and French, cardinal numbers are generally used:

CHAPTER 7: NUMBERS, TIME AND DATE

- **To count:**

    It. ***uno, due, tre…***

    Fr. ***un, deux, trois…***

    - *one, two, three…*

- **To indicate dates (See Dates p.359):**

In contrast with English, cardinal numbers are used in the Romance languages for days of the month except for the 1st when it is necessary to use the ordinal number: It. ***il primo***; Fr. ***le premier***. For example:

    It. ***Il primo*** di maggio;

    Fr. ***Le premier*** mai.

    - *The first of May.*

NOTE:

*A complete date in Italian and French is composed of the masculine definite article It. **il**, Fr. **le** + a cardinal number + month + year.*

Below is a table demonstrating the formation of a full date in the Romance languages:

Italian	il + *a cardinal number + month + year*
French	le + *a cardinal number + month + year*

Study the following example:

    It. Oggi è ***il 10 marzo 2018***;

    Fr. Aujourd'hui c'est ***le 10 mars 2018***.

    - *Today is the 10th of March, 2018.*

CHAPTER 7: NUMBERS, TIME AND DATE

- **To tell the time of day (See Time p.363):**

In Italian, hours are usually expressed using a form of **essere** + *the feminine definite article* It. **la, l'** or **le** (in order to agree with the number of unmentioned **ora** or **ore** (Italian) - *hour or hours*) + *a cardinal number*. In French, hours are normally expressed using the pronoun **il** + *a* form of the verb **être** + *a cardinal number* + *the word* **heure(-s)** - *hour(-s)*.

NOTE:

*In Italian, the appropriate form of the verb **ser** and **essere** must be selected, i.e. the 3rd person singular for "one o'clock" and plural for other hours except in French, where only the 3rd person singular of the verb **être** is used when indicating the time of day.*

The table below shows the idea of how to tell the time of day in the Romance languages:

Italian	**essere (è/sono)** + **la,l'/le** + *a cardinal number*
French	**il** + **être (est)** + *a cardinal number* + **heure(-s)**

Observe the following:

It. Che ora è? (Che ore sono?) - *È l'una* (*Sono le tre*);

Fr. Quelle heure est-il? - *Il est une heure* (*Il est trois heures*).

- *What time is it? It is one o'clock (It is three o'clock)*

In the Romance languages, minutes past the hour are usually added by the use of It. *e*, Fr. *et* + *cardinal number*. However, French *et* can be dropped. Minute(-s) is not normally used.

It. Sono le sei *e* dieci;

Fr. Il est six heures dix.

- *It's six ten (It's ten past six).*

- **To indicate age:**

In the Romance languages, one must conjugate the verb It. ***avere***, Fr. ***avoir*** - *have* to the subject in order to indicate the age of a person (literally, the number of years he/she has). For example:

> *Did you know?*
>
> *Perugia, an Italian city, is known as a university town, with the University of Perugia (over 34,000 students), the University for Foreigners (over 5,000 students), the Music Conservatory of Perugia and others. The city also hosts one of Europe's finest jazz festivals (July).*

It. ***Ho*** venticinque anni;

Fr. ***J'ai*** vingt cinq ans.

- *I am twenty five years old.*

It. Mio fratello ***ha*** trent'anni;

Fr. Mon frère ***a*** trente ans.

- *My brother is thirty years old.*

Ordinal Numbers

Ordinal numbers are numbers that indicate the order of nouns and just like cardinal numbers, ordinal numbers are also adjectives. However, unlike cardinal numbers, ordinal numbers must agree both in number and in gender with the noun they modify in Italian and French. Also, ordinal numbers usually precede nouns in the Romance languages. The Italian and French ordinal numbers are as follows:

	Italian	French
1st	**primo, prima, primi, prime**	**premier, première, premiers, premières**
2nd	**secondo(-a)**	**deuxième**
3rd	**terzo(-a)**	**troisième**
4th	**quarto(-a)**	**quatrième**
5th	**quinto(-a)**	**cinquième**

CHAPTER 7: NUMBERS, TIME AND DATE

	Italian	French
6th	sesto(-a)	sixième
7th	settimo(-a)	septième
8th	ottavo(-a)	huitième
9th	nono(-a)	neuvième
10th	decimo(-a)	dixième
11th	undicesimo(-a)/ undecimo	onzième
12th	dodicesimo(-a)/ duodecimo	douzième
13th	tredicesimo(-a)/ decimoterzo	treizième
14th	quattordicesimo(-a)/ decimoquarto	quatorzième
15th	quindicesimo(-a)/ decimoquinto	quinzième
16th	sedicesimo(-a)/ decimosesto	seizième
17th	diciassettesimo(-a)/ decimosettimo	dix-septième
18th	diciottesimo(-a)/ decimottavo	dix-huitième
19th	diciannovesimo(-a)/ decimonono	dix-neuvième
20th	ventesimo(-a)/ vigesimo	vingtième
21st	ventunesimo(-a)/ ventesimoprimo	vingt et unième
22nd	ventiduesimo(-a)	vingt-deuxième
23rd	ventitreesimo(-a)	vingt-troisième

CHAPTER 7: NUMBERS, TIME AND DATE

	Italian	French
24th	ventiquattresimo(-a)	vingt-quatrième
25th	venticinquesimo(-a)	vingt-cinquième
26th	ventiseiesimo(-a)	vingt-sixième
27th	ventisettesimo(-a)	vingt-septième
28th	ventottesimo(-a)	vingt-huitième
29th	ventinovesimo(-a)	vingt-neuvième
30th	trentesimo(-a)	trentième
31st	trentunesimo(-a)	trente et unième
32nd	trentaduesimo(-a)	trente-deuxième
33rd	trentatreesimo(-a)	trente-troisième
40th	quarantesimo(-a)	quarantième
50th	cinquantesimo(-a)	cinquantième
60th	sessantesimo(-a)	soixantième
70th	settantesimo(-a)	soixante-dixième
80th	ottantesimo(-a)	quatre-vingtième
90th	novantesimo(-a)	quatre-vingt-dixième
100th	centesimo(-a)	centième
101st	centounesimo(-a)	cent-unième
102nd	centoduesimo(-a)	cent-deuxième
103rd	centotreesimo(-a)	cent-troisième
200th	duecentesimo(-a)	deux-centième

CHAPTER 7: NUMBERS, TIME AND DATE

	Italian	French
201st	duecentounesimo(-a)	deux cent unième
202nd	duecentoduesimo(-a)	deux cent deuxième
300th	trecentesimo(-a)	trois-centième
400th	quattrocentesimo(-a)	quatre-centième
500th	cinquecentesimo(-a)	cinq-centième
600th	seicentesimo(-a)	six-centième
700th	settecentesimo(-a)	sept-centième
800th	ottocentesimo(-a)	huit-centième
900th	novecentesimo(-a)	neuf-centième
1000th	millesimo(-a)	millième
2 000	duemillesimo(-a)	deux millième
10 000	diecimillesimo(-a)	dix millième
100 000	centomillesimo(-a)	cent millième
1 000 000	milionesimo(-a)	millionième

Did you know?

Djibouti is a French- and Arabic-speaking country, located in the Horn of Africa. It is home to one of the saltiest bodies of water in the world, the Lake Assal, in the Danakil Desert in Central Djibouti.

It. È **la seconda** casa che ha comprato;

Fr. C'est **la deuxième** maison qu'elle a acheté.

- *It is **the second** house that she has bought.*

It. ***I primi*** giorni di lavoro;

CHAPTER 7: NUMBERS, TIME AND DATE

Fr. *Les premiers* jours de travail.

- ***The first*** *days of work.*

In Italian, in order to form ordinal numbers, the suffix **-esimo** is added to the cardinal numbers by dropping the final vowel of the cardinal number except for numbers ending in **-tré**. Those cardinal numbers that end in **-tré** must drop their accent **-tre** when **-esimo** is added (e.g. *trentatreesimo*).

In French, when the cardinal number ends in a mute *e*, the *e* must be dropped before adding the suffix **-ième** to form the ordinal number (e.g. mill*e* - mill**ième**). Also, the French **second/seconde** may replace **deuxième**. In some fixed expression, **tiers** and **tierce** are used in place of **troisième** (e.g. **le tiers-monde** - *the third world*; **une tierce personne** - *a third party*).

In the Romance languages, ordinals are usually used up to the 10th, since the 11th and higher are rather uncommon and leaves a strange impression when used in casual speech. Furthermore, for bigger numbers, it is far more common to utilize the ordinal numbers in speech. Observe the following:

It. Io vivo nella stanza (numero) **settanta** (not settantesimo);

Fr. Je vis dans la chambre (numéro) **soixante-dix** (not soixante-dixième).

- *I live in the room (number)* ***seventy***.

It is noticeable that if cardinal and ordinal numbers are used together, the cardinal number must precede the ordinal in French.

NOTE:

However, in Italian, the ordinals precede the cardinals in this case. For example:

It. i **primi due** giorni;
Fr. les **deux premiers** jours.
- *the first two days.*

Adverbial Ordinals in the Romance Languages

Most common adverbial forms and combinations of ordinals are as follows in the Romance languages:

Italian	French	English
primo	premièrement	*firstly*
in primo luogo	en premier lieu	*in the first place*

Fractions

Generally, fractions are used to express a portion or part of a whole. To form fractions, the cardinals and the ordinals are used together in the Romance languages. However, there are also special forms, which must be remembered.

	Italian	French
1/2 (a half)	un mezzo (una mezza)/ la metà	un demi(une demie)/ la moitié
1/3	un terzo (una terza)	un tiers (une tierce)
1/4	un quarto (una quarta)	un quart
1/5	un quinto (una quinta)	un cinquième (une cinquième)
1/6	un sesto (una sesta)	un sixième (une sixième)
1/7	un settimo (una settima)	un septième (une septième)
1/8	un ottavo (una ottava)	un huitième (une huitième)
1/9	un nono (una nona)	un neuv-ième (une neuvième)

CHAPTER 7: NUMBERS, TIME AND DATE

	Italian	French
1/10	un decimo (una decima)	un dixième (une dixième)
2/3	due terzi (due (terze)	deux tiers (deux tierces)
3/4	tre quarti (tre quarte)	trois quarts (trois quartes)

Did you know?

Switzerland's Gotthard tunnel is the longest in the world – measuring 57km in length, located 2.3km under the Alps, it is 7km longer than the Channel tunnel between England and France. It took 17 years to complete it.

It. Vorrei **mezzo** chilo di pomodori;

Fr. Je voudrais **un demi**-kilo de tomates.

*- I would like **half** a kilo of tomatoes.*

NOTE:

It. **la metà**; Fr. **la moitié** are primarily used in non-arithmetical context. Look at the example:

It. Hanno bevuto **la metà** della bottiglia;
Fr. Ils ont bu **la moitié** de la bouteille.
*- They drank **half** the bottle.*

In Italian and French, from 1/11 onwards fractions are formed by using ordinal numbers. Observe the following:

	Italian	French
1/12	un **dodicesimo**	un **douzième**
1/13	un **tredicesimo**	un **treizième**
1/14	un **quattordicesimo**	un **quatorzième**

	Italian	French
1/15	un **quindicesimo**	un **quinzième**
1/60	un **sessantesimo**	un **soixantième**

Arithmetical Operations

It must be remembered that in Italian and French the verb It. *fare*; Fr. *faire* - *to make/do* is used meaning *equals*. The following are the basic arithmetical calculations in the Romance languages:

	Italian	French
Addition	Addizione	Addition
5 + 4 = 9	5 **più** 4 **fa** 9	5 **et** 4 **font** 9
Subtraction	Sottrazione	Soustraction
6 - 2 = 4	6 **meno** 2 **fa** 4	6 **moins** 2 **font** 4
Multiplication	Moltiplicazione	Multiplication
5 x 10 = 50	5 **per** 10 **fa** 50	5 **fois** 10 **font** 50
Division	Divisione	Division
20 ÷ 2 = 10	20 **diviso** 2 **fa** 10	20 **divisé par** 2 **fait** 10

Collective Numbers

Collective numbers are considered to be nouns and are used to express an approximate quantity of something or specify groups in the Romance languages. It is noticeable that in order to form collective numbers, the following suffixes are added to most cardinal numbers in Italian and French:

Italian	French
-ina	*-aine*

CHAPTER 7: NUMBERS, TIME AND DATE

Below are some of the collective numbers:

	Italian	French
2	una coppia	une paire
10	una diecina	une dizaine
12	una dozzina	une douzaine
15	una quindicina	une quinzaine
20	una ventina	une vingtaine
40	una quarantina	une quarantaine
100	un centinaio	une centaine
1 000	un migliaio	un millier
1 000 000	un milione	un millon

NOTE:

*Such collective nouns as **a pair, a thousand** and **a million** are exceptions and no suffixes are added to them.*

*It. **quarantine** and Fr. **quarantaine** also means **quarantine**.*

When collective numbers are used before a noun, the preposition ***de*** (in French) and ***di*** (in Italian) is used. Observe the following:

It. Lei ha comprato **una dozzina di uova**;

Fr. Elle a acheté **une douzaine d'œufs**.

- *She bought **a dozen of eggs**.*

Multiple Numerals

The Romance languages do not have the English equivalent ending *-fold* (e.g. tenfold). Therefore, the combination of *cardinal number + times* can be used as an alternative:

CHAPTER 7: NUMBERS, TIME AND DATE

Spanish	Portuguese	Italian	French
cardinal number + **veces**	cardinal number + **vezes**	cardinal number + **volte**	cardinal number + **fois**

It. La popolazione della Spagna è **4 volte** più grande di quella del Portogallo;

Fr. La population de l'Espagne est **4 fois** plus grand que du Portugal.

- The population of Spain is **4 times** bigger than of Portugal.

Dates

Days

Italian	French	English
lunedì	lundi	*Monday*
martedì	mardi	*Tuesday*
mercoledì	mercredi	*Wednesday*
giovedì	jeudi	*Thursday*
venerdì	vendredi	*Friday*
sabato	samedi	*Saturday*
domenica	dimanche	*Sunday*

NOTE:

In Italian the days of the week are used with the definite article in order to express "on a certain day". However, in French no articles are used in this case. Once the article is used before the day of the week, it means an action happens every week (e.g. **mardi** - on Tuesday; **le mardi** - on Tuesdays).

It. Lo vedo **il** venerdì;

Fr. Je le vois vendredi (le vendredi - on Fridays).

- I see him on Friday.

Months

Italian	French	English
gennaio	janvier	*January*
febbraio	février	*February*
marzo	mars	*March*
aprile	avril	*April*
maggio	mai	*May*
giugno	juin	*June*
luglio	juillet	*July*
agosto	août	*August*
settembre	septembre	*September*
ottobre	octobre	*October*
novembre	novembre	*November*
dicembre	décembre	*December*

In order to say "*in a particular month*", the prepositions It. **in/a**, Fr. **en** are used in the Romance languages. Note that in Italian and French, it is also possible to use such combinations as Fr. **au mois de** + **a month**; It. **nel mese di** + **a month**. For example:

It. Vado in Argentina **in/a** febbraio (**nel mese di** febbraio);

Fr. Je vais en Argentine **en** février (**au mois de** février).

CHAPTER 7: NUMBERS, TIME AND DATE

*- I am going to Argentina **in** February.*

Did you know?

Belgian painters are credited to have invented oil painting in the 15th century. It's unsure who exactly the inventor was, but scientists presume it was Jan van Eyck.

Remember that the days of the week and the months of the year are not capitalized in Italian and French.

In the Romance languages dates are usually written as follows:

It. Che giorno è oggi? - **Oggi è domenica, 5 giugno**;

Fr. Quel jour sommes-nous aujourd'hui? - A**ujourd'hui est le dimanche, 5 juin**.

- What day is it today? - Today is Sunday, June 5.

NOTE:

In Italian a complete date is composed of a day of the week + a cardinal number + month + year. In French, the definite article must be put before a day of the week while forming the date.

Below is a table showing the formation of complete dates in the Romance languages:

Italian	day + a cardinal number + month + year
French	**le** + day + a cardinal number + month + year

Observe the following:

It. Oggi è **giovedì, 10 marzo 2016**;

Fr. Aujourd'hui c'est **le jeudi, 10 Mars 2016**.

- Today is Thursday, March 10, 2016.

CHAPTER 7: NUMBERS, TIME AND DATE

Ways to Ask the Date in the Romance Languages

In order to ask what day it is today one can use the following phrases in Italian and French:

Italian	French	English
Qual è la data di oggi?	Quelle est la date d'aujourd'hui?	What date is it today?
Che giorno è oggi?	Quel jour est-ce aujourd'hui?	What day is it today?
Che giorno siamo oggi?	Quel jour somme-nous aujourd'hui?	What day is it today?
Quanto ne abbiamo oggi?		What day is it today?

Seasons

Italian	French	English
l'estate	l'été	summer
l'autunno	l'automne	fall
l'inverno	l'hiver	winter
la primavera	le printemps	spring

Observe the prepositions used with the seasons in the Romance languages:

Italian	French	English
in estate	**en** été	in summer
in autunno	**en** automne	in fall
in inverno	**en** hiver	in winter

Italian	French	English
in primavera	**au** printemps	*in spring*

> **NOTE:**
>
> In Italian the word spring is feminine while in French all the seasons are masculine. In French **pringtemps** is used with the preposition **au** instead of **en**.

Time

The phrase for *What time is it?* is expressed as follows in the Romance languages:

Italian	French	English
Che ora è?/ Che ore sono?	Quelle heure est-il?	*What time is it?*

In Italian, hours are usually expressed using a form of **essere** + the feminine definite article It. **la, l'** or **le** (in order to agree with the number of unmentioned *ora* or *ore - hour* or *hours*) + a cardinal number.

In French, *hours* are normally expressed using the pronoun **il** + a form of the verb **être** + a cardinal number + the word **heure(-s)** - *hour(-s)*.

Remember that in Italian, the appropriate form of the verb **essere** must be selected, i.e. the 3rd person singular for *"one o'clock"* and plural for other hours except in French where only the 3rd person singular of the verb **être** is used when indicating the time of day.

The table below shows the idea of how to tell the time of day in the Romance languages:

Italian	**essere (è/sono)** + **la,l'/le** + *a cardinal number*
French	**il** + **être (est)** + *a cardinal number* + **heure(-s)**

Observe the following:

CHAPTER 7: NUMBERS, TIME AND DATE

It. Che ora è? (Che ore sono?) - *È l'una (Sono le tre)*;

Fr. Quelle heure est-il? - *Il est une heure (Il est trois heures)*.

- *What time is it?* ***It is one o'clock (It is three o'clock)***

It is worth mentioning that in Italy and France, as well as other countries where Italian and French are spoken, the 24-hour time is used widely. Study the entire 24-hour system:

	Italian	French	
1	È l'una	Il est une heure	It's 1 A.M.
2	Sono le due	Il est deux heures	It's 2 A.M
3	Sono le tre	Il est trois heures	It's 3 A.M.
4	Sono le quattro	Il est quatre heures	It's 4 A.M.
5	Sono cinque	Il est cinq heures	It's 5 A.M.
6	Sono le sei	Il est six heures	It's 6 A.M.
7	Sono le sette	Il est sept heures	It's 7 A.M.
8	Sono le otto	Il est huit heurs	It's 8 A.M.
9	Sono le nove	Il est neuf heures	It's 9 A.M.
10	Sono le dieci	Il est dix heures	It's 10 A.M.
11	Sono le undici	Il est onze heures	It's 11 A.M.
12	Sono le dodici	Il est douze heures	It's 12 A.M.
13	Sono le tredici	Il est treize heures	It's 1 P.M.
14	Sono le quattordici	Il est quatorze heures	It's 2 P.M.
15	Sono le quindici	Il est quinze heures	It's 3 P.M.
16	Sono le sedici	Il est seize heures	It's 4 P.M.
17	Sono le diciassette	Il est dix-sept heures	It's 5 P.M.
18	Sono le diciotto	Il est dix-huit heures	It's 6 P.M.
19	Sono le diciannove	Il est dix-neuf heures	It's 7 P.M.

CHAPTER 7: NUMBERS, TIME AND DATE

	Italian	French	
20	Sono le venti	Il est vingt heures	*It's 8 P.M.*
21	Sono le ventuno	Il est vingt et une heures	*It's 9 P.M.*
22	Sono le ventidue	Il est vingt-deux heures	*It's 10 P.M.*
23	Sono le ventitré	Il est vingt-trois heures	*It's 11 P.M.*
24	Sono le ventiquattro	Il est vingt-quatre heures	*It's 12 P.M.*

In the Romance languages, minutes are usually added to the hours by the use of It. *e*, Fr. *et* + cardinal number. However, French *et* can be dropped. Minute(-s) is not normally used.

It. Sono le sei *e* dieci (minuti);

Fr. Il est six heures dix (minutes).

- *It's six ten (It's ten past six).*

The half hour or 15 minutes can be expressed in two ways in Italian and French. Study the following:

Italian	French	English
quarto or **quindici**	**quart** or **quinze**	*quarter or fifteen*
mezza (mezzo) or **trenta**	**demie** or **trente**	*half or thirty*

NOTE:
In Italian, the masculine indefinite article is used before **quarto**.

It. Sono le tre e **un quarto** (Sono le tre e **quindici**);

Fr. Il est trois heures et **quart** (Il est trois heures **quinze**).

- *It's 3:15*

CHAPTER 7: NUMBERS, TIME AND DATE

> **Did you know?**
>
> Ravenna is a city in Northern Italy. It is known for its late Roman and Byzantine architecture. It was the capital of the Western Roman Empire from 402 until 476 - the collapse of the empire. Afterwards, the city was the center of Byzantine (East Roman) power in Italy from 584 to 751.

It. Sono le cinque e **mezza** (**mezzo**) (Sono le cinque e **trenta**);

Fr. Il est trois heures et **demie** (Il est trois heures **trente**).

- It's 5:30

Normally, after the half hour, the minutes must be subtracted from the next hour by utilizing the words It. **meno**; Fr. **moins** - *minus*. Observe the following:

It. Sono le quattro **meno** un quarto;

Fr. Il est quatre heures **moins** quart.

- It's quarter to four.

It. Sono le otto **meno** venti;

Fr. Il est huit heures **moins** vingt.

- It's twenty to eight.

In order to express A.M. or P.M., the following expressions are used in the Romance languages:

Italian	French	English
di mattina	du matin	in the morning (A.M.)
del pomeriggio	de l'après-midi	in the afternoon (from 12 P.M. to 5 P.M.)

Italian	French	English
di sera	du soir	*in the evening* *(5 P.M. till late P.M.)*

It. È l'una *di mattina*;

Fr. Il est une heure *du matin*.

- *It's one in the morning.*

It. Sono le due *del pomeriggio*;

Fr. Il est deux heures *de l'après-midi*.

- *It's two in the afternoon.*

It. Sono le otto *di sera*;

Fr. Il est huit heures *du soir*.

- *It's eight in the evening.*

In order to ask the question: *At what time?* one should say the following:

Italian	French	English
A che ora?	À quelle heure?	*At what time?*

While answering such question, it is necessary to utilize the preposition *a* (in Italian) and *à* (in French) - *at* before the specified time or such words as:

Italian	French	English
a mezzogiorno	à midi	*at noon*
a mezzanotte	à minuit	*at midnight*

It. A che ora arriva il treno? - Il treno arriva **a mezzogiorno**;

Fr. A quelle heure arrive le train? - Le train arrive **à midi**.

*- At what time does the train arrive? - The train arrives **at noon**.*

NOTE:
It is noticeable that the preposition **a** must be articulated with an appropriate feminine definite article while expressing the particular time in Italian. In French, there is no article used at all when expressing time.

Italian
a + le = **all'/alle**

It. A che ora arriva il treno? - Il treno arriva **all'**una (**alle** due);

Fr. A quelle heure arrive le train? - Le train arrive **à une heure** (à deux heures).

- At what time does the train arrive? - The train arrives at one (at two) o'clock.

Did you know?

French is the official language of the Democratic Republic of the Congo (DRC). It is accepted as the lingua franca to facilitate communication among the different ethnic groups. As many as 250 ethnic groups have been identified.

The expression *sharp* would be It. **in punto**; Fr. **précises** (or **juste**). Study the following:

It. Mi alzo alle sette **in punto**;

Fr. Je me lève à sept heures **précises (juste)**.

- I get up at seven A.M. sharp.

In order to express the time when an event starts and ends, one must use the following structure in the Romance languages:

Italian	French	English
dalle (ore) **alle (all')** (ore)	**de** (heures) **à** (heures)	*from (hour) to (hour)*

It. La lezione sarà **dalle** nove **alle** dodici (ore);

Fr. La leçon sera **de** neuf **à** douze (heures).

- *The lesson will be **from** nine **to** twelve.*

CHAPTER 8: PREPOSITIONS

Overview

Like the English prepositions *"with"*, *"of"*, *"to"*, *"from"*, Italian and French prepositions are used to express many types of connections or relationships between two words or different parts of the sentence by means of connecting them together. They normally demonstrate direction, location, time, purpose, means, cause and so on. Prepositions can be simple (consisting of only one word), and compound (consisting of several words). For example:

Simple preposition	*Compound preposition*
It. La casa **di** mio padre; Fr. La maison **de** mon père. *- The house of my father.*	It. **Vicino a** casa mia; Fr. **Près de** ma maison. *- Near my house.*

It is notable that Italian and French simple and compound prepositions must be followed by a noun or noun group, a pronoun or an infinitive, in contrast to English which utilizes the gerund (with *-ing* ending). Study the following:

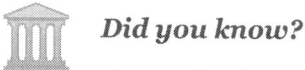

Did you know?

Switzerland was originally called Helvetia by Julius Caesar when he conquered the Helvetii, a group of Celtic tribes, who lived in the area between the Alps and the Jura Mountains.

It. Io gioco **con mio figlio**. > Io gioco **con lui**.

Fr. Je joue **avec mon fils**. > Je joue **avec lui**.

*- I play **with my son**. > I play **with him**.*

It. **Prima di dormire**, leggo un libro.

Fr. **Avant de dormir**, je lis un livre.

*- **Before sleeping** I read a book.*

CHAPTER 8: PREPOSITIONS

In the Romance languages, the prepositions, especially the most common ones, have several meanings in English, and the right translation usually depends on the context in the phrase. Therefore, the correct uses of different prepositions must be memorized and learned through practice since there are no strict rules. It is advised to learn each combination individually by means of using a dictionary to find more examples of the uses of prepositions.

Simple Prepositions

Below is a list of the most frequent simple prepositions in Italian and French:

Italian	French	English
a	à	*to, at, in*
di	de	*of, from*
in	en, dans	*in, by, into*
da	chez	*to, at the house of, at someone's place*
per	pour	*for, in order to*
da	par	*by*
con	avec	*with*
senza	sans	*without*
contro	contre	*against*
tra	entre	*between, among*
su	sur	*about, on, upon, above, over*
davanti a	devant	*before, in the presence of*

Italian	French	English
sotto	sous	under
da	depuis	since, from
durante	pendant (durant)	during
fino a	jusqu'à	until, toward
verso	vers	towards
eccetto, salvo	excepté, sauf	except
secondo, conforme, (conformemente a)	selon, d'après conformément à,	according to

Uses of Simple Prepositions

Preposition *a* (It.), *à* (Fr.)

The preposition It. *a* and Fr. *à* is very common and usually occurs in a wide spectrum of contexts and is used:

- **to express motion or direction *in*, *at* or *to* some place:**

    It. Loro vanno *al* cinema domani;

    Fr. Ils vont *au* cinéma demain.

    - *They go **to** the cinema tomorrow.*

- **to connect one verb to an infinitive (See also Use of the Infinitive p.301):**

    In this case this preposition is not translated directly. For example:

    It. Lei comincia *a* cantare;

CHAPTER 8: PREPOSITIONS

Fr. Elle commence *à* chanter.

- *She starts to sing.*

Below is a list of the most frequently used verbs which require the use of the preposition It. *a* and Fr. *à* before adding an infinitive.

Italian	French	English
aiutare a	aider à	to help to
apprendere a, imparare a	apprendre à	to learn how to
insegnare a	enseigner à	to teach how to
cominciare a, iniziare a	commencer à	to begin to, to start to
mettersi a	se mettre à	to start to, to set about
invitare a	inviter à	to invite to
prepararsi a	se préparer à	to prepare to
dedicarsi a	se consacrer à, se vouer à	to dedicate oneself to
decidersi a	se décider à	to decide to, to make up one's mind
tornare a	retourner à	to do something again
abituarsi a	s'habituer à	to become accustomed to
obbligare a	obliger à	to oblige

CHAPTER 8: PREPOSITIONS

- to imply manner or how something is performed (*with*, *by*, *on*):

>It. Vado *a* piedi;
>
>Fr. Je vais *à* pied.
>
>- *I go on foot.*

Here are some of the most common phrases expressing manner, which are used along with the preposition *a* (*à*) in the Romance languages:

Italian	French	English
alla cieca	à l'aveuglette	*blindly*
a cavallo	à cheval	*on horseback*
a matita	au crayon	*in pencil*
a mano	à la main	*by hand*
a piedi	à pied	*on foot*
alla sua maniera	à sa manière	*in one's own way*
but: <u>ad</u> alta/a bassa voce	à voix haute/basse	*loudly/in a low voice*

>It. Parlano *ad alta voce*;
>
>Fr. Ils parlent *à voix haute*.
>
>- *They speak loudly.*

NOTE:

However, French *de* must be used while expressing the noun modified by the indefinite article in adverbial clauses of manner (e.g. Ils parlent **d'une** voix inquiétante - They speak in an anxious voice; Elle chante **d'une** manière parfaite - She sings perfectly). And if the noun is not modified by an indefinite article, the preposition **avec** is always used (e.g. Ils parlent **avec anxiété** - They speak anxiously).

Remember that means of mechanical transportation are normally expressed by the preposition It. **in**; Fr. **en** in the Romance languages. For instance:

It. Vado **in** macchina oggi;

Fr. Je vais **en** voiture aujourd'hui.

- I go **by** car today.

NOTE: However, there are some means of travel which require the preposition **à** in French:

French	English
à cheval	on horseback
à moto	by motorcycle

The preposition It. **a** and Fr. **à** is also used to indicate a manner that is specifically a style:

It. Giardino **alla** francese;

Fr. Jardin **à** la française.

- French-style garden.

- **to introduce phrases which state location:**

    Here are some common expression which are used with the preposition ***a* (*à*)** when indicating location in Italian and French:

Italian	French	English
all'aria aperta	à l'extérieur; en plein air	in the open air
a destra	à droite	on the right
a sinistra	à gauche	on the left
al sole	au soleil	in the sun
da lontano	au loin	in the distance

NOTE:

Unlike in French, in Italian the expression <u>in the distance</u> is used with the preposition **da**.

- **to link such repeated words as:**

Italian	French	English
faccia a faccia, petto a petto	face à face	face to face
uno a uno	un à un	one on one
a poco a poco	peu à peu	little by little

CHAPTER 8: PREPOSITIONS

- **to express time and age (*at*):**

   It. Sono venuto **alle nove** ieri;
   Fr. Je suis venu **à neuf heures** hier.
   - *I came at nine o'clock yesterday.*

   It. **A quattordici anni** è diventata una ballerina;
   Fr. **À quatorze ans**, elle est devenue une ballerine.
   - *At age fourteen she became a ballerina.*

It is also used in such phrases of time as:

Italian	French	English
in/al/sul principio di	au début de	at the beginning of
a metà di, **nel** mezzo di	au milieu de	in the middle of
alla fine di	à la fin de	at the end of
all'arrivo di	à l'arrivée de	upon the arrival of

NOTE:

*The following irregularities must be remembered. Italian phrase **nel mezzo di** has the preposition **nel**. The Italian phrase **in/al/sul principio di** can be used with any of the mentioned above prepositions.*

However, the preposition ***a*** (It.) and ***à*** (Fr.) has several specific cases of usage in Italian and French, which will be considered below:

CHAPTER 8: PREPOSITIONS

*Italian **a** and French **à** prepositions*

There is a number of peculiarities of the Italian preposition ***a*** and French ***à*** in terms of usage, which are:

- Apart from expressing direction to a place, Italian and French preposition ***a*** (It.) and ***à*** (Fr.) can also be used to indicate location when used with names of places. It is advisable to learn Italian and French prepositions of places in context. Study the following:

    It. Studiamo ***all'***università;

    Fr. Nous étudions ***à*** l'université.

    - *We study **at** the university.*

    It. Mia figlia è ***a*** scuola;

    Fr. Ma fille est ***à*** l'école.

    - *My daughter is **in** school.*

- The preposition ***a*** (It.) and ***à*** (Fr.) is also used before the names of cities and towns in Italian and French. Study the following:

    It. Vado ***a*** Madrid;

    Fr. Je vais ***à*** Madrid.

    - *I go **to** Madrid.*

However, before the names of regions, countries, continents, or islands in Italian and French the prepositions ***in*** (It.) and ***en, dans*** (Fr.) must be used (**See Preposition *en* (Sp.), *em* (Port.), *in* (It.), *en*, *dans* (Fr.) p.562**). For instance:

It. Vado ***in*** Francia;

CHAPTER 8: PREPOSITIONS

Fr. Je vais **en** France.

- *I go **to** France.*

It. Vanno **in** Sicilia;

Fr. Ils vont **en** Sicile.

- *They go **to** Sicily.*

However, there are some islands that are used with the preposition ***à*** in French and must be memorized:

French	
à la Réunion	à Chypre
à la Martinique	à Madagascar
au Groenland	à Cuba

In French the preposition ***en*** is normally used before names of feminine countries or continents (most of the names of countries that end in a mute ***e*** are feminine, except **le Mexique** - *Mexico*); while the preposition ***au*** is used before masculine countries. Furthermore, the French preposition ***aux*** (*au + les*) and Italian ***negli*** (*in + gli*) are used before Fr. **États-Unis**; It. **Stati Uniti** - *The United States*. Study the following:

En
Fr. Elle va **en** France (Allemagne, Espagne, Italie, Europe, Afrique etc.).   - *She goes to France (Germany, Spain, Italy, Europe, Africa etc.)*
Au
Fr. Elle va **au** Mexique (Canada, Danemark, Portugal etc.).   - *She goes to Mexico (Canada, Denmark, Portugal etc.).*
Aux/ Negli

CHAPTER 8: PREPOSITIONS

> Fr. Elle va **aux** États-Unis;
> It. Lei va **negli** Stati Uniti.
> - *She goes to the United States.*

- The French preposition ***à*** can be used to mean *with*. Don't forget that ***à*** must be contracted with the definite article. For example:

Fr. du thé ***au*** lait.
- tea with milk.

Fr. l'homme ***aux*** yeux blue.
- the man with blue eyes.

NOTE:
In this case, in Italian, the preposition **con** (It.) are used in order to express <u>with</u>. Look at the same examples:

It. tè con latte.
- tea <u>with</u> milk.

It. l'uomo con gli occhi azzurri.
- the man <u>with</u> blue eyes.

- In French the preposition ***à*** can also introduce an infinitive and express the function of the preceding noun or the use of an object in the phrase or result or tendency. It corresponds to the English *for* and the infinitive is the equivalent of the gerund (*-ing*). Observe the following:

Fr. une salle ***à*** manger.
- a room for dining (a dining room).

Fr. une machine *à* écrire.

- *a machine **for** writing (a typewriter).*

Fr. une voiture *à* vendre.

- *a car **for** sale.*

NOTE:
In Italian, the preposition **da** (It.) are used in order to express <u>for</u>:

It. una sala **da** pranzo.
- *a room **for** dining (a dining room).*

It. una macchina **da** scrivere.
- *a machine **for** writing (a typewriter).*

It. una macchina **da** vendere.
- *a car **for** sale.*

- French *à* also expresses an infinitive which denotes some sort of action. The preposition *à* is used after an adjective in this case:

Fr. C'est facile *à* comprendre.

- *It's easy to understand.*

Fr. C'est difficile *à* prononcer.

- *It's difficult to pronounce.*

CHAPTER 8: PREPOSITIONS

NOTE:

In Italian, the preposition **da** must be used in order to introduce an infinitive that conveys the action. For instance:

It. È facile **da** capire.
- *It's easy to understand.*

It. È difficile **da** parlare.
- *It's difficult to speak.*

*Preposition **de** (Fr.), **di** (It.)*

This preposition is also rather frequent and has a lot of meanings. It can be used:

- **to express possession or ownership (*of*):**

The preposition **de** (Fr.), **di** (It.) usually corresponds to the English apostrophe s (*'s*) or the preposition *of*:

It. Parigi è la capitale **della** Francia;

Fr. Paris est la capitale **de** la France.

- *Paris is the capital **of** France.*

It. È la macchina **di** suo padre;

Fr. C'est la voiture **de** son père.

- *It is his father's car.*

- **to indicate a place of origin and departure (*from*):**

This preposition is usually equivalent to the English *from*:

CHAPTER 8: PREPOSITIONS

It. Di dove sei? - Sono **dell'**Ecuador (but Da dove vieni? - Vengo **dall'**Ecuador);

Fr. D'où es-tu? - Je suis **de** l'Equateur.

- *Where are you from? - I am **from** Ecuador.*

It. Diana è arrivata **dal** Cile;

Fr. Diana est arrivé **du** Chili.

- *Diana arrived **from** Chile.*

- **with geographical names (*of*):**

It. L'isola **della** Groenlandia;

Fr. L'île **du** Groenland.

- *The island **of** Greenland.*

It. La città **di** Londra;

Fr. La ville **de** Londres.

- *The city **of** London.*

- **to imply cause (*from*, *with*, *of*, *in*):**

It. Siamo stanchi **di** giocare a calcio;

Fr. Nous sommes fatigués **de** jouer au football.

- *We are tired **of** playing soccer.*

It. Sono pazzo **d'**amore;

Fr. Je suis fou **d'**amour.

*- I am crazy **in** love.*

- **to qualify or describe a noun which is used before another noun (*of*):**

  It. Una tazza ***di*** tè;

  Fr. Une tasse ***de*** thé.

  *- A cup **of** tea.*

  It. Il succo ***di*** mela;

  Fr. Le jus ***de*** pomme.

  - Apple juice.

- **to compare things (*than*) (See Comparison of Adjectives and Adverbs p.45):**

  It can also corresponds to English *of* or *in*, specifically in superlative phrases:

  It. Lei è la più bella ***del*** gruppo;

  Fr. Elle est la plus belle ***du*** groupe.

  *- She is the most beautiful **of** the group.*

- **to express the material from which something is made:**

  It. una casa ***di/in*** legno;

  Fr. une maison ***de/en*** bois.

  - A wooden house.

CHAPTER 8: PREPOSITIONS

> **NOTE:**
> *Italian preposition **di** and **in**; and French **de** and **en** are interchangeable and either preposition can be used to express the material from which something is made. However, It. **di** and Fr. **de** are normally used to point out the sort of object a person is talking about, while It. **in** and Fr. **en** underline the material from which something is made.*
>
> *Observe the following:*

It. calzature **di** pelle;	It. calzature **in** pelle;
Fr. chaussures **de** cuir.	Fr. chaussures **en** cuir.
- leather shoes.	- shoes made of leather.

- **to connect one verb to an infinitive or an object (See also Use of the Infinitive p.301).**

The preposition *de* (Fr.), *di* (It.) is not translated. Study the following:

It. Ha finito *di* leggere il libro;

Fr. Il a fini *de* lire le livre.

- He finished reading the book.

Below is a list of the most common verbs which take the preposition *de* (Fr.), *di* (It.) before an infinitive.

Italian and French verbs

Italian	French	English
accettare di	accepter de	to accept

CHAPTER 8: PREPOSITIONS

Italian	French	English
accontentarsi di	**se contenter de**	*to content oneself with*
accorgersi di	**s'apercevoir de**	*to become aware of*
accusare di	**accuser de**	*to accuse of*
ammettere di	**admettre de**	*to admit*
arrischiarsi di	**risquer de**	*to risk*
arrossire di	**rougir de**	*to blush*
astenersi di	**s'abstenir de**	*to abstain from*
augurare di	**souhaiter de**	*to wish*
avere bisogno di	**avoir besoin de**	*to need*
avere paura di, temere di	**avoir peur de, craindre de**	*to be afraid of, to fear*
avere voglia di	**avoir envie de**	*to feel like doing something*
avere l'intenzione di	**avoir l'intention de**	*to intend to do something*
avere ragione di	**avoir raison de**	*to be right to do smth.*
aver torto di	**avoir tort de**	*to be wrong to do smth.*
avvertire di	**avertir de**	*to warn*
cercare di <u>provare a</u>	**essayer de, tâcher de**	*to try*
cessare di	**cesser de**	*to cease*
chiedere di	**demander de**	*to ask*

CHAPTER 8: PREPOSITIONS

Italian	French	English
comandare di	commander de	to order
consigliare di	conseiller de	to advise
consolarsi di	se consoler de	to take comfort
convincere di	convaincre de	to convince
credere di	croire de	to believe, count oneself
decidere di	décider de	to decide
detestare	détester de	to hate, to detest
dimenticare di	oublier de	to forget
dire di	dire de	to say, to tell
dispensare di	dispenser de	to release from
domandare di	demander de	to ask
dubitare di	douter de	to doubt
evitare di	éviter de	to avoid
fingere di, far finta di	feindre de, faire semblant de	to pretend
finire di	finir de	to finish
giurare di	jurer de	to swear
godere di, fruire di	jouir de, profiter de	to enjoy, take an advantage of
impedire di	empêcher de	to prevent
indignarsi per	s'indigner de	to be indignant

CHAPTER 8: PREPOSITIONS

Italian	French	English
infischiarsi di	se foutre de, (s'en foutre de)	to not give a hoot about
lagnarsi di, lamentarsi di	se plaindre de	to complain
mancare di	manquer de	to lack
meravigliarsi di, stupirsi di	s'émerveiller de, s'étonner de	to be surprised
meritare di	mériter de	to deserve
minacciare di	menacer de	to threaten someone to do smth.
occuparsi di	s'occuper de	to busy oneself with
offrire di	offrir de	to offer
ordinare di	ordonner de	to order
pensare di	<u>penser à</u>	to plan
pentirsi di	se repentir de	to regret
permettere di	permettre de	to permit
persuadere di	persuader de	to persuade
pregare di	prier de, supplier de	to beg
privare di	priver de	to deprive
proibire di	prohiber	to prohibit
promettere di	promettre de	to promise
progettare di, aver in vista di	projeter de, envisager de	to plan on doing smth

CHAPTER 8: PREPOSITIONS

Italian	French	English
proporre di	proposer de	to propose
proporsi di	se proposer de	to intend to, be about to
raccomandare di	recommander de	to recommend
rendersi conto di	se rendre compte de	to realize
ricordare di, ricordarsi di	se souvenir de, se rappeler (de)	to remember
rifiutare di	refuser de	to refuse
rimproverare di	reprocher de	to reproach for
rincrescere di	regretter de	to regret
ringraziare di	remercier de	to thank
ripetere di	répéter de	to repeat
risolvere di	résoudre de	to resolve
sbagliare a	se tromper	to make a mistake
sbrigarsi a	se dépêcher de, se hâter de	to hurry
scommettere di	parier de	to bet
scusarsi di	s'excuser de	to apologize
sforzarsi di	s'efforcer de	to try hard to do
smettere di	arrêter de	to stop
sognare di	rêver de	to dream of
sperare di	espérer de	to hope

CHAPTER 8: PREPOSITIONS

Italian	French	English
stancarsi di	**se fatiguer de**	*to get tired of*
sospettare di	**soupçonner de**	*to suspect*
suggerire di	**suggérer de**	*to suggest*
supplicare di	**supplier de**	*to beseech, to beg*
tentare di	**tenter de**	*to attempt*
terminare di	**terminer de**	*to end, to stop*
vantarsi di	**se vanter de**	*to flaunt, to brag about*
vergognarsi di	**se gêner**	*to be ashamed of*
vietare di, interdire dal,	**défendre de, interdire de**	*to forbid*
———	**venir de**	*to have just done smth.*

NOTE:

Unlike French, Italian doesn't have the verb meaning *to have just done*, instead the following expression is used: **aver/essere appena fatto** (e.g. **Sono appena arrivato** - *I have just arrived*).

Italian verbs **provare**, **sbagliare** and **sbrigarsi** are used with the preposition **a**. The verb **indignarsi** is used with **per**. The verb **detestare** is used without prepositions.

The following is a list of verbs which take the preposition **de** (Fr.), **di** (It.) before an object (noun or pronoun).

Italian and French verbs

Italian	French	English
accorgersi di	s'apercevoir de	to notice
approssimarsi	s'approcher de	to get closer to
avere bisogno di	avoir besoin de	to need
avere paura di	avoir peur de	to be afraid of
avere voglia di	avoir envie de	to want someone or something badly
dimenticarsi di, dimenticare di	oublier de	to forget
dipendere da	dépendre de	to depend on
dubitare di	douter de	to doubt
ereditare di	hériter de	to inherit
fare a meno di	se passer de	to do without
farsi beffe di	se moquer de	to make fun of
fidarsi di	se fier à	to trust
godere di, fruire di	jouir de, profiter de	to enjoy, take an advantage of
indignarsi di	s'indigner de	to be indignant
innamorarsi di	tomber amoureux de	to fall in love
lamentarsi di	se plaindre de	to complain
mancare di	manquer de	to lack
meravigliarsi di, stupirsi di	s'émerveiller de, s'étonner de	to be surprised

CHAPTER 8: PREPOSITIONS

Italian	French	English
nutrirsi di	se nourrir de	to feed on
occuparsi di	s'occuper de	to take care of
partire di	partir de	to leave
ricordarsi di	se souvenir de, se rappeler (de)	to remember
ridere di	rire de	to laugh at
riguardarsi da	se méfier de	to beware of
servirsi di	se servir de	to make use of
soffrire di	souffrir de	to suffer from
trattare di	traiter de	to deal with, treat

- with time and dates (See Time and Dates p.482):

NOTE:

In the Romance languages the preposition **de** (Fr.), **di** (It.) can also be used in several time expressions.

Observe the following:

Italian	French	English
di/<u>la</u> mattina	<u>le</u> matin, <u>dans la</u> matinée	in the morning
di giorno	<u>de</u> jour, <u>dans la</u> journée	in the daytime
di sera	<u>le</u> soir, <u>dans la</u> soirée	in the evening

CHAPTER 8: PREPOSITIONS

Italian	French	English
di notte	la nuit	at night
di buon'ora	de bonne heure	early
d'/in estate	en été	in the summer
d'/in inverno,	en hiver	in the winter
di/in primavera	au printemps	in the spring
d'/in autunno	en automne	in the fall

NOTE:

With some phrases, in Italian and French different prepositions are used, especially with seasons. In Italian the preposition **in** is interchangeable with **di** in phrases designating seasons. Some French time expressions require the definite article. All the irregularities must be learned by heart.

It. **Di mattina** (**La mattina**) mio marito legge spesso il giornale;

Fr. **Le matin** (**Dans la matinee**) mon mari lit souvent le journal.

- My husband often reads the newspaper **in the morning**.

- **in the expressions with indefinite pronouns:**

The preposition **de** (Fr.), **di** (It.) is normally used before an adjectives and after the following indefinite pronouns:

Italian	French	English
qualcosa	quelque chose	something
niente, nulla	rien	nothing

It. Ho qualcosa *di* nuovo;

Fr. J'ai quelque chose *de* nouveau.

- *I have something new.*

It. Non c'è niente *di* speciale;

Fr. Il n'y a rien *de* spécial.

- *There is nothing special.*

- **to construct adverbial phrases and idioms:**

   The most common adverbial phrases and idioms used with the preposition *de* (Fr.), *di* (It.) in Italian and French are:

Italian	French	English
di quando in quando	de temps en temps	*from time to time*
di colpo, d'un tratto	d'un coup	*suddenly*
di buona voglia, di buona volontà, di buon grado	de bonne grâce	*willingly*
di mala voglia, di mala volontà	de mauvaise grâce	*reluctantly*
di nuovo	de nouveau	*again*

It. Lo ha fatto *di buona voglia*;

Fr. Il l'a fait *de bonne grâce*.

- *He did it **willingly**.*

CHAPTER 8: PREPOSITIONS

Preposition in (It.), en, dans (Fr.)

This common preposition has a range of meanings and usually means in, by, into or about, which depends on the context. It is used:

- **to denote location (*in*, *at*, *on*):**
  This preposition usually means inside of or at a place.

  It. Le chiavi sono **nella** borsa;
  Fr. Les clés sont **dans** le sac.
  - *The keys are **in** my bag.*

*French Prepositions **en/dans***

There are two French prepositions **en** and **dans**, which are used to indicate location. The difference between them is that **dans** is normally used with an article, while **en** is never used with an article. For instance:

French	
Je suis **dans la voiture.** - *I am in the car.*	Je suis **en classe.** - *I am in class.*

The preposition **dans** denotes place more precisely then **en** and designates *inside*.

French	
dans la ville. - *in the city, inside the city.*	**en ville.** - *in city, to city.*
dans la classe d'espagnol. - *in Spanish class.*	**en classe.** - *in class.*

Moreover, in French the preposition **en** is normally used before names of feminine countries or continents (most of the names of countries that end in a mute e are feminine, except *le Mexique* - Mexico);

> Fr. Il va *en* Espagne.
>
> - *He goes to Spain.*

The French preposition ***dans*** must be used with names of continents which are qualified by another phrase:

> Fr. Il va ***dans*** le Nord de l'Amérique.
>
> - *He goes **to North of America**.*

Nevertheless, the preposition **en** may be used before names of continents in spoken languages:

> Fr. Il va *en* Amérique du Nord.
>
> - *He goes to North America.*

Remember that if the name of a country is used with a complement, the form ***dans le*** (*l'*, ***la***, ***les***) must be used rather than ***en***.

> Fr. Vous allez ***dans le Nord de l'Espagne***.
>
> - *You go **to the North of Spain**.*

It should be mentioned that before names of islands the preposition can differ in French. Thus, below is the list of some common islands which require the preposition ***en***:

French

en Islande - *in Iceland*	en Haïti - *in Haiti*
en Sardaigne - *in Sardinia*	en Nouvelle-Guinée - *in New Guinea*

It is quite interesting that *en* is usually used before names of American states and Canadian provinces, when those names end in *e* or *ie* in French (including *Ontario* and *Saskatchewan*). Observe some of the examples:

French

en Floride - *in Florida*	en Ontario - *in Ontario*
en Californie - *in California*	en Nouvelle-Écosse - *in Nova Scotia*

In all other cases, the forms *dans le*, *dans le territoire de*, *dans la province de* or *dans l'État de* are normally used, for example:

French

dans le territoire du Nunavut - *in the territory of Nunavut*	dans la province du Québec - *in the province of Quebec*

NOTE:

But **au Nouveau-Mexique** - *New Mexico*, **au Nouveau-Brunswick** - *New Brunswick*,

à Terre-Neuve - *Newfoundland*.

- **with means of mechanical transportation (*by*)**

It. *in*; Fr. *en* (sometimes *par*) are used with means of mechanical transportation in order to express how someone is moving around in the Romance languages. These prepositions are equivalent to *by* in English. For instance:

CHAPTER 8: PREPOSITIONS

It. Vado *in* macchina oggi;

Fr. Je vais *en* voiture aujourd'hui.

- *I go **by** car today.*

There are some of the most common phrases which describe means of transportation and which require the preposition It. *in*; Fr. *en*:

Italian	French	English
in automobile/ macchina	en auto/voiture	by car
in autobus	en autobus	by bus
in taxi	en taxi	by taxi
in aereo	en avion	by plane/air
in metro	en métro	by the underground
in nave	en bateau	by boat
in treno	en train and **par le train** (when arriving)	by train

> **NOTE:**
> In French **par** must be used with the definite article in comparison with **en**, which doesn't require it.

In order to to express how a person enters or leaves transport, the following verbs can be used in Italian and French:

CHAPTER 8: PREPOSITIONS

Italian	French	English
montare in/a/su; salire su	monter en/dans (le,la)	*to get on*
scendere da	descendre de	*to get off; to descend from*
imbarcarsi in	embarquer dans	*to embark*
sbarcare da	débarquer de	*to disembark from*

It. *montare in* (*imbarcarsi in*) una macchina (un treno, un autobus, una nave etc.);

Fr. *monter en/dans* (*embarquer dans*) (une) voiture (un train, un autobus, un bateau etc.);

- *to get on (to embark) a car (a train, a bus, a ship etc.).*

It. *scendere da* (*sbarcare da*) una macchina (un treno, un autobus, una nave etc.);

Fr. *descendre d'* (*débarquer d'*) une voiture (un train, un autobus, un bateau etc.);

- *to get off a car (a train, a bus, a ship etc.).*

➤ **to indicate time (in):**

It. **in**; Fr. **en** are used to indicate the time after which a thing is done or completed. It corresponds to English *in*. Observe the following:

It. Lo farà *in* due ore;

Fr. Il le fera *en* deux heures.

- *He will do it in two hours.*

CHAPTER 8: PREPOSITIONS

To mean *within* regarding the time during which an action can be done is expressed by using the following prepositions in Italian and French:

Italian	French	English
fra	**dans** (+ article)	*within*

It. Posso farlo *fra* un'ora;

Fr. Je peux le faire *dans* l'heure.

- *I can do it **within** an hour.*

It. *in*; Fr. *en* are also used to indicate when something is going to happen:

It. Vado in Argentina *in* estate;

Fr. Je vais en Argentine *en* été.

- *I go to Argentina **in** the summer.*

➤ **in certain expressions:**

It. *in*; Fr. *en* are used in the following idioms and expressions:

Italian	French	English
but: <u>per</u> scherzo;	en plaisantant; en riant; en badinant	*as a joke*
in casa	but: <u>à la</u> maison; <u>chez</u> soi	*at home*
in caso di	en cas de	*in the event of; in case*
in effetti; infatti	en effet	*in fact; in effect*

Italian	French	English
in realtà	en réalité	*in reality*
in luogo di; invece di	*but:* <u>au</u> lieu de; <u>à la</u> place	*instead of*
in breve; in succinto	en bref; en résumé en abrégé	*in short*
in conclusione	en conclusion	*in conclusion*
insomma	en somme	*in sum*
in poche parole	en quelques mots; en peu de mots	*in a few words*
in totale	*but:* au total	*in total*

Verbs with Italian **in** and French **en**

The following is a list of verbs which take the preposition It. ***in*** and Fr. **en** *before an object* (*noun* or *pronoun*).

Italian	French	English
agire in	**agir en**	to act like/as
avere fiducia *di*	**avoir confiance en**	to trust
irrompere in	**casser en** (morceaux)	to break into (pieces)
cambiarsi in	**se changer en**	to change into
convertire in	**convertir en**	to convert into
tagliare in	**couper en**	to cut in
credere in	**croire en**	to believe in

CHAPTER 8: PREPOSITIONS

Italian	French	English
degenerare in	dégénérer en	to degenerate into
mascherarsi da	se déguiser en	to disguise oneself as
scrivere in	écrire en	to write in (Chinese)
erigersi *a*	s'ériger en	to set oneself up as
misurare in	mesurer en	to measure in (meters)
andare in collera	se mettre en colère	to get angry
mettersi in cammino	se mettre en route	to set out
partire in	partir en	to leave for
tingere in	peindre en	to paint in
ridurre in	réduire en	to reduce to
tradurre in	traduire en	to translate into (Spanish)
trasformare qualcosa in	transformer quelque chose en	to transform smth. into
vendersi in	se vendre en	to be sold in (bottles)
viaggiare in	voyager en	to travel by (taxi)

NOTE:

In Italian, the verbs **avere fiducia** and **erigersi** are used with the preposition **di** and **a**.

Verbs with French *dans*

The following is a list of French verbs which take the preposition Fr. ***dans*** *before an object* (*noun* or *pronoun*).

French	English
apprendre qqch dans (un livre)	to learn smth. from (a book)
avoir dans l'esprit/l' idée que	to have a feeling that
avoir dans l' idée/la tête que	to have in mind
boire qqch dans (une tasse)	to drink smth out of (a cup)
chercher dans (un carton)	to look in (a box)
copier qqch dans (un livre)	to copy smth from (a book)
courir dans	to run through
coûter dans (les 10 dollars)	to cost about (10 dollars)
entrer dans (une salle)	to to enter (a room)
errer dans (une ville)	to wander around/through (a town)
fouiller dans	to look through
lire dans (un journal)	to read in (a paper)
manger dans (une assiette)	to eat off (a plate)
mettre son espoir dans	to pin one's hopes on
partir dans (10 minutes)	to leave in (10 minutes)
réduire en	to reduce to
traduire en	to translate into (Spanish)
transformer qqch en	to transform smth. into
se vendre en	to be sold in (bottles)

French	English
voyager en	to travel by (taxi)

Preposition *da* (It.), *chez* (Fr.)

It. *da* and Fr. *chez* are usually used with a person, a person's name or pronoun in order to express *at, to, in the house of* in the English language, for example:

It. Vai *da* Peter domani?

Fr. Vas-tu *chez* Peter demain?

- Are you going to Peter's house tomorrow?

This also extends to places of work, business, shops, groups as well as a person's profession or society in Italian and French. Study the following:

It. Andiamo *dal* medico la prossima settimana?

Fr. Nous allons *chez* le médecin la semaine prochaine.

- We are going to the doctor's next week.

Preposition *per* (It.), *pour* (Fr.)

The prepositions It. *per* and Fr. *pour* are rather common and have an extensive variety of meanings and exceptions, which must be memorized. Generally it can be translated as *for* in English. These prepositions are used to indicate:

- **purpose (in order to):**

The prepositions It. *per* and Fr. *pour* indicate a purpose or an aim that will be attained and are equivalent to English *in order to* or *to*:

CHAPTER 8: PREPOSITIONS

It. L'ho fatto *per* aiutarti;

Fr. Je l'ai fait *pour* t'aider.

- *I have done it **to** help you.*

It. Imparo francese *per* parlare con la mia zia dalla Francia;

Fr. J'apprends le français *pour* parler avec ma tante de France.

- *I learn french **to** speak with my aunt from France.*

- **recipient (for):**

The prepositions It. *per* and Fr. *pour* are also used to indicate the person or the object who will receive the action and correspond to *for* in English:

It. Ho un regalo *per* te;

Fr. J'ai un cadeau *pour* toi.

- *I have a gift **for** you.*

It. Lui lavora *per* IKEA;

Fr. Il travaille *pour* IKEA.

- *He works **for** IKEA.*

- **opinion or point of view (for, according to):**

It. *per* and Fr. *pour* can be used to express an opinion, which is equivalent to *for* or *according to* in English:

It. *Per* me, il cinese è la lingua più difficile;

Fr. *Pour* moi, le chinois est la langue la plus difficile.

- ***For** me, the Chinese is the most difficult language.*

It. ***Per*** il mio amico, è una buona opzione;

Fr. ***Pour*** mon ami, c'est une bonne option.

- ***According to*** my friend, it is a good option.

- **direction or destination (for):**

It. ***per*** and Fr. ***pour*** are also used to express the destination for a person or object:

It. Partono ***per*** la Repubblica Dominicana domani;

Fr. Ils partent ***pour*** la République Dominicaine demain.

- They leave ***for*** Dominican Republic tomorrow.

It. Questo è il bus ***per*** Guayaquil;

Fr. Ceci est le bus ***pour*** Guayaquil.

- This is the bus ***to*** Guayaquil.

- **deadline (for, on, by):**

This preposition can be used to express when something must be done by the particular time in the future. In this case the prepositions It. ***per*** and Fr. ***pour*** imply particular dates in the future and are equivalent to *for*, *on* or *by* in English:

It. Devo preparare la lezione ***per*** domani;

Fr. Je dois préparer la leçon ***pour*** demain.

- I must prepare the lesson ***for*** tomorrow.

- **comparison (for, although, despite, in spite of):**

CHAPTER 8: PREPOSITIONS

This preposition is used to compare inequalities or disparities of someone or something in order to differentiate him/her/it from others. In this case the prepositions It. **per** and Fr. **pour** are equivalent to *for, although, despite, in spite of* in English:

It. **Per** essere spagnolo, conosce la cultura cinese molto bene;

Fr. **Pour** être espagnol, il connaît très bien la culture chinoise.

- **For** a Spaniard, he knows Chinese culture very well.

- **reason or cause (because of, for):**

The preposition It., **per**, Fr. **pour** expresses the reason or motive which brought about the action. It means *because of* or *for* in English:

It. E 'stato punito **per** aver mentito;

Fr. Il a été puni **pour** avoir menti.

- He was punished **because of** lying.

It. Lei lo adora **per** il suo coraggio;

Fr. Elle l'adore **pour** sa bravoure.

- She adores him **for** his bravery.

*Preposition **da** (It.), **par** (Fr.)*

The prepositions Sp., Port. **por**, It. **da** and Fr. **par** can be translated as *by* in English. These prepositions are used to indicate:

- **passive voice:**

The prepositions It. **da** and Fr. **par** indicate the agent or the doer *by whom* or *by which* an action is started, which means that such phrases are usually used in passive constructions:

It. La porta è stata aperta ***da*** lui;

Fr. La porte a été ouverte ***par*** lui.

- *The door was opened **by** him.*

It. Il villaggio è stato distrutto ***dall'***inondazione;

Fr. Le village a été détruit ***par*** l'inondation.

- *The village was destroyed **by** the flood.*

- **direction or location (through, along):**

The prepositions It. ***da*** or ***per*** and Fr. ***par*** also designate a place or a direction through which movement takes place and are equivalent to English *through* or *along*:

It. Andiamo ***da*** quella parte!

Fr. Allons-y ***par*** là!

- *Let's go that way!*

It. Abbiamo dovuto passare ***per*** questa strada;

Fr. Nous avons dû passer ***par*** cette rue.

- *We had to pass **through** this street.*

NOTE: *That in Italian the preposition **per** is used in this case.*

- **manner or means (by, through, out of or by means of):**

The prepositions It. ***da*** or ***per*** and Fr. ***par*** also can express the manner or means by which something is done. It is equivalent to *by, through, out of* or *by means of* in English. Below are several of the phrases which denote manner:

CHAPTER 8: PREPOSITIONS

Italian	French	English
per caso; **per** accidente	par hazard; par accident	by accident
per abitudine	par habitude	out of habit

NOTE: in Italian the preposition **per** is used in this case.

It. Lo fa **per** abitudine;

Fr. Il le fait **par** habitude;

- He does it **out of** habit.

It. Parleremo **al** telefono più tardi;

Fr. Nous allons parler **au** téléphone plus tard.

- We will talk **on** the phone later.

NOTE:
Italian preposition **al** and French **au** are used in this case.

- **amount and rate (per, a):**

The prepositions Fr. **par** translates quantity per unit of measurement and rate. It is equivalent to English *per* or *a*:

It. Lei guadagna 20 dollari **all'**ora.

Fr. Elle gagne 20 dollars **de l'**heure.

- She earns 20 dollars **per** hour.

CHAPTER 8: PREPOSITIONS

> **NOTE:**
> Italian preposition **a** and French **de** are used in this case.

It. Studio francese tre volte **_alla_** settimana;

Fr. J'apprends le français trois fois **par** semaine.

- I learn French three times **per** week.

> **NOTE:**
> In Italian, the preposition **a** is used in this case.

Verbs with *per* (It.) and *pour* (Fr.)

Below is the list of the most common verbs that require It. **per** and Fr. **pour** before an infinitive:

> **NOTE:**
> However, there are verbs which are used with different prepositions. They are all italicized and underlined. Pay attention to them and try to memorize them carefully.

Italian	French	English
scusarsi per	s'excuser _de_/pour	to apologize for
sforzarsi _di_/_a_	s'efforcer _de_/_à_	to struggle to
essere per/_da_	être pour	to be in favor of
lottare per	lutter pour	to struggle for
optare per	opter pour	to opt for

The following is a list of verbs which take the preposition It. **per** and Fr. **pour** before an object (noun or pronoun).

Italian	French	English
spaventarsi per	s'effrayer _à_	to get frightened about
scambiare _con_	échanger _contre_/ troquer _contre_	to exchange for
iniziare _col_/_da_	commencer par / _avec_	to begin by/with
inquietarsi per	s'inquiéter _de_/ se soucier _de_	to be very concerned about
scusarsi per	s'excuser _de_/pour	to apologize for
essere per/_da_	être pour	to be in favor of
interessarsi _a_	s'intéresser _à_	to be interested in
lottare per	lutter pour	to struggle for
giurare per/_su_	jurer par/_sur_	to swear by/on
optare per	opter pour	to opt for
pagare per/_con_	payer pour/_avec_	to pay by/with
chiedere _di_	demander _de_	to ask about/after
preoccuparsi per	se préoccuper _de_	to worry about
pregare per	prier pour	to pray for
uscire per	sortir par	to leave via
prendere per	prendre pour	to take for
viaggiare per	voyager par	to travel by (train)
votare per	voter pour	to vote for

*Preposition **con** (It.), **avec** (Fr.)*

CHAPTER 8: PREPOSITIONS

The prepositions It. **con** and Fr. **avec** mean *with* and are basically used like its English equivalent. These prepositions are used to express:

- **accompaniment (with):**

    It. Lui va al cinema **con** Anna;

    Fr. Il va au cinéma **avec** Anna.

    - *He is going to the cinema **with** Anna.*

    It. Lei vuole sposarsi **con** uno straniero;

    Fr. Elle veut se marier **avec** un étranger.

    - *She want to get married **to** a foreigner.*

- **instrument, means (with):**

    The prepositions It. **con** and Fr. **avec** are also used to indicate the instrument *with* which something is done in Spanish, Portuguese, Italian and French. It corresponds to *with* in English:

    It. Ho scritto questa lettera **con** una matita;

    Fr. J'ai écrit cette lettre **avec** un crayon.

    - *I wrote this letter **with** a pencil.*

    It. L'ho visto **con** i miei propri occhi;

    Fr. Je l'ai vu **avec** mes propres yeux.

    - *I saw it **with** my own eyes.*

- **reason, cause (with):**

CHAPTER 8: PREPOSITIONS

It. E 'impossibile lavorare **con** questo rumore;

Fr. Il est impossible de travailler **avec** ce bruit.

- *It is impossible to work **with** this noise.*

It. Ci sono cose che la gente non si dimentica mai **con** il tempo;

Fr. Il y a des choses qu'on n'oublie jamais **avec** le temps.

- *There are things that one never forgets **with** time.*

- **attribute (with):**

In order to express the attribute or describe a person's appearance the prepositions It. **con** are used in Italian.

NOTE:
Remember that in French, the preposition Fr. **à** is used in this sense. For example:

It. Quella è una ragazza **con** i capelli lunghi;

Fr. C'est une fille **aux** cheveux longs.

- *That is a girl **with** long hair.*

However, in the Romance languages, the prepositions It. **con** and Fr. **avec** can be found in a number of other meanings depending on the context. Below are the most common examples where the prepositions It. **con** and Fr. **avec** are used differently from the use of *with* in the English language:

- **used to form adverbial phrases:**

The prepositions It. **con** and Fr. **avec** can be used to compose phrases that function like adverbs. It is possible to do the same English using with and other preposition, but nevertheless it is more common to do so in the Romance languages. Observe the following:

CHAPTER 8: PREPOSITIONS

It. Lei ha detto questo **con** entusiasmo;

Fr. Elle a dit ça **avec** enthousiasme.

- *She said it enthusiastically.*

It. Aspetto la tua lettera **con** pazienza;

Fr. J'attends ta lettre **avec** patience.

- *I am waiting for your letter patiently.*

- **used to indicate conditions (in spite of, despite):**

Sometimes Fr. **avec** can occur in the phrases with the meanings of *despite, in spite of*, for instance:

It. **Nonostante/Dopo** tutto questo, è ancora felice;

Fr. **Avec** tout cela, elle est toujours heureuse.

- ***Despite** everything, she is still happy.*

NOTE:
Italian **nonostante** or **dopo** should be used, since these expressions sound more natural in this case.

Preposition *senza (It.), sans (Fr.)*

The prepositions It. **senza** and Fr. **sans** stand for *without* and are placed before nouns or verbs. These prepositions are used to indicate:

- **a lack (without):**

It. Io preferisco il tè **senza** zucchero;

Fr. Je préfère le thé **sans** sucre.

- *I prefer the tea **without** sugar.*

It. Non posso prendere una decisione ***senza*** di voi;

Fr. Je ne peux pas prendre une décision ***sans*** vous.

- *I can't make a decision **without** you.*

- **constructions with an infinitive:**

The preposition It. ***con*** and Fr. ***avec*** - *without* is also followed by an infinitive. It should be noted that in English a gerund used in this case (**See Infinitive p.301**). Observe the following:

It. Lei è entrato ***senza*** guardarmi;

Fr. Elle est entrée ***sans*** me regarder.

- *She entered **without** looking at me.*

*Preposition **contro** (It.), **contre** (Fr.)*

The preposition It. ***contro*** and Fr. ***contre*** literally and figuratively means against in all contexts. It is used to express:

- **location or juxtaposition (against, next to):**

It. Il tavolo sta ***contro*** la parete;

Fr. La table est ***contre*** le mur.

- *The table is **against** the wall.*

- **opposition (against):**

It. Sono ***contro*** la guerra;

CHAPTER 8: PREPOSITIONS

Fr. Ils sont **contre** la guerre.
- *They are **against** the war.*

- **protection (against, from):**

It. Questa è la medicina **contro** l'influenza;
Fr. C'est le médicament **contre** la grippe.
- *That is the medicine for the flu.*

*Preposition **tra** (It.), **entre** (Fr.)*

The preposition It. **contro** and Fr. **contre** generally means *between, among*. It is used the way one uses its English equivalent:

It. Non c'è nessuna differenza **tra** te e me;
Fr. Il n'y a aucune différence **entre** toi et moi.
- *There is no difference **between** you and me.*

It. Devo scegliere **tra** questi due prodotti;
Fr. Je dois choisir **entre** ces deux produits.
- *I have to choose **between** those two products.*

*Preposition **su** (It.), **sur** (Fr.)*

The preposition It. **su** and Fr. **sur** normally means *on, about* or *over*. It can be used in a number of ways depending on the context. Thus, It. **su** and Fr. **sur** is used:

- **to mean location (on, upon, over):**

CHAPTER 8: PREPOSITIONS

It. Ho messo un libro **sul** tavolo;

Fr. J'ai mis un livre **sur** la table.

- *I put a book **on** the table.*

It. Puoi sederti **sulla** sedia;

Fr. Tu peux t'assoir **sur** la chaise.

- *You can sit **on** the chair.*

- **to mean subject or topic (about, on, concerning, with regard to):**

The preposition It. **su** and Fr. **sur** is used to show formal treatment of a subject or topic:

It. Questo autore ha scritto un libro **sulla** cucina orientale;

Fr. Cet auteur a écrit un livre **sur** la cuisine orientale.

- *This author wrote a book **about/on** oriental cuisine.*

It. Lei ha partecipato a una conferenza **sulla** pedagogia;

Fr. Elle a participé à une conférence **sur** la pédagogie.

- *She participated in a conference **on** pedagogy.*

- **to express approximation of time (about, around, over):**

It. Arriveremo <u>**verso le**</u> cinque;

Fr. Nous arriverons **sur** les cinq heures.

- *We will arrive **at around** five o'clock.*

NOTE:
In Italian, **verso le** should be used in this case.

It. **Sul** 2012, l'economia del paese ha iniziato a crescere;

Fr. **<u>Autours de</u>** 2012, l'économie du pays a commencé à croître.

- **Around** 2012 the economy of the country started to grow.

NOTE:
In French, the preposition **autours de** should be used in this case.

Preposition *davanti a (It.), devant (Fr.)*

The preposition It. **davanti a** and Fr. **devant** means *in front of* or *before* and designates a location or position. This preposition is used with nouns or pronouns. It is notable that in Italian the preposition **davanti** is used with **a**. Observe the following:

It. Sono **davanti alla** scuola;

Fr. Je suis **devant** l'école.

- I am **in front of** the school.

It. Lei è passato **davanti a** me;

Fr. Elle a passé **devant** moi.

- She passed **before** me.

Preposition *sotto (It.), sous (Fr.)*

The preposition It. **sotto** and Fr. **sous** means *under*. It can be used literally when indicating position (e.g. under the sky), or figuratively (e.g. under the pressure):

It. Il cane è **sotto** la pioggia;

Fr. Le chien est **sous** la pluie.

- The dog is **in** the rain.

CHAPTER 8: PREPOSITIONS

It. La situazione è **sotto** controllo;

Fr. La situation est **sous** contrôle.

- *The situation is **under** control.*

But In Italian and French, the preposition It. **sotto** and Fr. **sous** is still used in this sense:

It. Il cane è **sotto** l'albero;

Fr. Le chien est **sous** l'arbre.

- *The dog is **under** the tree.*

*Preposition **da** (It.), **depuis** (Fr.)*

The preposition It. **da** and Fr. **depuis** expresses *from* or *since*. It is used in order to emphasize:

- **range or distance (from):**

It. Vorrei viaggiare **da** Napoli fino a Milano;

Fr. Je voudrais voyager **depuis** Naples jusqu'à Milan.

- *I would like to travel **from** Naples to Milan.*

It. Ci sono scarpe **da** venti fino a settanta euro;

Fr. Il y a des chaussures <u>**de**</u> vingt à soixante-dix euros.

- *There are shoes **from** twenty to seventy euros.*

NOTE:
French preposition **de** should be used in this case.

CHAPTER 8: PREPOSITIONS

- **time (from, since):**

> It. Egli cerca un lavoro **da** giugno;
>
> Fr. Il cherche un travail **depuis** Juin.
>
> - *He has been looking for a job **since** June.*

> It. Mi conoscono **dall'**infanzia.;
>
> Fr. Ils me connaissent **depuis** l'enfance.
>
> - *They have known me **since** childhood.*

*Preposition **durante** (It.), **pendant** (**durant**) (Fr.)*

The preposition It. ***durante*** and Fr. ***pendant*** (***durant***) means *during* or *for*. It is used to indicate:

- **duration of time (from):**

> It. Abbiamo parlato **durante** tutta la notte;
>
> Fr. Nous avons parlé **pendant** toute la nuit.
>
> - *We talked **during** all night.*

> It. **Durante** ottobre, il clima è diventato più freddo;
>
> Fr. **Pendant** (**Durant**) octobre, le temps est devenu plus froid.
>
> - ***In (during)*** *October, the weather became colder.*

*Preposition **fino a** (It.), **jusqu'à** (Fr.)*

CHAPTER 8: PREPOSITIONS

The prepositions It. *fino a* and Fr. *jusqu'à* generally express *until* or *up to*. These prepositions are used to demonstrate:

- **time (until, up to):**

    It. Voglio visitare la Colombia fino **alla** fine dell'anno;

    Fr. Je veux visiter la Colombie *jusqu'à* la fin de l'année.

    - *I want to visit Colombia **until** the end of the year.*

- **place (until, up to, as far as):**

    It. Ha viaggiato *fino a* Barranquilla;

    Fr. Il a voyagé *jusqu'à* Barranquilla.

    - *He travelled **as far as** Barranquilla.*

Preposition *verso* (It.), *vers* (Fr.)

The prepositions It. *verso* and Fr. *vers* literally and figuratively mean *towards* or *around* or *about*. These prepositions are used to indicate:

- **direction of movement (towards, to):**

    It. L'ho visto andare *verso* il parco;

    Fr. Je l'ai vu aller *vers* le parc.

    - *I saw him going **towards** the park.*

NOTE:

In French, the preposition <u>towards</u> in figurative meaning is Fr. *envers*. While in Italian, the prepositions It. *verso* are still used. Observe

CHAPTER 8: PREPOSITIONS

the following:

> It. Qual è il tuo atteggiamento **verso** il femminismo?
> Fr. Quelle est votre attitude **envers** le feminisme?
> - What is your attitude **towards** feminism?

- **approximation of time (around, about):**

> It. Ha promesso di venire **verso** le sette;
> Fr. Elle a promis de venir **vers** sept heures.
> - She promised to come **around** seven o'clock.

Preposition **eccetto** *(salvo) (It.),* **excepté** *(sauf) (Fr.)*

The prepositions It. **eccetto** (**salvo**) and Fr. **excepté** (**sauf**) mean *except*. These prepositions are used basically like their English equivalent. For example:

> It. Ognuno è venuto **eccetto** (**salvo**) Mario;
> Fr. Tout le monde est venu **excepté** (**sauf**) Mario.
> - Everybody came **except** Mario.

It should be mentioned that It. **salvo** and Fr. **sauf** are much more frequent in everyday language.

Preposition **secondo** *(conforme; conformemente a) (It.),* **selon** *(conformément à; d'après) (Fr.)*

422

The prepositions It. *secondo* (*conforme*; *conformemente a*) and Fr. *selon* (*conformément à*; *d'après*) corresponds to *according to*. These prepositions are used the same way as their English equivalent. For example:

It. *Secondo* lui, non è importante;

Fr. *Selon* lui, c'est pas important.

- *According to him*, it's not important.

It. *Conforme* le previsioni, sta per piovere domani;

Fr. *D'après* les prévisions, il va pleuvoir demain.

- *According to* the forecast, it will rain tomorrow.

It should be remembered that in the Romance languages, the prepositions It. *secondo* and Fr. *selon* are also widely used in speech meaning *depending on*. Study the following:

It. *Secondo* le circostanze, decideremo cosa fare;

Fr. *Selon* les circonstances, nous allons décider quoi faire.

- *Depending on* the circumstances, we will decide what to do.

Compound Prepositions (Prepositional Phrases)

Below is a list of the most frequent compound prepositions in Italian and French:

Italian	French	English
nella parte bassa	au bas de	below; at the foot/bottom of

CHAPTER 8: PREPOSITIONS

Italian	French	English
al di sopra di; *but:* sopra	au-dessus de; par-dessus	above, over
attraverso	à travers	across, through
al lato di; accanto a	à côté de	next to
al di là di	au delà de	beyond
circa a; a proposito di	au sujet de; à propos de	about, as regards, concerning
attorno a; intorno a	autour de	around
vicino a	près de	near
but: verso	*but:* envers	towards
but: lungo	au long de	along
ai piedi di	au pied de	next to; nearby
invece di; in luogo di	au lieu de; à la place de	instead of, in place of
but: malgrado, a dispetto di	*but:* malgré, en dépit de	in spite of, despite
a scopo di; affinché; al fine di	afin que/de	in order to
prima di	avant de	before
but: dopo	*but:* après	after
dinnanzi a; di fronte a	en face de;	in front of

CHAPTER 8: PREPOSITIONS

Italian	French	English
dietro a	*but*: **derrière**	behind
lontano da	loin de	away from
dentro; all'interno di	à l'intérieur de	inside, in
rispetto a; riguardo a; in quanto a; in merito a	par rapport à; quant à	with respect to, in relation to, concerning
in conformità con	conformément à; en conformité avec	according to; in accordance with
fuori di	hors de; en dehors de	outside, out of
grazie a	grâce à	thanks to
a causa di	à cause de	because of

Prepositions *nella parte bassa* (It.), *au bas de* (Fr.)

The prepositions It. **nella parte bassa** and Fr. **au bas de** mean *below, at the foot/bottom of*:

Did you know?

The name for the Euro currency was proposed by Belgium, as was the design for the € symbol.

It. Troverai la risposta **nella parte bassa della** pagina;

Fr. Tu vas trouver la réponse **au bas de** la page.

- You will find the answer **at the bottom of** the page.

CHAPTER 8: PREPOSITIONS

Prepositions ***al di sopra di (sopra) (It.), au-dessus de (par-dessus) (Fr.)***

The prepositions It. ***al di sopra di*** (***sopra***) and Fr. ***au-dessus de*** (***par-dessus***) mean *above*. Look at the example:

It. L'aereo stava volando ***al di sopra della*** (***sopra***) città;

Fr. L'avion volait ***au-dessus*** (***par-dessus***) ***de*** la ville.

- *The plane was flying* ***above*** *(****over****) the city.*

Prepositions ***attraverso (It.), à travers (Fr.)***

The prepositions It. ***attraverso*** and Fr. ***à travers*** express *across, through*:

It. Hanno deciso di passare ***attraverso*** la foresta;

Fr. Ils ont décidé de passer ***à travers*** la forêt.

- *They decided to go* ***through*** *the forest.*

Prepositions ***al lato di (accanto a) (It.), à côté de (Fr.)***

The prepositions It. ***al lato di*** (***accanto a***) and Fr. ***à côté de*** mean *next to*:

It. Il ristorante sta ***al lato della*** (***accanto alla***) mia casa;

Fr. Le restaurant est ***à côté de*** ma maison.

- *The restaurant is* ***next to*** *my house.*

CHAPTER 8: PREPOSITIONS

Prepositions *al di là di* (It.), *au delà de* (Fr.)

The prepositions It. *al di là di* and Fr. *au delà de* mean *beyond*:

It. Gli esploratori non hanno mai viaggiato *al di là dei* mari;

Fr. Les explorateurs n'ont jamais voyagé *au-delà des* mers.

- *The explorers have never travelled **beyond** the seas.*

Prepositions *circa a (a proposito di)* (It.), *au sujet de (à propos de)* (Fr.)

The prepositions It. *circa a* (*a proposito di*) and Fr. *au sujet de* (*à propos de*) stand for *about, as regards, concerning*:

It. Voglio sapere tutto *circa a* (*a proposito di*) questa storia;

Fr. Je veux tout savoir *au sujet de* (*à propos de*) cette histoire.

- *I want to know everything **about** this story.*

Prepositions *attorno a (intorno a)* (It.), *autour de* (Fr.)

The prepositions It. *attorno a* (*intorno a*) and Fr. *autour* de express *around*:

It. Sogna di viaggiare *attorno al* (*intorno al*) mondo;

Fr. Il rêve de voyager *autour du* monde.

- *He dreams of travelling **around** the world.*

Prepositions *vicino a* (It.), *près de* (Fr.)

CHAPTER 8: PREPOSITIONS

The prepositions It. **vicino a** and Fr. **près de** mean *near*:

It. Il mio amico vive **vicino alla** scuola.;
Fr. Mon ami vit **près de** l'école.
- *My friend lives **near** the school.*

Prepositions *verso (It.), envers (Fr.)*

The prepositions It. **verso** and Fr. **envers** mean *towards*:

It. L'insegnante è molto gentile **verso** gli alunni;
Fr. Le professeur est très gentil **envers** les élèves.
- *The teacher is very kind **towards** the students.*

Prepositions *lungo (It.), au long de (Fr.)*

The prepositions It. **lungo** and Fr. **au long de** mean *along, throughout, during* and can indicate:

- **time (throughout, during):**

    It. Il festival durerà **lungo** una settimana;
    Fr. Le festival va durer **au long de** la semaine.
    - *The festival will last **throughout** a week.*

- **movement over or for the length of (along):**

    It. Due uomini hanno camminato **lungo** il fiume;

CHAPTER 8: PREPOSITIONS

Fr. Deux hommes ont marché **le long de** la rivière.

- *Two men walked **along** the river.*

*Prepositions **ai piedi di** (It.), **au pied de** (Fr.)*

The prepositions It. ***ai piedi di*** and Fr. ***au pied de*** express *next to; nearby; at the bottom of*:

It. Stavano ***ai piedi di*** una montagna;

Fr. Ils étaient ***au pied d****'une montagne.

- *They were **at the bottom of** a mountain.*

*Prepositions **invece di** (**in luogo di**) (It.), **au lieu de** (**à la place de**) (Fr.)*

The prepositions It. ***invece di*** (***in luogo di***) and Fr. ***au lieu de*** (***à la place de***) express *instead of, in place of*:

It. ***Invece di*** (***in luogo di***) guardare la televisione, lei ha deciso di leggere un libro;

Fr. ***Au lieu de*** (***à la place de***) regarder la télévision, elle a décidé de lire un livre.

- ***Instead of*** *watching TV, she decided to read a book.*

*Prepositions **malgrado** (**a dispetto di**) (It.), **malgré** (**en dépit de**) (Fr.)*

The prepositions It. ***malgrado*** (***a dispetto di***) and Fr. ***malgré*** (***en dépit de***) designate *in spite of, despite*:

It. Sono uscito ***malgrado*** (***a dispetto della***) la pioggia;

Fr. Je suis sorti **malgré** (**en dépit de**) la pluie.

- *I went out **despite** the rain.*

Prepositions *a scopo di (affinché) (It.), afin que/de (Fr.)*

The prepositions It. **a scopo di** (**affinché, al fine di**) and Fr. **afin que/de** stand for *in order to*:

It. È andato in un negozio **a scopo di** (**affinché/ al fine di**) comprare una nuova giacca;

Fr. Il est allé dans un magasin **afin d'**acheter une nouvelle veste.

- *He went to a store **in order to** buy a new jacket.*

Prepositions *prima di (It.), avant de (Fr.)*

The prepositions It. **prima di** and Fr. **avant de** stand for *before*:

It. **Prima di** uscire, ho spento la luce;

Fr. **Avant de** sortir, j'ai éteint la lumière.

- ***Before*** *going out I switched off the light.*

Prepositions *dopo (It.), après (Fr.)*

The prepositions It. **dopo** and Fr. **après** mean *after*:

It. **Dopo** aver cenato, è andato dormire;

Fr. **Après** avoir dîné, il est allé dormir.

- ***After*** *having dinner he went to sleep.*

Prepositions *dinnanzi a (di fronte a) (It.)*, *en face de (Fr.)*

The prepositions It. **dinnanzi a** (*di fronte a*) and Fr. **en face de** mean *in front of*:

It. **Dinnanzi alla** (***di fronte alla***) nostra casa c'è un grande parco;

Fr. **En face de** notre maison il y a un grand parc.

- *In front of* our house there is a big park.

Prepositions *dietro a (It.)*, *derrière (Fr.)*

The prepositions It. **dietro a** and Fr. **derrière** stand for *behind*. It is used when referring to position (e.g. behind the house):

It. La scuola si trova **dietro al** parco;

Fr. L'école se trouve **derrière** le parc.

- *The school is **behind** the park.*

NOTE:
Take into consideration that Italian and French prepositions It. **dopo di** and Fr. **après** can be used to express <u>after</u> (meaning being in pursuit of) when following the verbs of motion:

It. L'uomo è uscito **dopo di** lei.
Fr. L'homme est sorti **après** elle.
- *The man went out **after** her.*

Prepositions *lontano da (It.)*, *loin de (Fr.)*

CHAPTER 8: PREPOSITIONS

The prepositions It. **lontano da** and Fr. **loin de** mean *away from*:

It. Mia sorella vive **lontano dal** centro della città;

Fr. Ma soeur vit **loin du** centre-ville.

- My sister lives *far from* the city center.

Prepositions *dentro (all'interno di) (It.), à l'intérieur de (Fr.)*

The prepositions It. **dentro** (**all'interno di**) and Fr. **à l'intérieur de** mean *inside, in*:

It. La bambola è **dentro** la (**all'interno della**) scatola;

Fr. La poupée est **à l'intérieur de** la boîte.

- The doll is **inside** the box.

Prepositions *rispetto a (riguardo a, in quanto a, in merito a) (It.), par rapport à (quant à) (Fr.)*

The prepositions It. **rispetto a** (**riguardo a, in quanto a, in merito a**) and Fr. **par rapport à** (**quant à**) mean *with respect to, in relation to, concerning*:

It. Ho già sentito la notizia **rispetto alla** celebrazione;

Fr. Je l'ai déjà entendu les nouvelles **par rapport à** la célébration.

- I have already heard the news **regarding** the celebration.

Prepositions *in conformità con (It.), en conformité avec (conformément à) (Fr.)*

The prepositions It. *in conformità con* and Fr. *en conformité avec* (*conformément à*) designate *according to, in accordance with*:

It. *In conformità con* questo cartello stradale, dobbiamo girare a sinistra;

Fr. *En conformité avec* ce panneau de signalisation de route, nous devons tourner à gauche.

- *In accordance with* this road sign, we must turn left.

Prepositions *fuori di (It.), hors de (en dehors de) (Fr.)*

The prepositions It. *fuori di* and Fr. *hors de* (*en dehors de*) mean *outside, out of*:

It. I bambini giocano *fuori dalla* casa;

Fr. Les enfants jouent *hors de* (*en dehors de*) la maison.

- The children play *outside* the house.

Prepositions *grazie a (It.), grâce à (Fr.)*

The prepositions It. *grazie a* and Fr. *grâce à* express *thanks to*:

It. *Grazie al* mio insegnante, io so l'italiano molto bene;

Fr. *Grâce à* mon professeur, je connais très bien l'Italien.

- *Thanks to* my teacher, I know Italian very well.

Prepositions *a causa di (It.)*, *à cause de (Fr.)*

The prepositions It. *a causa di* and Fr. *à cause de* stand for because of:

Did you know?

Reggio Calabria or simply Reggio is a city in southern Italy. Reggio has several popular nicknames: "The city of Bronzes", because of the Riace Bronzes - ancient, life-size Greek statues; "the city of bergamot", which is cultivated in the region; and "the city of Fata Morgana", which is an optical phenomenon observed in Italy only from the Reggio coastal side.

It. La lezione è stata annullata *a causa della* forte nevicata;

Fr. La leçon a été annulée *à cause de* fortes chutes de neige.

- *The lesson was canceled **because of** the heavy snowfall.*

Contraction of Prepositions with Article

See Contraction of the Article p.63.

CHAPTER 9: CONJUNCTIONS

Overview

Like the English conjunctions *"and"*, *"or"*, *"if"*, *"as well as"*, *"but"* Spanish, Portuguese, Italian and French conjunctions are the words which connect two parts of a sentence together. Observe the following:

>It. Lei parla francese *e* italiano molto bene;
>
>Fr. Elle parle très bien français *et* italien.
>
>- *She speaks French **and** Italian very well.*

Conjunctions are divided into three major groups, **coordinating**, **subordinating** and **correlative**, in the Romance languages:

Coordinating Conjunctions

Coordinating conjunctions join similar words or group of words, for example:

>It. Io leggo *ma* lei dorme;
>
>Fr. Je lis *mais* elle dort.
>
>- *I read **but** she sleeps.*

Note that the two parts of the clause bare independent of each other and could easily be separated by punctuation, in the Romance languages. Study the following:

>It. Io leggo, lei dorme;   It. Io leggo. Lei dorme;
>Fr. Je lis, elle dort.   Fr. Je lis. Elle dort.
>- *I read, she sleeps.*   - *I read. She sleeps.*

Below is a list of the most common *coordinating* conjunctions in the Romance languages:

Italian	French	English
e	et	and
ma	mais	but
o	ou	or
allora	alors	so

Subordinating Conjunctions

Subordinating conjunctions connect a dependent clause to a main clause. It is noticeable that dependent clause cannot be used alone as its meaning is not complete without the main clause. Observe the following:

Did you know?

Lyon is the 3rd largest city in France, located around 470 km (292 mi) south from Paris. It has a long culinary arts tradition. Lyon is considered "the gastronomic capital of the world". Popular local dishes are: coq au vin, quenelle, gras double, salade lyonnaise, rosette lyonnaise and others.

It. **Come** lui non ha tempo, non può farlo;

Fr. **Comme** il n'a pas le temps, il ne peut pas le faire..

- **Since** he doesn't have time, he cannot do it.

The main clause is "*he cannot do it*". The clause "*Since he doesn't have time*" is a dependent one and is not complete without the main one. In fact the idea is not that he doesn't want to do it, but he cannot do it since he doesn't have enough time.

CHAPTER 9: CONJUNCTIONS

It is noticeable that Subordinating conjunctions are usually placed at the beginning of the sentence they introduce in Italian and French.

Below is a list of some frequently used subordinating conjunctions in Italian and French:

Italian	French	English
a condizione che	à condition que	on the condition that
a causa di	à cause de	because of;
grazie al fatto che; per il fatto che	grâce au fait que; dû au fait de/que	owing to the fact that; thanks to
affinché	afin de/que	so that
a meno che	à moins de/que	unless
piuttosto	plutôt que	rather, on the contrary
prima che (di)	avant de/que	before
dopo che; dopoché	après que	after
perciò; dunque; e così	comme ça; aussi (with invertion)	thus
appena che	aussitôt que; dès que; à peine (with invertion)	as soon as, after,
è per questo; è perciò;	c'est pourquoi; voilà pourquoi	that is why
cosicché; ebbene	donc; ainsi donc	therefore

CHAPTER 9: CONJUNCTIONS

Italian	French	English
nonostante che, malgrado che	malgré que	despite that
anche se	même si	even if
però; anche se; benché; sebbene; ciò nonostante; cionondimeno; nondimeno; comunque; tuttavia	quoique; bien que; cependant; toutefois; néanmoins; pourtant	however; yet; nevertheless
come; giacché siccome; poiché	comme; dès lors que; puisque	as, for, since
con l'obiettivo di; allo scopo di che; al fine di/che	dans le but de/que; aux fins de/que; à l'effet de/que	with the purpose of
purché	pourvu que	provided that, as long as
quando	quand	when
dato che	étant donné que	given that
in maniera che; in modo che	de (telle) manière que; de telle sorte que; de telle façon que	in such a way that
in caso di/che; nel caso di/che	en cas de; au cas où; dans le cas où	in case that
in considerazione del fatto che	compte tenu du fait que	in view of the fact that
eccetto che	excepté que; sauf que	except that

CHAPTER 9: CONJUNCTIONS

Italian	French	English
oltre che; oltre a ciò; oltreché	outre que; hormis que	apart from that
finché; fino a quando	avant de; jusqu'à ce que	until
piuttosto che	plutôt que	rather than
mentre (che)	pendant que; tandis que	while
allora	alors	then
perché	pour que	in order that; so that
in quanto	(pour) autant que; puisque	inasmuch as
per quanto	pour autant que	(as) much as
pertanto	pourtant; par suite; par conséquent	so, therefore
per la ragione che	pour la raison que	for the reason that
perché	parce que; car	because
che	que	that
se	si	if
visto che	vu que	seeing that
supposto che	supposé que; à supposer que	assumed that

Italian	French	English
dal momento che	une fois que	once
come	comme	as (comparative)
...che; ...di	...que	...than
così come	ainsi que; aussi bien que	as well as
come se	comme si	as if
tanto quanto	autant que; autant	as far as; as much as

Remember that in the Romance languages, the conjunctions which are used with Fr. *que* and It. *che* need the subjunctive following them. Otherwise the indicative is used.

Correlative Conjunctions

Correlative conjunctions are pairs of conjunctions.

Below is a list of some commonly used correlative conjunctions in Italian and French:

Italian	French	English
sia...che	et...et	both...and
non...né...né	ni...ni...ne	neither...nor
non solo...ma anche	non seulement... mais aussi	not only...but also
o...o; sia...sia	ou (bien)...ou (bien); soit...soit	either...or (else)

CHAPTER 9: CONJUNCTIONS

Functions of Conjunctions

All the conjunctions in the Romance languages perform different functions, which are presented below:

Copulative conjunctions

Copulative conjunctions join two or more words, word groups or sentences which have similar function in Italian and French. The most frequent copulative conjunctions are:

Italian	French	English
e	et	*and*
non solo...ma anche	non seulement... mais aussi	*not only...but also*
non...né...né	ne...ni...ni	*neither...nor*
sia...che	et...et	*both...and*

Did you know?

The Swiss eat more chocolate than any other nation in the world, over 11 kg per year.

It. Il mio collega è molto abile **e** competente;

Fr. Mon collègue est très qualifiée **et** compétent.

- *My colleague is very skilled **and** competent.*

It. Ho comprato questa casa, **non solo** perché era a buon mercato, **ma anche** perché era in buone condizioni;

Fr. J'ai acheté cette maison **non seulement** parce qu'elle était bon marché, **mais aussi** parce qu'elle était en bon état.

- *I bought this house **not only** because it was cheap, **but also** because it was in good condition.*

CHAPTER 9: CONJUNCTIONS

Adversative conjunctions

These conjunctions demonstrate opposition among the units they connect. Below is a list of the most frequent adversative conjunctions in Italian and French:

Italian	French	English
ma	**mais**	*but*
però; anche se, benché; sebbene; ciò nonost-ante; cionondi-meno; nondimeno; comunque; tuttavia	**quoique; bien que; cependant; toutefois; néan-moins; pourtant**	*however; yet; nevertheless*
piuttosto	**plutôt**	*rather*
piuttosto che	**plutôt que**	*rather than*
oltre che; oltre a ciò; oltreché	**outre que; hormis que**	*apart from that*
eccetto (che); tranne (che)	**excepté (que); sauf (que)**	*except (that)*
quand-anche	**même si**	*even if*
prima che (di)	**avant que**	*before*

It. La giornata era calda, **comunque (*però, ciò nonostante* etc.)** non siamo andati in spiaggia;

Fr. La journée était chaude, **cependant (*quoique, néanmoins* etc.)** nous ne sommes pas allés à la plage.

- *It was a hot day,* **however (*yet, nevertheless*)** *we didn't go to the beach.*

CHAPTER 9: CONJUNCTIONS

Did you know?

The world's first recorded lottery took place in Belgium. It was held to raise money for the poor.

It. Egli va a fare una passeggiata ogni giorno, **tranne** quando è freddo;

Fr. Il se promène chaque jour, **sauf** quand il fait froid.

- He goes for a walk every day, **except** when it is cold.

Disjunctive conjunctions

Disjunctive conjunctions connect words or sentences in order to indicate different opinions or alternatives. Below are some frequently used disjunctive conjunctions in the Romance languages:

Italian	French	English
o	ou	or
o...o; sia...sia	ou (bien)...ou (bien); soit...soit	either...or
non...né...né	ni...ni...ne	neither...nor

NOTE:

In Spanish, if **o** precedes a word which begins with an *o*, it changes to a **u** in order to differentiate the words (e.g. Uno **u** otro plato me va – Either dish is ok for me).

It. Cucinerai **o** pulirai la casa?

Fr. Tu vas cuisiner **ou** nettoyer la maison?

- Will you cook **or** clean the house?

It. **O** vieni con me, **o** rimani;

Fr. **Ou** (**soit**) tu viens avec moi, **ou** (**soit**) tu restes.

- **Either** you go with me **or** you stay.

Consecutive conjunctions

Consecutive conjunctions connect words or sentences in order to indicate the result of an action. The most frequent ones are the following:

Italian	French	English
dunque; ebbene	donc; ainsi donc; alors	therefore
allora	alors	then
cosicché; e così	comme ça, aussi (with invertion)	thus
è per questo; è perciò;	c'est pourquoi; voilà pourquoi	that is why
perciò; pertanto	donc; par suite; par conséquent	so, therefore
di (tale) maniera che; in (tale) modo che	de (telle) manière que; de (telle) sorte que; de (telle) façon que	in such a way that

It is noticeable that consecutive conjunctions are usually placed at the beginning of the clause they represent in the Romance languages.

Did you know?

Parma, a city in northern Italy, is famous for its proscicutto (cured ham), cheese, music and architecture. In 2004 Parma has a food tourism sector, which represented by Parma Golosa and Food Valley.

It. Egli non ha studiato, **perciò** non ha passato l'esame;

Fr. Il n'a pas étudié, **donc** il n'a pas passé l'examen.

- He did not study, **therefore** he did not pass the exam.

It. Lei l'ha detto **di maniera che** mi arrabbiassi;

Fr. Elle l'a dit **de telle manière que** je me suis fâché.

- She said it **in such a way that** I got angry.

CHAPTER 9: CONJUNCTIONS

Causal conjunctions

These conjunctions subordinate one clause to another, where one causes the other to happen. Below is a list of the most common causal conjunctions:

Italian	French	English
perché	parce que; car	because
come; giacché siccome; poiché	comme; dès lors que; puisque	as, for, since
che	que	that
in considerazione del fatto che	compte tenu du fait que	in view of the fact that
visto che	vu que	seeing that
dal momento che	du moment que	once
supposto che	supposé que; à supposer que	assumed that
per la ragione che	pour la raison que	for the reason that
dato che	étant donné que	given that
in quanto	(pour) autant que; puisque	inasmuch as

It. Mark non è venuto **perché** era occupato;

Fr. Mark n'était pas venu **parce qu'**il était occupé.

- Mark didn't come **because** he was busy.

It. **Come** non hai chiamato, sono partito;

Fr. **Comme** tu n'as pas appelé, je suis partie.

- **Since** you didn't call, I left.

CHAPTER 9: CONJUNCTIONS

Concessive conjunctions

These conjunctions express an idea that implies the opposite of the main part of the sentence. Below is a list of adversative conjunctions in the Romance languages:

Italian	French	English
nonostante; malgrado che	**malgré le fait que**	*despite the fact that*
anche se	**même si**	*even if*
però; anche se, benché, sebbene; ciò nonostante; ciononondimeno; nondimeno; comunque; tuttavia	**bien que; cependant; toutefois; néanmoins; pourtant**	*however; yet; nevertheless; although*
per quanto che	**pour autant que**	*(as) much as*

It. Le piace cucinare, **anche se** (**però** and etc.) lei non cucina spesso;

Fr. Elle aime cuisiner, **bien qu'**elle (**néanmoins** and etc.) ne cuisine pas souvent.

- She likes to cook, **although** she doesn't cook often.

Did you know?

Lille, a city in northern France, close to the border with Belgium, is distinguished by Flemish architectural style. It features 17th-century red brick town houses aligned in a row, cobbled pedestrian streets. This architectural style is uncommon in France.

It. **Nonostante** ci siamo sforzati molto, non abbiamo vinto il concorso;

Fr. **Malgré le fait que** nous nous sommes efforcés beaucoup, nous n'avons pas gagné la compétition.

- **Despite the fact that** we have tried hard, we have not won the competition.

CHAPTER 9: CONJUNCTIONS

Conditional conjunctions

Conditional conjunctions describe the condition that needs to be met in order to fulfil what is implied in the main clause. Below is a list of some frequently used conditional conjunctions in Italian and French:

Italian	French	English
a condizione che	à condition que	on the condition that
se	si	if
come; giacché siccome; poiché	comme; dès lors que; puisque	as, for, since
in caso di che; nel caso	en cas que; au cas où; dans le cas où	in case that
purché	pourvu que	provided that, as long as

Note that Conditional conjunctions usually take the verb either in the Subjunctive or in the Infinitive.

Did you know?

The World Wide Web was invented by Tim Berners Lee in Switzerland in 1989.

It. **Nel caso** ti perda, chiama questo numero;

Fr. **Au cas où** tu te perdes, appelle ce numéro.

- **In case that** you get lost, call this number.

It. **Se** lei vuole essere un medico, deve studiare molto;

Fr. **Si** elle veut être un médecin, elle doit beaucoup étudier.

- **If** she wants to be a doctor, she must study a lot.

Final conjunctions

Final conjunctions are coordinating conjunctions and are used to express a clause that indicate the purpose or aim of the main clause, such as:

Italian	French	English
affinché	afin que	so that
con l'obiettivo di; allo scopo di che; al fine di che	dans le but de/que; aux fins de que; à l'effet de que	with the purpose of
perché	pour que	in order that; so that

Note that final conjunctions must be followed by the Subjunctive.

It. Ti ricordo *affinché* non dimentichi di comprare un regalo;

Fr. Je te rappelle *pour que* tu n'oublies pas d'acheter un cadeau.

- *I remind you so that you will not forget to buy a gift.*

It. Lavora sodo *affinché* (*perché*) possa comprare una casa;

Fr. Elle travaille dur *afin qu'* (*pour qu'*) elle puisse acheter une maison.

- *She works hard so that she can buy a house.*

Temporal conjunctions

These conjunctions indicate the time and tells us when something has happened. Below is a list of some common temporal conjunctions in the Romance languages:

CHAPTER 9: CONJUNCTIONS

Italian	French	English
quando	quand	*when*
appena che	aussitôt que; dès que; à peine (with invertion)	*as soon as, after*
purché	pourvu que; du moment que	*as long as*
prima che (di)	avant que/de	*before*
dopo che; dopoché	après que	*after*
mentre (che)	pendant que; tandis que	*while*
a meno che	à moins que	*unless*
finché; fino a quando	jusqu'à ce que	*until*

It. **Quando** sono arrivato, lei stava già dormendo;

Fr. **Quand** je suis arrivé, elle dormait déjà.

- **When** I arrived she was already sleeping.

Did you know?

There is no other country in Europe with as many street and music festivals all year round as Belgium

It. **Mentre** lui leggeva il giornale, sua moglie parlava al telefono;

Fr. **Pendant qu'**il lisait le journal, sa femme parlait au téléphone.

- **While** he was reading the newspaper, his wife spoke on the phone.

CHAPTER 9: CONJUNCTIONS

Comparative conjunctions

Comparative conjunctions are used to compare two ideas. Below are some common comparative conjunctions:

Italian	French	English
come	comme	as (compa-rative)
...che; ...di quello que	...que	...than
così come	ainsi que; aussi bien que	as well as
come se	comme si	as if
tanto quanto	autant que; autant autant	as far as; as much as

Did you know?

Messina is a city in norths Sicily. It is famous for the Norman Messina Cathedral (12 century), with the 3 late Gothic portals, the early 15th century windows and an astronomical clock on the bell tower.

It. Lei guadagna più soldi **di quelli che** ha guadagnato due anni fa;

Fr. Elle gagne plus d'argent **qu'**elle en a gagné il y a deux ans.

- She earns more money **than** she earned a couple of years ago.

It. Parla **come se** fosse il mio capo;

Fr. Il parle **comme s'**il était mon patron.

- He talks **as if** he were my boss.

CHAPTER 9: CONJUNCTIONS

Complementizer

These conjunctions are used to subordinate one sentence to another. The most frequent is:

Italian	French	English
che	que	that

It. Gabriela ha detto **che** stava per venire alla festa di stasera;

Fr. Gabriela a dit **qu'**elle allait venir à la fête ce soir.

- Gabriela said **that** she was going to come to the party tonight.

CHAPTER 10: INTERJECTIONS

Overview

Did you know?

Strasbourg, a French city, is the official seat of the European Parliament. The city is located near the border with Germany. Strasbourg is also one of the capitals of the European Union (along with Brussels, Luxembourg).

Like in English, in the Romance languages an interjection is a word that is used to express emotion, feeling or spontaneous reaction in the spoken language and can indicate exclamations (*wow!*), greetings (*hey!*), curses (*bloody hell!*) and etc. The use of these short words will make a speaker sound more natural and authentic.

Types of Interjections

Below are the most common interjections that are used:

- **To express greetings and farewell** in Italian and French:

Italian	French	English
Buongiorno! Buondì!	Bonjour!	Good day! Good morning!
Buon pomeriggio!	Bon après-midi!	Good afternoon!
Buonasera!	Bonsoir!	Good evening!
Buonanotte!	Bonne nuit!	Good night!
Ciao! Salve!	Bonjour!	Hello!
Ciao!	Salut!; Ciao! Tchao! Coucou! (informal)	Hi! Bye!

CHAPTER 10: INTERJECTIONS

Italian	French	English
Come sta?	**Comment allez-vous?**	*How are you? (formal)*
Come stai?	**Ça va?**	*How are you? (informal)*
Arrivederci! (informal) **Arrivederla!** (formal) **Addio!**	**Au revoir! Adieu! Babaille!** (colloquial Canada)	*Goodbye!*
A più tardi! A dopo! Di nuovo! Ci vediamo!	**À plus! À plus tard!**	*See you later!*
A presto!	**À bientôt!**	*See you soon!*
Alla prossima!	**À la prochaine!**	*See you next time!*
A domani!	**À demain!**	*See you tomorrow!*

- Used as a polite formula when the speaker is introduced to somebody:

Italian	French	English
Piacere! Molto lieto(-a)!	**Enchanté(-e)!**	*Nice to meet you!*

- Used to answer the telephone:

Italian	French	English
Pronto!	**Allô!**	*Hello! Speaking!*

CHAPTER 10: INTERJECTIONS

- **Used as greeting upon someone's arrival:**

Italian	French	English
Benvenuto(-a;-i;-e)!	Bienvenue!	*Welcome!*

- **To indicate gratitude or politeness in the Romance languages:**

Italian	French	English
Grazie!	Merci!	*Thank you! Thanks!*
Grazie mille!	Merci beaucoup!	*Thank you very much!*
Di niente! Prego! Di nulla!	De rien! Service! (Switzerland)	*You're welcome!*
Non c'è di che!	Il n'y pas de quoi!	*Don't mention it!*
Per favore! Per piacere! Prego!	S'il te plait! (informal) S'il vous plait! (formal)	*Please!*

- **To express: 1) a regret or sorrow; 2) a request for attention or request to pass; 3) a request for someone to repeat something:**

Italian	French	English
Mi dispiace	Je suis désolé(-e)	*I'm sorry*
Con permesso	Excusez-moi (formal) Excuse-moi (informal)	*Excuse me (request for attention or request to pass)*

CHAPTER 10: INTERJECTIONS

Italian	French	English
Mi scusi (formal) **Scusami** (informal)	**Pardon**	*Pardon me* (request for attention or request to pass)
Come? Prego?	**Comment? Quoi?** (informal)	*Pardon?* (interrogative) (expressing of surprise or asking to repeat)

- To mean praise and approval:

Italian	French	English
Congratulazioni! Auguri! Felicitazioni!	**Félicitations!**	*Congratula-tions!*
Bravo/a/i/e!	**Bravo!**	*Bravo! Well done!*

- To say or write to someone who is celebrating something (his or her birthday or some other holiday) in order to express the good wishes:

Italian	French	English
Congratulazioni! Auguri! Complimenti!	**Félicitations!**	*Congratula-tion!*
Buon natale!	**Joyeux noël!**	*Merry Christmas!*
Buon anno!	**Bonne année!**	*Happy New Year!*

CHAPTER 10: INTERJECTIONS

Italian	French	English
Buona Pasqua!	**Joyeuses Pâques!**	*Happy Easter!*

- To wish something (e.g.: a nice day, safe trip, good night and etc.):

Italian	French	English
Buona giornata!	**Bonne journée!**	*Have a nice day!*
Buona serata!	**Bonne soirée!**	*Have a good evening!*
Dormi bene!	**Dormez bien!** (formal) **Dors bien!** (informal)	*Sleep well!*
Sogni d'oro!	**Faites de beaux rêves!** (formal) **Fais de beaux rêves!** (informal)	*Sweet dreams!*
Buon viaggio!	**Bon voyage!**	*Have a safe journey!*
Buona fortuna!	**Bonne chance!**	*Good luck!*
Buone vacanze!	**Bonne vacances!**	*Have a good holiday!*
Salute!	**À tes (vos) souhaits!** **À tes amours!**	*Bless you! (said after a sneeze)*
Salute! **Alla salute!**	**Santé!** **À la tienne!** (formal) **À la vôtre!** (informal) **À ta (votre) santé!**	*Cheers! (toast when drinking alcohol)*
Cin cin! (Cincin!)	**Tchin-tchin!**	*Chin chin (toasting)*

CHAPTER 10: INTERJECTIONS

Italian	French	English
Buon appetito!	Bon appétit!	*Enjoy your meal!* *Bon appetit!*

- To express agreement or disagreement:

Italian	French	English
Sì!	Oui! Ouais! (colloquial) Si! (contradict a negative statement)	*Yes!*
No!	Non!	*No!*
Va bene! D'accordo! Ebbene!	D'accord! Bien! C'est bien! C'est bon!	*Okay!*
Certamente! Ma certo!	Bien sûr!	*Of course!*
È vero!	C'est vrai!	*That's true!* *True!*
Proprio così! Appunto! Giust'appunto!	C'est cela! C'est ça (colloquial) Ça y est! C'est cela même!	*That's it!* *That's right!*
Esatto! Esattamente!	Exact! Exactement!	*Exact!* *Exactly!*
Infatti!	En effet!	*Indeed!*

- To indicate that someone does not consider the matter important enough:

CHAPTER 10: INTERJECTIONS

Italian	French	English
Dici sciocchezze! Dici fesserie! Parli a vanvera!	Tu dis n'importe quoi! Tu dis des bêtises!	*Nonsense!* *Whatever!*
Non importa!	Peu importe! Cela (Ça) ne fait rien!	*It doesn't matter!*

- Used as a reply to an unimportant statement, which indicates indifference on the part of the speaker:

Italian	French	English
E allora?	Et alors?	*So what?*

- To express astonishment, admiration or surprise:

Italian	French	English
Caspita! Bah! Wow!	Waouh! Ouah! Oh là là! Ayoye! (Canada)	*Wow!*
Ahi! Ahime!	Ah! Coudonc! (Canada)	*Oh!*

CHAPTER 10: INTERJECTIONS

Italian	French	English
Bah! Va'! Accidem-poli! Accidenti! Ma! Acciderba! Ammazza! Cribbio! Diamine! Osteria! Per la miseria! Porca vacca! Porca miseria! Porca troia! Porca puttana!	Aweille!\Enweille! (Quebec) Mazette! Mince! Mais! Malepeste! (dated) Viarge! (Canada, vulgar, slang) Nom de bleu! (Switzerland) La vache! Nom d'un chien! Nom d'une pipe! Nom de Dieu! Bon sang!	*Damn! Come on!* (expres-sion surprise, in either a positive or negative sense)
Dio mio!	Mon Dieux!	*My God!*
Gesù Cristo!	Mon Dieu!	*Jesus Christ! Good Lord!*
Cielo!	Ciel!	*Good heavens!*
Signore!	Seigneur!	*Lord!*
Per l'amor di Dio Caspita! Per carità! Perdio!	Pour l'amour de Dieu! Nom de Dieu!	*For God's sake!*
Mamma mia!	Mamma mia!	*Mamma mia!*

CHAPTER 10: INTERJECTIONS

- To express pain or sorrow:

Italian	French	English
Ahi!	Aïe! Ayoye !\Ouille! (Canada)	Ouch!
Ahimè! Aimè!	Ha! Hélas!	Ah! Alas!

- To express encouragement:

Italian	French	English
Dai! Andiamo! Alé! Avanti! Orsù! Su! Suvvia!	Allez! Allez-y! Vas-y! Aweille/Enweille! (Canada)	Let's.. Let's go!

- To indicate exclamation to get attention:

Italian	French	English
Ehi! Ehilà! Ohilà!	Ohé!	Hey!

- To express irritation, anger or annoyed remark:

CHAPTER 10: INTERJECTIONS

Italian	French	English
Vai a farti friggere! Vai a fare in culo! Fanculo! Vaffanculo!	Va te faire foutre! Vas te faire enculer!	*F*ck you, F*ck off, Go to hell* (vulgar)
Diavolo!	Diable! Diantre!	*Bloody hell! Damn!*
Accidenti! Mannaggia!	Zut!\ Zut alors! Punaise!	*Damn!*
Merda!	Merde!	*Shit!* (vulgar)
Cazzo!\Sticazzi! Cazzo duro!	Putain! Putain de merde! Bordel de merde! Bordel! (Canada) Câlisse!Tabarnak! Crisse!Calvaire!	*F*ck!* (vulgar)
Figlio di puttana!	Fils de pute! Fils de garce!	*Son of a bitch* (vulgar)
Tua madre!	Ta mère!	*lit.: Your mother; Shut the f*ck up* (an insult, especially in reply to another insult) (vulgar, offensive)
Basta! Abbastanza!	Ça suffit!	*Enough!*
Pst! Sst!	Chut!	*Shh! Hush!* (requesting silence)

CHAPTER 10: INTERJECTIONS

Italian	French	English
Silenzio!	**Silence!**	*Silence!*
Taci! **Zitto!**	**Tais-toi!** **La ferme!** **Ferme ta gueule!** **\Ta gueule!** (slang, vulgar, offensive)	*Shut up! Shut your mouth!*

- To tell someone to use his\her caution:

Italian	French	English
Fate attenzione! (formal) **Fa' attenzione!** (informal)	**Faites attention!** (formal) **Fais attention!** (informal)	*Be careful!*

- Used as a cry of distress or a request for assistance:

Italian	French	English
Aiuto!	**Au secours!**	*Help!*

- Used as acknowledgement of a mistake:

Italian	French	English
Ops!	**Oups!**	*Oops!*

CHAPTER 10: INTERJECTIONS

- Used as a pause for thought to introduce a new topic or reinforcement of a question or filler, which expresses hesitation or pause in speech:

Italian	French	English
Ehm... Ecco...	Euh...	Uh..., Um...
Allora...	Alors...	So..
Ba\Beh!\Bè... Bene\Ben...	Bah!\Ben! Bien!\Bon!	Well..
Tipo...	Comme...	Like..
Sai...	Tu sais (T'sais)...	You know...
Cioè...	C'est-à-dire...	That is (to say)..
Capito?	Compris? Tu vois?	Understood?
Neh?	Hein? Pigé? Hé? (Canada)	Huh? (a tag question)
No?	Non?	OK? isn't it?\doesn't it? (used as filler at the end of a sentence)
Vero? Nevvero?	Vrai? N'est-ce pas?	Right?

- To express the sound of a sneeze:

Italian	French	English
Eccì!	Atchoum!	Artishoo! Achoo!

- **To express animal sounds:**

Italian	French	English
Miao!	Miaou!	*Meow!* (cat's sound)
Bau-bau! Arf-arf!	Wouaff-wouaff!	*Bow-bow! Woof-woof* (dog's sound)
Chip-chip!	Cui-cui!	*Tweet! Chirp!* (bird's sound)

Interjections with Exclamatory Words

(See Exclamations with Interrogative Pronouns p.113)

VERB CHARTS

Regular Verbs

	Italian	French
\multicolumn{3}{c}{**Indicative mood**}
\multicolumn{3}{c}{*Present tenses*}
Present tense	lavoro	je travaille
Present Perfect	ho lavorato	j'ai travaillé
\multicolumn{3}{c}{*Past tenses*}
Preterite	lavorai	je travaillai
Imperfect	lavoravo	je travaillais
Past Perfect	ebbi lavorato	j'eus travaillé
Pluperfect	avevo lavorato	j'avais travaillé
\multicolumn{3}{c}{*Future tense*}

VERB CHARTS

	Italian	**French**
Future	lavorerò	je travaillerai
Future Perfect	avrò lavorato	j'aurai travaillé
	Conditionals	
Conditional present	lavorerei	je travaillerais
Conditional Perfect (Past)	avrei lavorato	j'aurais travaillé
	Subjunctive mood	
	Present tenses	
Present tense	lavori	je travaille
Present Perfect	abbia lavorato	j'aie travaillé
	Past tenses	
Past tense	lavorassi	je travaillasse
Past Perfect	avessi lavorato	j'eusse travaillé

VERB CHARTS

	Italian	**French**
	Future tenses	
Future tense	—	—
Future Perfect	—	—
	Imperative mood	
	lavora (tu) lavori (Lei) lavoriamo (noi) lavorate (voi) lavorino (Loro)	travaille (tu) travaillez (vous) travaillons (nous) travaillez (vous) travaillez (vous)
	Infinitive	
	lavorare	travailler
	Compound infinitive	
	avere lavorato	avoir travaillé
	Participle	
Present Participle (gerund)	(gerund) lavorando (part.pres) lavorante	travaillant

VERB CHARTS

	Italian	French
Compound Present Participle	—	—
Past Participle	*lavorato*	*travaillé*

Irregular Verbs

Italian	French	English
Present Tense		
Avere (ho, hai, ha, abbiamo, avete, hanno)	**Avoir** (j'ai, tu as, il\elle a, nous avons, vous avez, ils\elles ont)	To have
Tenere (tengo, tieni, tiene, tengono)	**Tenir** (tiens, tiens, tient, tiennent)	To hold, To keep
Essere (sono, sei, è, siamo, siete, sono)	**Être** (suis, es, est, sommes, êtes, sont)	To be
Stare (stai, stanno)	—	To be
Andare (vado, vai, va, vanno)	**Aller** (vais, vas, va, allons, allez, vont)	To go
Dare (dai, dà, danno)	**Donner** (regular)	To give
Fare (faccio, fai, facciamo, fanno)	**Faire** (faisons, faites, font)	To do

VERB CHARTS

Italian	French	English
Dire (dico, dici, dice, diciamo, dicono)	**Dire** (disons, dites, disent)	*To say*
Potere (posso, puoi, può, possiamo, possono)	**Pouvoir** (peux, peux, peut, peuvent)	*Can*
Volere (voglio, vuoi, vuole, vogliamo, vogliono)	**Vouloir** (veux, veux, veut, veulent)	*To want*
Sapere (so, sai, sa, sappiamo, sanno)	**Savoir** (sais, sais, sait)	*To know*
Porre (pongo, poni, pone, poniamo, ponete, pongono)	**Mettre** (mets, mets, met)	*To put*
Conoscere (regular)	**Connaître** (connais, connais, connaît, connaissons, connaissez, connaissent)	*To get to know*
Venire (vengo, vieni, viene, vengono)	**Venir** (viens, viens, vient, viennent)	*To come*
Dormire (regular)	**Dormir** (dors, dors, dort)	*To sleep*
Sentire (regular)	**Sentir** (sens, sens, sent)	*To feel*
Morire (muoio, muori, muore, muoiono)	**Mourir** (meurs, meurs, meurt, meurent)	*To die*

Preterite

469

VERB CHARTS

Italian	French	English
Essere (fui, fosti, fu, fummo, foste, furono)	**Être** (fus, fus, fut, fûmes, fûtes, furent)	*To be*
Stare (stetti, stesti, stette, stemmo, steste, stettero)	*(no equivalent)*	*To be*
Avere (ebbi, avesti, ebbe, avemmo, aveste, ebbero)	**Avoir** (eus, eus, eut, eûmes, eûtes, eurent)	*To have*
Mettere (misi, <u>mettesti</u>, mise, <u>mettemmo</u>, <u>metteste</u>, misero)	**Mettre** (mis, mis, mit, mîmes, mîtes, mirent)	*To put*
Fare (feci, facesti, fece, facemmo, faceste, fecero)	**Faire** (fis, fis, fit, fîmes, fîtes, firent)	*To do*
Dire (dissi, dicesti, disse, dicemmo, diceste, dissero)	**Dire** (dis, dis, dit, dîmes, dîtes, dirent)	*To say*
Venire (venni, venne, vennero)	**Venir** (vins, vins, vint, vînmes, vîntes, vinrent)	*To come*
Sapere (seppi, seppe, seppero)	**Savoir** (sus, sus, sut, sûmes, sûtes, surent)	*To know*
Prendere (presi, prese, presero)	**Prendre** (pris, pris, prit, primes, prîtes, prirent)	*To take*
Conoscere (conobbi, conobbe, conobbero)	**Connaître** (connus, connus, connut, connûmes, connûtes, connurent)	*To know*

VERB CHARTS

Italian	French	English
Leggere (lessi, lesse, lessero)	**Lire** (lus, lus, lut, lûmes, lûtes, lurent)	*To read*
Scrivere (scrissi, scrisse, scrissero) vedere	**Écrire** (écrivis, écrivis, écrivit, écrivîmes, écrivîtes, écrivirent)	*To write*
Tenere (tenni, tenne, tennero)	**Tenir** (tins, tins, tint, tînmes, tîntes, tînrent)	*To have\to hold*
Portare (regular)	**Apporter** (regular)	*To bring*

INDEX

a (It.) **à** (Fr.)
   to express motion or direction *in, at* or *to* some place, 372
   before an infinitive, 303, (See Infinitive p.301), 372
   with expressions of manner (*with, by, on*), 374,
   with some means of travel in French, 375
   to indicate a manner that is a style, 375
   with phrases stating location, 376
   to link some repeated words, 376
   to express time and age, 377
   with time phrases, 377
   with names of places in Italian and French, 378
   before names of cities and towns in Italian and French, 378
   before names of some islands in French, 378-379
   to mean *with* in French, 380
   to express the use of an object in French, 380
   to express an infinitive which denotes an action, 381
   to express manner or means (It., Fr.), 408-409
   to denote amount and rate (It.), 409
   to express the attribute (Fr.), 413
a causa di (It.), 434
à cause de (Fr.), 434
a dispetto di (It.), 429
a proposito di (It.), 427
a scopo di (It.), 430
à côté de (Fr.), 426
à la place de (Fr.), 429
à l'intérieur de (Fr.), 432
à propos de (Fr.), 427
à qui (Fr.), 108
à travers (Fr.), 426
abbastanza (It.), 133
accanto a (It.), 426
adjectives:
   gender agreement, 26
   feminine of, 27
   special forms of feminine in French, 27-31
   position of, 32-34
   plural of, 31
   use of, 32-34
   comparison of, 45-46
   superlative of, 46-47
   irregular comparatives and superlatives of, 48-50
adverbs:
   use of, 37
   formation of (ending in –*mente, -ment*), 37
   special forms in Italian and French, 38
   manner, 38
   place, 39
   time, 40
   intensity, 41
   doubt, 42
   expressing affirmation, 42
   expressing exclusion, 42
   composed of several words, 43
   adverbial phrases, 43
   position of, 44
   comparison of, 45-46
   superlative of, 46-47
   irregular comparatives and superlatives of, 48-50
affinché (It.), 430
afin que/de (Fr.), 430
ai piedi di (It.), 429
al di là di (It.), 427
al di sopra di (It.), 426
al fine di (It.), 448
alcuno (It.), 128
al lato di (It.), 426
aller (Fr.):
   present tense of, 158

INDEX

replacing the future tense, 182
all'interno di (It.), 432
allora (It.), 436
alors (Fr.), 436
ambedue (It.), 143
andare (It.):
    present tense of, 158
    replacing the future tense, 182
apprendre (Fr.):
    past participle of, 185
après (Fr.), 430, 431
aprire (It.):
    past participle of, 185
-are verbs (It.),
    past participle, 184
    present tense, 148-150, 151-154
arithmetical operations, 357
article:
    definite, 51-53
        contraction of, 63-64
        singular forms of, 52
        plural forms of, 52
        use of, 54-60
            with days of the week, seasons, time expressions and dates, 359-369
            in specific situations, 54
            with the unique object, 54
            to refer to a category people or things, 55
            with abstract nouns, 55
            with a certain object mentioned earlier, 55
            before a noun specifying the object, 55
            with a noun referring to an idea, colors or phenomenon, 56
            omission of, 59
    indefinite, 51-54
        singular forms of, 52
        plural forms of, 52
        use of, 53-54
            to express only one thing, 53
            to refer to someone or something not yet known, 53
            to mean *some*, 54
        omission of, 60
    partitive in Italian and French, 61-63
    contraction of, 63-64
assez (Fr.), 44, 133
attorno a (It.), 427
attraverso (It.), 426
au bas de (Fr.), 425
au delà de (Fr.), 427
au lieu de (Fr.), 429
au long de (Fr.), 428
au pied de (Fr.), 429
au sujet de (Fr.), 427
aucun (Fr.), 141
au-dessus de (Fr.), 426
autour de (Fr.), 427
avant de (Fr.), 430
avec, 43, 412-414
avoir (Fr.):
    agreement of the past participle with in French, 189-190
    versus *être* as an auxiliary verb, 188-189
    past participle of, 184
    present tense of, 157
    preterite of, 194
avere (It.):
    versus *essere* as an auxiliary verb, 188-189
    past participle of, 184
    present tense of, 157
    preterite of, 194

bastante (It.), 133
beau (Fr.), 31
beaucoup (de) (Fr.), 44, 49, 133
bello (It.), 35
bene (It.), 39, 49
bien (Fr.), 39, 44-45; 49
bon (Fr.), 33, 48
buono (It.), 33, 36, 48

ça fait...que (Fr.), 182-183
cattivo (It.), 33, 48

INDEX

capire (It.):
   past participle of, 184
cardinal numbers, 340
causative constructions, 312
ce (cet)/cette/ces (Fr.), 100-101
ce qui/ce que (Fr.), 122
ceci/cela (Fr.), 101
certain (Fr.), 129
certo (It.), 129
chacun (Fr.), 130
chaque (Fr.), 130
che (It.), 106, 110, 114, 118, 120
chez (Fr.):
   with a person, a person's name or pronoun, 404
   with places of work and person's profession, 404
chi (It.), 107
ciò che (It.), 122
circa a (It.), 427
colui che/colei che/coloro che (It.), 122
come (It.), 112, 115
comment (Fr.), 112, 115
combien (Fr.), 111, 115
comparative:
   of adjectives and adverbs, 45
   irregular, 48
compound tenses, 186-206
   asking questions, 206
   negation of, 209
   in the past, 229-246
comprendre (Fr.):
   past participle of, 184
con (It.), 43, 380, 412-414
conditional tense:
   formation of, 246
   irregular verbs in, 247
   use of, 250
   conditional perfect tense, 251
   conditional clauses, 254
conforme (It.), 423
conformément à (Fr.), 423, 433
conformemente a (It.), 423
conjunctions: 435–451
   functions of conjunctions, 441-451
      coordinating, 435
      correlative, 440
      subordinating, 436
connaître (Fr.):
   past participle of, 185
   present tense of, 158
   preterite of, 195
conoscere (It.):
   past participle of, 185
   preterite of, 195
continuous tenses, 298-300
contre (Fr.), 415
contro (It.), 415
croire (Fr.):
   past participle of, 185
cui (It.), 119

d'après (Fr.), 423
da (It.):
   in the imperfect tense, 228
   in the present tense, 182-183
   to mean in the distance, 376
   to express *for*, 381
   with a person, a person's name or pronoun, 404
   with range or distance, 419
   with time, 419
   with passive voice, 407
   with places of work and person's profession, 404
   to denote direction or location, 408
   to express manner or means, 408
dans (Fr.):
   to denote location, 395
   to indicate time, 400
   verbs with in French, 403
   with article, 395
   with geographical names, 395-397
dare (It.):
   present tense of, 158
dates, 359-363
davanti a (It.), 418
days, 359
de (Fr.):
   in adverbial clauses of manner, 43
   French passive with de, 337

INDEX

to express possession or ownership, 382
to indicate a place of origin and departure, 382
with geographical names, 383
to imply cause, 383
to qualify a noun, 384
to compare things, 384
to express the material from which something is made, 34, 384
to connect one verb to an infinitive or an object, 385
with time and dates, 392
with indefinite pronouns, 393
in adverbial phrases and idioms, 394
to denote amount and rate (Fr.), 409
to express range or distance (Fr.), 419

definite article:
contraction of, 63-64
singular forms of, 52
plural forms of, 52
use of, 54-60
   with days of the week, seasons, time expressions and dates, 359-369
   in specific situations, 54
   with the unique object, 54
   to refer to a category people or things, 55
   with abstract nouns, 55
   with a certain object mentioned earlier, 55
   before a noun specifying the object, 55
   with a noun referring to an idea, colors or phenomenon, 56
   omission of, 59

demonstrative adjectives, 98-102
indefinite, 126-143

demonstrative pronouns, 102-104
indefinite, 126-143

dentro (It.), 432

depuis (Fr.):
in the imperfect tense, 228
in the present tense, 182-183
with range or distance, 419
with time, 419

derrière (Fr.), 431

devant (Fr.), 418

di (It.):
in adverbial clauses of manner, 43
to express possession or ownership, 382
to indicate a place of origin and departure, 382
with geographical names, 383
to imply cause, 383
to qualify a noun, 384
to compare things, 384
to express the material from which something is made, 34, 384
to connect one verb to an infinitive or an object, 385
with time and dates, 392
with indefinite pronouns, 393
in adverbial phrases and idioms, 394

di chi (It.), 108
di dove (It.), 113
di faccia a (It.), 431
di fronte (a) (It.), 39, 431
dietro (a) (It.), 39, 431
différent (Fr.), 131
differente (It.), 131
dinnanzi a (It.), 431
dire (It., Fr.):
past participle of, 184
present tense of, 158
preterite of, 194

direct object pronouns, 72-76
lo, la, l', li, le (It.); le, la, l', les (Fr.), 72-76
mi, ti, ci, vi (It.); me/m', te/t', nous, vous (Fr.), 72-76
use of, 74
word order of, 75-76

disjunctive (prepositional) pronouns, 89–91

divers (Fr.), 131

INDEX

dont (Fr.), 123
dopo (di) (It.), 414, 430, 431
dormir (Fr.):
    present tense of, 158
d'où (Fr.), 113
dove (It.), 112, 124
durant (Fr.), 420
durante (It.), 420

e (It.), 436
eccetto (It.), 422
écrire (Fr.):
    past participle of, 185
    preterite of, 195
en (Fr.):
    to denote location, 395
    to express the material from which something is made (Fr.), 384-385
    with expressions, 400-401
    with geographical names, 395-397
    with means of transportation, 397-399
    to indicate time, 399-400
    with verbs, (Fr.), 401-402
en conformité avec (Fr.), 433
en dehors de (Fr.), 433
en dépit de (Fr.), 429
en face de (Fr.), 39, 431
entrambi (It.), 143
entre (Fr.), 416
envers (Fr.), 422, 428
-er verbs:
    past participle, 184
    present tense, 148-150, 151-154
-ere verbs:
    past participle, 184
    present tense, 148-150, 155-156
essere (It.):
    imperative mood, 288
    imperfect tense of, 224
    past participle of, 184
    present tense of, 157
    preterite of, 193
    with the passive voice, 330-337
    with reflexive and intransitive verbs in present perfect, 188
et (Fr.), 436

être (Fr.):
    imperative mood of, 288
    imperfect tense of, 224
    past participle of, 184
    present tense of, 157
    preterite of, 193
    with the passive voice, 330-337
    with reflexive and intransitive verbs in present perfect, 188
    passive with *de*, 337
excepté (Fr.), 422

fa...che (It.), 182-183
faire (Fr.):
    in causative constructions, 312-315
    past participle of, 184
    present tense of, 158
    preterite of, 194
fare (It.):
    in causative constructions, 312-315
    past participle of, 184
    present tense of, 158
    preterite of, 194
finir (Fr.), 151
finire (It.), 151
fino a (It.), 421
fra (It.), 400
fractions, 355-357
fuori di (It.), 433
future perfect tense, 242-246
future tense, 236-242

gerund, 291-298
grâce à (Fr.), 433
grand (Fr.), 33, 48
grande (It.), 33, 35, 48
grazie a (It.), 433

hors de (Fr.), 433

il cui (It.), 123
il quale (It.), 122
il resto (It.), 140
imparare (It.):
    past participle of, 185
imperative, 286-291

INDEX

imperfect subjunctive, 279-281
imperfect tense, 222-229
in (It.):
  in adverbial clauses of manner, 43
  to denote location, 395
  to express the material from which something is made, 384-385
  with expressions, 400-401
  with means of transportation, 397-399
  to indicate time, 399-400
  with verbs, 401-402
in conformità con (It.), 433
in luogo di (It.), 429
in merito a (It.), 432
in quanto a (It.), 432
indefinite adjectives, 126-143
indefinite article, 51-54
indefinite pronouns, 126-143
indirect object pronouns, 76-80
infinitive, 301-312
interrogative pronouns, 104-125
intorno a (It.), 427
invece di (It.), 429
inversion,
-ir verbs (Fr.):
  past participle, 184
  present tense, 148-150, 156-157
-ire verbs (It.):
  past participle, 184
  present tense, 148-150, 156-157
irregular verbs:
present tense of, 157-159
past participle of, 184-185
preterite of, 193-195
imperfect of, 224

jusqu'à (Fr.), 421

laisser (Fr.), 315-317
lasciare (It.), 315-317
lavorare (It.), 145-146
le reste (Fr.), 140
leggere (It.):

past participle of, 185
preterite of, 195
lequel (Fr.), 110, 119, 120
les deux (Fr.), 143
lire (Fr.):
  past participle of, 185
  preterite of, 195
loin (de) (Fr.), 39, 432
lontano (da) (It.), 39, 432
lungo (It.), 428
ma (It.), 436
mais (Fr.), 436
malgrado (It.), 429
malgré (Fr.), 429
mal (Fr.), 39, 49
male (It.), 39, 49
malo (It.), 33
mauvais (Fr.), 33, 48
mettere (It.):
  past participle of, 185
  preterite of, 194
mettre (Fr.):
  past participle of, 185
  present tense of, 158
  preterite of, 194
molto (It.), 41, 44, 47, 49, 133, 212
months, 512
morire (It.):
  past participle of, 185
  present tense of, 159
mourir (Fr.):
  past participle of, 185
  present tense of, 159

na parte de baixo de (Port.),
negation, 209-221
ne...aucun (Fr.), 219-220
ne...jamais (Fr.), 217-218
ne...même pas (Fr.), 221
ne...ni...ni (Fr.), 216-217
ne...pas (Fr.), 209-212
ne...pas du tout/ne...point (Fr.), 220
ne...personne (Fr.), 214-215
ne...plus (Fr.), 218-219
ne...que (Fr.), 221
ne...rien (Fr.), 215-216

INDEX

non...affatto/non...punto (It.), 220
non...che (It.), 221
non...mai (It.), 217-218
non...neanche (nemmeno/neppure) (It.), 221
non...nessun (It.), 219-220
non...nessuno (It.), 214-215
non...niente/non...nulla (It.), 215-216
non...né...né (It.), 216-217
non...più (It.), 218-219
nella parte bassa (It.), 425
nessuno (It.), 36, 141, 142
niente (It.), 142
nonostante (It.), 414
nouns, 10-25
nouveau (Fr.), 33
nuovo (It.), 33
numbers, 340-359

o (It.), 436
ogni (It.), 130
ognuno (It.), 130
ordinal numbers, 350-355
ou (Fr.), 436
où (Fr.), 112, 124
ouvrir (Fr.):
  past participle of, 185

par (Fr.):
  with means of transportation, 397-399
  with passive voice, 407
  to denote direction or location, 408
  to express manner or means, 408
  to denote amount and rate, 409
par rapport à (Fr.), 432
par-dessus (Fr.), 426
parlare (It.):
  present tense of, 149
  imperfect tense of, 223
parler (Fr.):
  present tense of, 149
  imperfect tense of, 223
partir (Fr.):
  present tense of, 150
  imperfect tense of, 223
partire (It.):
  present tense of, 150
  imperfect tense of, 223
partitive (It., Fr.), 61-63
passive voice, 330-339
past participle, 183-186
pendant (Fr.), 420
per (It.):
  to denote purpose, 404
  to mean recipient, 405
  to express opinion or point of view, 405
  to denote direction or destination, 406
  to designate deadline, 406
  to make comparison, 406
  to denote direction or location, 407-408
  to express manner or means, 408
  to mean reason or cause, 407
  with verbs, 410-411
perché (It.), 113
personne (Fr.), 142
peu (Fr.), 44, 49-50, 133
pluperfect subjunctive, 281-284
pluperfect tense, 230-232
poco (It.), 44, 49-50, 133
porre (It.):
  past participle of, 185
  present tense of, 158
possessive adjectives, 93-96
possessive pronouns, 97-98
potere (It.):
  present tense of, 158
pour (Fr.):
  to denote purpose, 404
  to mean recipient, 405
  to express opinion or point of view, 405
  to denote direction or destination, 406
  to designate deadline, 406
  to make comparison, 406
  to mean reason or cause, 407
  with verbs, 410-411
pourquoi (Fr.), 113

INDEX

pouvoir (Fr.):
  present tense of, 158
prendere (It.):
  past participle of, 185
  preterite of, 194
prendre (Fr.):
  past participle of, 185
  preterite of, 194
prepositions, 300
present participle, 291-298
present perfect, 186-191
present tense:
  of -are verbs (It.), 148-150, 151-154
  of -er verbs (Fr.), 148-150, 151-154
  of -ere verbs (It.), 148-150, 155-156
  of first conjugation verbs, 148-150, 151-154
  formation, 148-150
  of -ir verbs (Fr.), 148-150, 156-157
  of -ire verbs (It.), 148-150, 156-157
  of irregular verbs, 157-159 (see also Verb Chart, 465-471)
  of -re verbs (Fr.), 148-150, 155-156
  of reflexive verbs, 318-330
  of second conjugation verbs, 148-150, 155-156
  of spelling-change verbs, 159-180
  of third conjugation verbs, 148-150, 156-157
près de (Fr.), 428
present continuous tense, 300
prima di (It.), 430
pronouns, 65-143

qualcosa (It.), 127
qualcuno (It.), 128
quale (It.), 109, 110
quand (Fr.), 112, 125
quando (It.), 112, 125
quant à (Fr.), 432
quanto (It.), 111, 115
que (Fr.), 106, 110, 118

quel (lequel) (Fr.), 109, 110, 114, 119
quello/quella/quei (quegli/quelle (It.), 100-101
quello che/quell che (It.), 122
quelque (Fr.), 128
quelque chose (Fr.), 127
quelqu'un (Fr.), 128
questo/questa/questi/queste (It.), 100-101
qui (Fr.), 107, 120
quoi (Fr.), 106

-re verbs:
  past participle, 184
  present tense, 148-150, 155-156
reflexive pronouns, 91-93
reflexive verbs, 318-330
relative pronouns, 116-125
rien (Fr.), 142
riguardo a (It.), 432
rispetto a (It.), 432

salvo (It.), 422
sans (Fr.), 43, 414
sapere (It.):
  present tense of, 158
  preterite of, 194
sauf (Fr.), 422
savoir (Fr.):
  past participle of, 185
  present tense of, 158
  preterite of, 194
scrivere (It.):
  past participle of, 185
  preterite of, 195
seasons, 362-363
second conjugation verbs, 148-150, 155-156
secondo (It.), 423
selon (Fr.), 423
sentir (Fr.):
  present tense of, 159
senza (It.), 43, 414
seul (Fr.), 132, 275
solo (It.), 42, 132, 275
sono...che (It.), 182-183
sopra (It.), 426
sotto (It.), 418

INDEX

sous (Fr.), 418
stare (It.):
  imperative mood of, 288
  present tense of, 157
  preterite of, 194
su (It.), 416
subjunctive, 256-285
sufficiente (It.), 133
suffisant (Fr.), 133
superlative of adjectives and adverbs, 46-47
sur (Fr.), 416

tale (It.), 129
tel (Fr.), 129
tenere (It.):
  present tense of, 157
third conjugation verbs, 148-150, 156-157
time, 363-369
tout (Fr.), 137, 140
tous les deux (Fr.), 143
tra (It.), 416
travailler (Fr.), 145-146
très (Fr.), 41, 47, 212
trop (Fr.), 136
troppo (It.), 136
tutti e due (It.), 143
tutto (It.), 137, 140

unico (It.), 132, 275
unique (Fr.), 275

vario (It.), 131
vedere (It.):
  past participle of, 185
vendere (It.):
  present tense of, 150
  imperfect tense of, 223
vendre (Fr.):
  present tense of, 150
  imperfect tense of, 223
venir (Fr.):
  past participle of, 185
  present tense of, 158
  preterite of, 194
venir de (Fr.), 191
venire (It.):
  past participle of, 185
  present tense of, 158
  preterite of, 194
verbs:
  asking questions, 206-209
  compound tenses in the past, 229-246
  conditional perfect tense, 251-254
  conditional clauses, 254-256
  conditional tense, 246-256
  future perfect tense, 242-246
  future tense, 236-242
  imperative, 286-291
  imperfect tense, 222-229
  irregular (see Verb Charts, 468-471)
  mood:
    indicative, 147-256
    subjunctive, 256-285
    imperative, 286-291
  passive voice, 330-339
  pluperfect tense, 230-232
  present perfect, 186-191
  present tense,
    of -are verbs (It.), 148-150, 151-154
    of -er verbs (Fr.), 148-150, 151-154
    of -ere verbs (It.), 148-150, 155-156
    of first conjugation verbs, 148-150, 151-154
    formation, 148-150
    of -ir verbs (Fr.), 148-150, 156-157
    of -ire verbs (It.), 148-150, 156-157
    of irregular verbs, 157-159
    (see also Verb Chart, 465-471)
    of -re verbs (Fr.), 148-150, 155-156
    of reflexive verbs, 318-330
    regular (see Verb Charts, 465-468)
    subjunctive, 256-285
      imperfect, 279-281
      pluperfect, 281-284
      present, 258-276
      present perfect, 276-278

sequence of tenses with the subjunctive, 284-285
vers (Fr.), 421
verso (It.), 417, 421, 428
vicino a (It.), 428
voir (Fr.):
   past participle of, 185
volere (It.):
   present tense of, 158
vouloir (Fr.):
   present tense of, 158

Printed in Great Britain
by Amazon